People in Social Organisations and Enterprises

Motivation, Knowledge Transfer and Situated Learning in Their Communities of Practice

People in Social Organisations and Enterprises

Motivation, Knowledge Transfer and Situated Learning in Their Communities of Practice

Christopher Whitworth, Zbigniew Zontek

West Yorkshire 2018

The reviewer: Professor Branislav Mičieta, University of Zilina, Slovakia

Authors of chapters:

Christopher Whitworth: 4.2, 4.3, 5.1, 5.2, 5.3, 5.4, Appendix
Zbigniew Zontek: 2, 4.4, 4.5, 5.5, 5.6, 6.4, 6.5, 8
Christopher Whitworth & Zbigniew Zontek: Summary, 1, 3, 4.1, 4.6, 6.1, 6.2, 6.3, 7,

First Printing: 2018

ISBN 978-1-387-56384-5

Lulu Press, Inc.
www.lulu.com

ISBN 978-1-387-56384-5
90000

9 781387 563845

Contents

Summary

Choosing the title for this book proved more difficult than writing it. Is this text about social enterprise, social organisations, non-government organisations, volunteers, charities or something else entirely? The final decision was made by deciding that the aim was really to study people, their behaviours and interactions, and the structures they work in to create a social good. So, this book is about some of these people and the tasks they set themselves. Their motivation, their chosen processes, and their group achievements are addressed. The topic is wide, so the chosen focus was restricted to people, and their interactions, specifically forms of knowledge transfer, when they work together in small communities of practice, for a social purpose. Communities of practice have been studied by many, and this is discussed in depth later. The concept was an ideal foundation for limiting this study's study boundaries.

An unexpected outcome was a clear division by the importance of monetary consideration. The priority and emphasis of funding and fund-raising could be placed in a spectrum. Thus a label for this was sought. "Organisations" and "enterprises" are labels that can each be used to describe groups of individuals, working in many ways, and using widely different processes. The labels have subtly different meanings in different cultures, so definition of what is meant by them here is essential, and addressed in depth later. Briefly though, Enterprise, as used here, and capitalized, to stress its importance, means that the community of practice has monetary priorities, whilst organisation, as used here, applies when money is very much a secondary consideration to a knowledge sharing role.

Thus, in some cases, the focus is on social enterprise, learning about and operationalizing fund-raising via some forms of business "enterprise" operation, to raise money for their social good. The study of the Yorkshire Air Ambulance group exemplifies this "enterprise" fund-raising role. At the other extreme, study of a medical support "organisation" demonstrated that it exists to share knowledge, with "enterprise", in a financial sense almost non-existent. In between are organisations campaigning, and thus sharing and disseminating knowledge, for a cause. The differences are discussed and underpinned by a review of relevant literature. Some academic work points to "phases" of social organisations. Most seem to believe that only financed work exists, and that groups operating without structured income from donations, work or sale of product or services are "beginners". This book illustrates that it's not true, over half the cases considered are almost totally funded by the members themselves. Therefore, a key finding is that social organisations can exist in the long term, with almost no hegemony, structure or income stream. What these disparate groups have in common is that they are all motivated people, voluntarily operating in communities of practice, and involved in knowledge transfer processes.

So, this book is about people. Specifically why and how do people help others? What do they do, how and why do they get involved, who do they learn from, and teach, also what do they learn and share? Restating this in academic English: What motivates individuals to join and take part in social enterprise's and other organisations, what behaviours do they exhibit, do they join or form groups that can be labelled as "communities of practice", and do they undertake and deliver situated learning, as part of their knowledge transfer processes?

The topic has been studied qualitatively via interpretative phenomenological analysis and related methodologies. Over 30 interviews, from disparate groups in the UK and Poland have been analysed in depth. The outcome has been to identify common factors in individuals behaviours, motivations and interactions. Where differences exist they have been noted and, unless they could be clearly attributed to the "technical purpose", or immediate environment of the group, studied in depth.

Chapter 1: Introduction

The topic of social organisations, and the people therein, as exemplified by their behaviours, have interested the authors for many years. When the opportunity to study it in depth arose, this collaborative work emerged, with the aim of analysing, documenting and evaluating the behaviour of groups of volunteers. Between 2009 and 2016 the authors joined forces to interview and evaluate the behaviour of a large number of individuals, when involved with communities of practice ("CoPs" is used where space is limited) operating as social organisations and enterprises[1], Qualitative techniques were an obvious choice. Initially an interpretative phenomenological analysis (IPA is used where space is at a premium) methodology was used. The transcripts were analysed and mined for "meaning units". This reduced over 20 hours of interviews and hundreds of pages of text, to around 100 pages of analysis and summation. This was then further mined, with constant referral back to its original sources, and analysed further using other tools, to create summary conclusions. Finally these conclusions were compared between groups, countries and technical purposes.

Thus, this book considers over 30 people's attitudes, many more than is usual for interpretative phenomenological analysis. All the groups were purposively selected to be independent -not controlled, limited or trained by a central charity or "Head Office". This ensured that they made their own decisions on how to operate. Some of the groups had umbrella organisations, but all worked independently, and devised their own processes. This was a prerequisite of inclusion. One interesting quote, from the Guardian (UK) newspaper in March 2015, illustrates the point about small and independent. An extract is here, a fuller quote is in the literature chapter, and discussed there: „Two weeks after launching my small charity, I was invited to meet the chief executive of the largest and oldest charity in my space. 'You're doing the wrong thing', I was told, 'you're fragmenting the charitable space. You should just raise money for us as we know best how to spend it. You don't know what you're doing.' (…) My response? 'If I truly thought you were doing a good enough job, I wouldn't be doing this'"[2]. This sums up many views heard during primary research for this book. Thus, all the groups (10 were finally used, in England and Poland) were purposively chosen as being self-starting communities of practice, operating with specific social agenda's[3].

The motivations, behaviour and achievements of these purposively selected individuals working in their community of practice have been identified. The book documents and evaluates many stories, obtained by qualitative semi-structured interview of individuals, all interviewed in the last few years, and from groups resident and working in 2 countries, and from very different sectors. The chosen communities of practice include campaigners to achieve a change in society (or avoid one), health and social care support and even a village festival. The interviews were transcribed very carefully, from duplicated digital audio

---

[1] The term „organisation" and „enterprise" has specific meaning in this book. The usage is defined later in this chapter.
[2] http://www.theguardian.com/voluntary-sector-network/2015/mar/15/why-i-believe-small-charities-are-better-than-big-ones, Accessed 27 May 2017.
[3] N.B.: The terms „group", „CoP" and (in the Polish examples) „association", when used in the context of the 10 studied „groups" are used interchangeably. The choice is only to make the English text flow better, so ... „A medical support CoP and a village festival group..." Both are CoPs in this text.

recordings. The subsequent evaluation via interpretative phenomenological analysis, followed by other qualitative techniques allowed conclusions to be drawn and reported for each group and its individuals. An overview is then given, of common and distinctive features. The entire study is underpinned by a very extensive literature review, citing papers in English and Polish

1.1 Structure

This book is structured to be read in page order, with only essential underpinning from the academic literature in the main text, so as not to confuse the reader. To more fully justify the main text, extra supporting information is provided in a separate 20 page literature chapter, with further details, such as fuller examples of transcripts and analyses, in appendices. This "cascade" style allows the reader to be led through the authors thought processes, but to dig deeper if required. The authors believe that the book is for people with a practical, interest in the topics of motivation and knowledge transfer, so it will be read to help them further understand community of practice operation in these social groups, in an academically sound way.

Thus it details, for 10 groups, represented by 31 individuals:
- Firstly, how and why people say they were motivated to form or join communities of practices, to help themselves and others;
- Secondly, their resulting acquisition and sharing of situated learning, and subsequent knowledge transfer in these communities. Part of this is their reuse of situated learning from prior life experiences, and how the implicit knowledge resulting from this is transferred tacitly into their community of practice;
- Finally, how to answer the question: Why are situated learning and knowledge transfer key factors, does their use in this way create a reward, a return on investment for their time, and sometimes money, when used as part of their commitment and activity in the group.

All this output was mined from their own words, via full transcripts of semi or unstructured interviews. More than 20 hours of interviews were recorded. The investigation of the transcripts and its outcomes therefore forms the core text. To defend the decisions that led to the research and its outcomes, an extensive literature review was obviously required, and the essential parts of this are embedded in the core text itself. To fully explicate this literature would be confusing, so further detail, that some readers may not need, is situated after the discussion and conclusions. Inevitably, this separation leads to some duplication, because a basic discussion of the literature is required to introduce the analysis approach and methodology. The authors have sought to manage this, in a way that allows a reading of the core text, without too much detail. Interested and academically minded readers can then move on to the literature review chapter to question or otherwise agree with the authors usage of the concepts. Similarly some footnote references are duplicated.

As discussed later, 4 social groups exemplify the process used, whilst 6 others are only reported briefly. However, all were analysed to the same depth and are reported with equal value in the results. The 4 fully discussed, in Chapter 4, are: A medical support CoP and a village festival group in the UK, plus a vegan campaign CoP and group of motorcyclists who banded together to support the children's home - in Poland. These are asserted to provide saturation of the relevant information. The 6 other groups reported in Chapter 5, were mainly only sampled, to complement or contrast the findings. However, the transcripts were analysed in the same way, at the same depth. These groups include a supporter of the Air Ambulance CoP in Yorkshire, UK, a branch of an international running club, that exists mainly for social reasons, but has an occasional "enterprise" role, a UK CoP campaigning to save a Victorian heritage site, and a Northern UK theatre charity. In Poland there were: a theatre group which supports disabled young people and a group of parents, who built a house for their disabled children and helpers. Figure 1 shows the structure of the book and work processes. Each section in the book contains a textual description of these processes, with examples.

Figure 1. The overall plan of the book

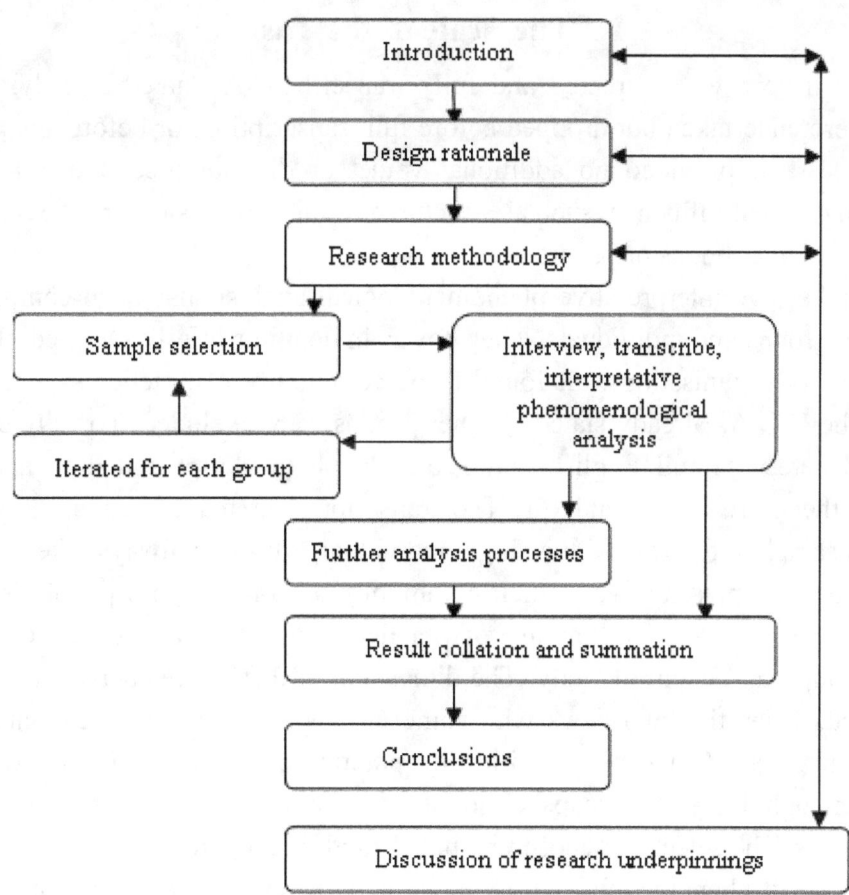

Source: Authors' study.

Thus, 31 individual interviews, from 10 communities of practice were mined for this book. All were analysed in equal detail, but those in Chapter 5 were sampled more lightly, sometimes via only 1 interview. To save space the discussion is also lighter, but the full detail is held by the authors and may be used elsewhere. 14 groups were originally considered for inclusion, but 4 were excluded because they did not fully fit the criteria of self-starting community of practice, that were not externally controlled or influenced - external training provision was a key exclusion factor. Some common or contrasting views from other published material illustrates the core analysis. A follow up volume is planned to cover some of the original research in other ways, including other research on this topic undertaken in the last few years.

After extensive research, some of which is detailed in chapter 8, the processes shown in Figure 1 above were planned and designed in depth. The arrows illustrate the sequence of work. The book is structured in the same way. These processes are described in the methodology section.

1.2 The Scale of the Task

31 interviews have been completed and fully transcribed. As stated already, some other interviews were undertaken but dropped before full transcription, or before analysis, as they proved unnecessary, provided no additional value, or did not meet the criteria, usually because of an external influence, such as structured training provision or other control. They may be used for other books or papers.

A comprehensive interpretative phenomenological analysis has been completed for all the compliant groups and individuals. They cover, in depth or briefly sampled, the 10 social enterprises and/or organisations, all found to be community of practice's, in 2 countries - Poland and the UK. As already stated, 4 other groups were excluded. To fully evidence the process used here, one full English and 1 full Polish transcript and their analyses, plus samples of others, are in Appendix 1. The transcripts that made up the analysis sources range from a sample interview with a single individual, who was always a key, experienced and fully involved representative of their community of practice, to 6 people from 1 social enterprise or organisation's community of practice. This gives a wide coverage, in both breadth of groups, and depth of study. The dimension of differences between countries was also evaluated. Thus, the interviews with some groups achieve theoretical saturation, and this is demonstrated. Other communities of practice are only represented by 1 or 2 interviews, enough for just a snapshot to use to evaluate and demonstrate common or differing features. The selections chosen in the UK and Poland are balanced.

This volume of phenomenological research, undertaken over 7 years, is unusually large and more than enough for a definitive study. It provides a basis for very thorough conclusions and reflections on the motivational drivers for, and subsequent situated learning that occurred in each organisation's community of practice, and of each individual therein. The motivation and rationale for their presence in a community of practice, and the situated learning acquired from other group members and outside, is demonstrated, as is how it allowed new or peripheral members to move to full participation in their social enterprises or organisations community of practice.

The initial interpretative phenomenological analysis was fluid and unconstrained, with in depth textual summaries of its outcomes for each interviewee made. To save space these are not fully presented in the results chapters. However, these, plus the raw data, were then re-examined to build some further analysis, which is reported for each community of practice, rather than individually. This has allowed in-depth comparison between groups, and also between countries. The sample of community of practice's was purposive, to enable these comparisons. Broadly similar aims were found to be present in both Polish and UK groups, and a range of aims is also present in each set.

Chapter 2: Study Design And Research Methodology

2.1 Principles

The study was designed to record, understand, and evaluate qualitatively, the situated learning[4] and knowledge transfer that occurs in the key managers and supporters of a selection of groups. As stated already, they were purposively selected to contain functioning communities of practice[5]. The original concept of situated learning in a community of practice came from Lave and Wenger, but has been extended significantly, by many other workers, including, in the last decade, Cox[6]. The community of practice concept is only discussed briefly here, to explain the rationale for its use as a limited to the scope. Its theoretical value is covered in depth, and referenced fully, in the literature review chapter.

The authors used and built on the community of practice concept by undertaking a large qualitative study. Many groups, initially believed to meet the community of practice criteria, both in the UK and Poland, were initially selected and a sample of key members interviewed. In the 10 cases where the clear presence of a community of practice, and occurrence of situated learning within it was found, the interviews were transcribed fully and evaluated in depth.

The study was designed to, and has, identified how and why members joined their respective groups and communities, their motivations and their subsequent situated, social and cognitive learning. This has been used to demonstrate the knowledge transfer that occurred inside the organisations, or is acquired from outside, in this social enterprise or organisational context.

2.2 Design Detail

The design started by identifying key terms. They are discussed and referenced briefly here. More depth can be found in the literature review chapter. Some boundaries to study are always needed. The authors here chose to study motivation and knowledge, but only in social enterprise CoPs, to limit the scope. CoPs were chosen because their members have to find, create and transfer knowledge on the issues they study. Wenger[7], and Wenger *et al.*[8] define as being made from a group or network of people, and sometimes organisations, often working informally, and sharing their knowledge. They state that these groups share common interests, which, with their concern about social issues, processes and practices, create a context. They define practice as coordinated activities of people undertaking tasks, and informed by a particular organisational context[9]. These activities are related to a

---

[4] Lave, J., Wenger, E., *Situated Learning: Legitimate Peripheral Participation*, Cambridge University Press 1991.
[5] Lave, J., *Cognition in Practice: Mind, mathematics, and culture in everyday life*, Cambridge University Press. Cambridge 1988.
[6] Cox, A., *What are communities of practice? A comparative review of four seminal works*, „Journal of Information Science" 2005, Vol. 31, No. 6, pp. 527-540.
[7] Wenger, E., *Communities of Practice: Learning, Meaning and Identity*, Cambridge University Press, Cambridge 1998.
[8] Wenger, E., McDermott, R., Snyder, W., *Cultivating Communities of Practice: A Guide to Managing Knowledge*, Harvard Business School Press, Cambridge 2002.
[9] Lave, J., Wenger, E., *Situated Learning...*, op. cit

particular topic or theme, with a common style of activities and tasks referred to as "shared practice". Later, Wenger et al. say: "communities of practice are groups of people who share a concern or a passion for something they do and learn how to do it better as they interact regularly[10]. These key definitions, although mostly paraphrased here, form the basis of this usage of the groups under study, as CoPs.

The topic of "social enterprise" and "social organisation" has been widely studied but not well defined. The authors needed some limits, so chose to define social enterprise or organisation participants as "individuals that form and/or join groups, that then labour to develop social products or services, then give them away, or just recover their costs"[11]. In some cases their labour is directed to fundraising for money that is then donated to the "cause", or "technical purpose" - thus social enterprise is the best label. An example used later is the Yorkshire Air Ambulance CoP. In other cases their labour is solely directed to knowledge acquisition and sharing, thus "social organisation" is a better label. The medical group exampled later fits this definition well. These definitions, and how the participating groups were chosen, were informed by Salamon & Sokolowski[12], who provided a definition used in the selection of groups for study. They looked at a broad range of entities that meet the following five key criteria:

– They have some kind of formal organisational structure (e.g., a set of rules, formal or informal, that define goals, activities, membership, selection and competencies of officers, the use of resources, etc.);

– They are self-governing (i.e., are not a subordinate part or agency of another organisation);

– They are not profit distributing (i.e., any income or surplus generated by their operations is ploughed back into the organisation, not distributed among the organisation's officers or owners);

– They are private (i.e., are not a part or an agency of their government);

– They are voluntary (i.e., membership is not coerced or mandated by law, and they customarily receive donations of money, other property, or labour to be used for the social good).

All the groups selected meet this criteria. They were purposively chosen, and tested via the interviews, to demonstrate that their interactions could be described as communities of practice - being a group where *soft or subtle* (so implicit rather than tacit) knowledge is created, shared and sustained[13]. As already mentioned the concept was originally introduced by Lave & Wenger, who originally used it to explore situated learning[14]. Here it is used as a

---

[10] Wenger-Trayner, E., *Introduction to communities of practice: A brief overview of the concept and its uses,* http://wenger-trayner.com/introduction-to-communities-of-practice/, Accessed 18 August 2017.

[11] Authors definition, built from the work cited and other reading.

[12] Salamon L., M., Sokolowski, W., *Volunteering in Cross-National Perspective: Evidence From 24 Countries.* "Working Papers of the Johns Hopkins Comparative Nonprofit Sector Project", No. 40. Baltimore, The Johns Hopkins Center for Civil Society Studies, 2001.

[13] Hildreth, P., M., Kimble, C., *Knowledge Networks: Innovation through Communities of Practice,* Idea Group, Hershey 2004.

[14] Lave, J., Wenger, E., *Situated Learning...,* op. cit.

theoretical framework from which to explore motivation, situated learning, other forms of knowledge transfer and storage, both tacit and explicit, and their drivers. Specifically the study only considers social enterprises and organisations. The authors can demonstrate that, in each group studied, the managers, and other members, work as a community of practice. More detail on these concepts and their limiting criteria will be found in chapter 8, the literature discussion.

2.3 Sampling Criteria

As already stated, all 10 organisations finally used here were communities of practice, and met the given definition of not-for-profit enterprises. All are formally constituted, but not externally controlled or influenced, and each has a different, well defined social enterprise or organisational aim. The sample is thus purposive: of similarly sized groups from different sectors, chosen and interviewed in 2 European countries. The organisations were chosen to cover a range of activities, similarly in the UK and Poland, with aims from caring for long-term illness, or healthy eating, to theatre groups and clubs. This is to enable the motivations and other factors common to the social CoP and its situated learning, to be separated from those specific to the declared "technical" purpose of each group.

In coming together to provide a social service, the members inevitably find, create and transfer knowledge internally, on the issues they study. This work studies the phenomena in an original and new, social enterprise organisational context, extending it further outside the original in-firm situations from which community of practice study grew, as described initially by Lave & Wenger[15] and extended by many, including Hildreth & Kimble[16]. The work by Cox already cited, although it questions the community of practice concept in the "tightly managed 21st century" actually supports the author's usage of it in this study of situated learning by individuals, because "Wenger's 1998 book treats communities of practice as the informal relations and understandings that develop in mutual engagement on an appropriated joint enterprise, but his focus is the impact on individual identity (…)"[17].

2.4 Data Capture Processes

Qualitative inquiry into motivations and subsequent situated learning was the chosen approach. By semi-structured, one off (in most cases) interviews, the authors have established when and how this occurred between members, or was learned from outside.. As described by Cresswell[18], qualitative study represents "a legitimate mode of social and human science exploration (…). Good models of qualitative enquiry demonstrate the rigour, difficulty and time-consuming nature of this approach". The researcher "gathers words, analyses them inductively, focused on the meaning of participants, (to) describe a process (…)"[19]. From the author's prior experience they recognise the "multiple dimensions of the

---

[15] Ibidem.
[16] Hildreth, P M. and Kimble, C., *Knowledge Networks...*, op .cit.
[17] Cox, A., *What are communities of practice...*, op.cit.
[18] Cresswell, J., *Qualitative Inquiry and Research Design: Choosing among Five Traditions*, Sage 1998, pp. 14-20.
[19] Cresswell, J., *Qualitative Inquiry and Research Design...*, op. cit., p. 9.

problem or issue, and wishes to display it in all its complexity"[20].

The authors of this book took the ontological position that human reality is subjective, and that generalising is difficult - "variables cannot be easily identified, theories are not available to explain behaviour of participants"[21]. This approach, using concepts discussed by Cresswell above, defined the research design, with detail emergent from the initial research outcomes.

It was clearly necessary to experience the perceptions of the participants under study, and look for meaning - from their viewpoint. The overall objective was to understand the motivation to become involved in, and eventually manage and contribute to, the members situated learning, and subsequent knowledge base. Each individual's perceptions and recollections of their initial motivations, and the subsequent interactions between members, was explored. In doing this the authors discovered, and demonstrate that the individual's own transition from new peripheral membership to eventual mature core legitimacy, in community of practice managerial roles. Hegemony, a concept used often by Fairclough but best seen in a paper in "Organisational Studies"[22], was a prominent feature of many interviews. Their focus of this aspect, and repeated stress of their situated learning, both in the community of practice under study, and in their earlier life, and how it helped them, clearly shows that the study needed a perspective to inform it and give it some rigour, phenomenology was thus the obvious and appropriative choice for this study, because it allowed an "orienting framework".

To summarise and reiterate, the authors undertook and extracted significance via interpretative phenomenological and other narrative analysis, of over 30 open ended interviews, and supporting material supplied by the interviewees. 10 CoPs (from an original list of 14), were studied, in some cases only one individual from their group, in others the complete "management" or senior members of the team. In each of the cases studied, the individual's original motivation, subsequent situated learning, and its drivers, were assessed.

The authors have analysed the essences of the interviews and, from the transcripts and associated notes, drew out common themes. The process is described in depth, and extensively exampled, later. They were helped in this by a large literature review, extending well outside the IPA framework. This review is detailed in the literature chapter, as already explained, only key points are outlined here. The project concludes with the production of an integrated narrative, which demonstrates the essence or invariant structure of the interactions and behaviours.

2.5 Interview Management

The activities, behaviours and cultures of group members, were captured and reflected upon, by story acquisition and analysis (see figures 1 and 2 for the overall process). Using a single, or occasionally two, phenomenological open ended interviews separated in time, each

---

[20] Ibidem, p. 15.
[21] Ibidem, p. 18.
[22] Humphreys, A., Brown, B., *Narratives of Organizational Identity and Identification: A Case Study of Hegemony and Resistance*, "Organizational Studies" 2002, Vol. 23, No. 3, pp. 421-447.

individual's recollections and understanding of what drives or drove them to participate in their group, was captured. Interviews were mostly help 1 to 1, but in a few cases, 2 or more individuals from a group, had to be interviewed together- the consequence of this and its effect on possible storytelling, has been carefully considered. The interviews usually lasted between 30 and 70 minutes. All interviews here are only identified by a code for the group and interviewee number (C1, M3 etc.). This allows total anonymity. There are only 2 exceptions, the Air Ambulance group, specifically identified at the request of the interviewee, and the running club, where the interviewees wished to promote the concept. In these cases the interviewees are anonymised, but not the CoP.

The purpose of the interviews was explained and the use of the recording devices pointed out. Consent forms were obtained in all cases and are stored securely. All participants have agreed to give full access for the research and subsequent publication. As stated above, all relevant ethical conditions are met and documented. As far as possible, the interviewers restricted themselves to encouraging noises and unfocused prompts, once the interview was under way, to minimise "steering".

The specific context of the interviewee's CoP and its purpose was thus addressed in each case. All interviews were very carefully transcribed, word for word, with pauses and hesitancy noted, as required by the research method. Where interviewees identified other group members, their names were replaced by the appropriate code. In most cases associated organisations and towns are also anonymised to protect the interviewees.

The authors then documented, transcribed and finally analysed, the narrative data using interpretative phenomenological analysis techniques, followed by, in some cases, a secondary study of the outcomes. The data is extremely rich, still current and relevant, so further analysis is intended, and will be reported in papers and possibly a later volume. The source data acquired comprises well over 20 hours of audio and over 400 pages of transcripts. There is also a body of secondary data. This comprises leaflets, booklets, handouts, videos and Facebook site links. Its use has been documented, but to preserve anonymity, not fully referenced.

Although the interviews were open and relatively unstructured the interviewers ensured that all relevant areas were addressed. The initial brief outlined the purpose and requirements. Where the interviewer identified important gaps, questions were asked, but only after the interviewee "dried up", and the questions were carefully crafted to be open: "tell me more about that?" etc.

The situated learning that facilitated the individual's individual journey, from peripheral to full legitimised participation, was always explored. The specific context and technical purpose of their group was addressed in each case. Although the words "community of practice" were not usually used or explained, the authors ensured that the groups and individuals interviewed met the criteria for this. 4 of the original groups in the selection did not, and are excluded, leaving 10 for study here.

Chapter 3: Rationale for use of Interpretative Phenomenological Analysis, and the Process Used

"Interpretative phenomenological analysis is a qualitative research approach committed to the examination of how people make sense of their major life experiences"[23]. This is taken from page 1 of the introduction to the book which defined the authors final approach, clearly ideally suited to the authors purposes here. A second quote from the same source also illustrates this" "Interpretative phenomenological analysis researchers are especially interested in what happens when the everyday flow of lived experience takes on a particular significance for people"[24].

The applicability of this is best defended by a quote from the authors primary data collection "I would hate, hate, hate, anyone else to go through what I did unnecessarily…" (taken from interview L1). This quote, by an individual whose parent was suffering from the disease that caused the group to form and share experiences about the medical problem they all faced, is used to illustrate the rationale for this choice of research approach. The experience of this community of practice member is clearly an event with real meaning, and the life experience which prompted it, of great importance to the interviewee.

Smith et al. go on to quote the example of how "someone makes sense of a major transition in their life"[25]. In addressing their 2nd major theoretical axis, an interpretative endeavour informed by hermeneutics, the theory of interpretation, they assert that, as sense making creatures, the narrative that interviewees provide, reflects their attempts to make sense of the events.

A further example, not from the author's group selection, but from the Facebook page of a newly diagnosed cancer sufferer, who had not had time to find, join or form a community of practice to help him with situated learning, demonstrates the opposite: *After a terrible day of feeling like I cannot even finish the last three days of radiotherapy, I have had a simple but profound revelation. I have not been taking in enough water for the past week. And have been going downhill at a rate of knots. So, I am now sitting sending water into my stomach …straight into my tummy… and I feel 500 percent better. I just thought I would pass this simple realisation and cure to my two friends-in-throat cancer…"* (Used with the writers approval 11/2014).

The authors further defend their choice of approach by further quoting from Smith: "The aim is to find a reasonably homogeneous sample to examine convergence and divergence in some detail… Immediate claims are therefore bounded by the group but an extension can be considered through theoretical generalisability(…)"[26].

Although interpretative phenomenological analysis derives from the field of psychology, this book takes the view quoted by Smith *et al.*, that "interpretative

---

[23] Smith, J. A., Flowers, P., Larkin, M., *Interpretative Phenomenological Analysis: Theory, Method and Research*, Sage, London 2009, p. 1.
[24] Ibidem, p. 3.
[25] Ibidem.
[26] Smith, J. A., Flowers, P., Larkin, M., Interpretative Phenomenological Analysis, op. cit., p. 3

phenomenological analysis's core interest group is people concerned with the human predicament...engaging with the world"[27]. In summary, therefore, appropriate techniques have been used to evaluate individual's motivational drivers and the situated learning that occurred, in their chosen communities of practice. The primary data from these semi-structured interviews was supplemented by analysing relevant secondary data available from the group. This material included minutes, websites and newsletters. They are used but not fully referenced, to aid in anonymity, as requested by most interviewees.

The findings were then considered against, and are underpinned by, published literature, summarised briefly here and detailed in the literature chapter. This study therefore builds and applies a literature resource of situated learning in social enterprise organisations, and their communities of practice.

3.1 Data Analysis

From the literature review the authors undertook, it is clear that there is no single, commonly accepted methodology for this type of qualitative study and analysis of attitudes, behaviours and paradigms. However, the process required is an inductive, phenomenological process of observations "enabling a thorough understanding of the research sample and context" but not allowing *"the meaning of events to individuals to be ignored"*. This quote is from Bryman & Bell[28], and led to the final choice of phenomenological data capture, followed by analysis of the captured narrative and a final process of integration.

The authors note that this qualitative, interpretative approach, albeit with considerable variation in detail, is outlined in many of the papers and books reviewed. For example Smith, Flowers and Larkin state, quoting Husserl: "The founding principle of phenomenological inquiry is that experience should be examined in the way it occurs (…) then Husserl reasoned that these essential features of an experience (…) and might then illuminate a given experience for others too"[29]. The majority of the relevant texts seen and documented here and in the literature chapter, have adopted inductive and theory building styles, addressing attitude, behaviour, cultural issues and related factors.

So, for this book a "rich picture" of these attitudinal and culturally influenced behaviours was required. Using IPA and unstructured interviews allows exploration of the meaning and deeper nuances of questions and answers, "employing a combination of exploratory and conclusive research strategies"[30]. The interviewees choose what to say and they prioritize their remarks and focus. Thus the study is led by authors understanding and belief that knowledge and the processes that lead to its production are always very much context specific[31]. The authors go on to discuss why non-numeric data is necessary to provide a rich description and allow possible explanations of peoples meaning-making- how the interviewees make sense of the world and experience the events important to them[32].

---

[27] Smith, J. A., Flowers, P., Larkin, M., *Interpretative Phenomenological Analysis...*, op. cit, p. 5.
[28] Bryman, A., Bell, E., *Business Research Methods,* Oxford University Press 2003, p. 86.
[29] Smith, J. A., Flowers, P., Larkin, M., *Interpretative Phenomenological Analysis...*, op. cit., p. 12.
[30] Robson, C., *Real World Research*, Blackwell, Oxford 2002, p. 31.
[31] Lyons, E. and Coyle, A. *Analysing Qualitative Data in Psychology*, Sage 2007, p. 4.
[32] Ibidem.

Figure 2 illustrates the first stage of the process used. Once the groups were selected and interviewees found, this shows the full process, from initial interview, to summary text supported by meaning units. A full explanation follows. Examples of transcripts are in Appendix 1.

Figure 2. The interpretative phenomenological analysis process - as used here. Stage 1.

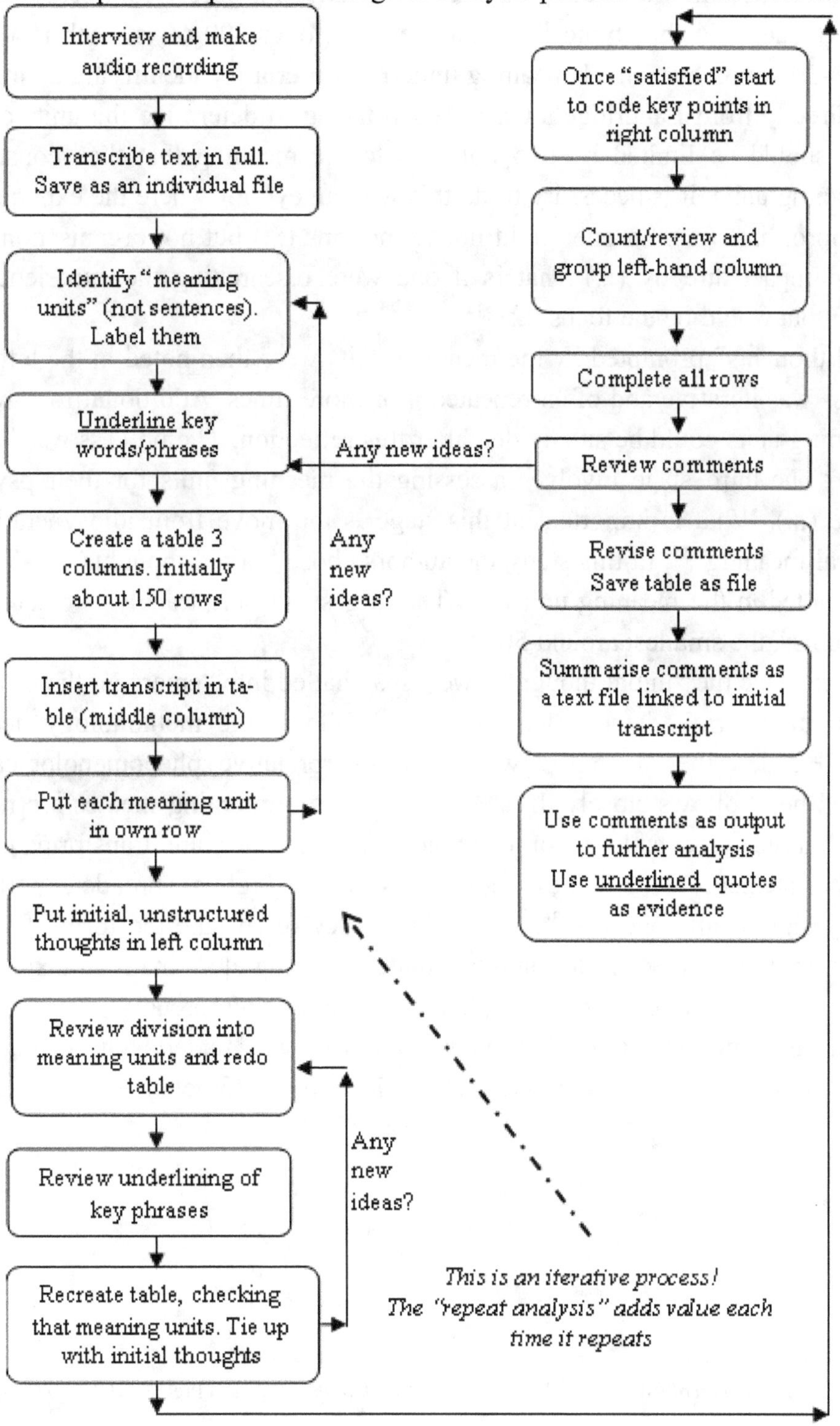

Interview and make audio recording

Transcribe text in full. Save as an individual file

Identify "meaning units" (not sentences). Label them

Underline key words/phrases

Create a table 3 columns. Initially about 150 rows

Insert transcript in table (middle column)

Put each meaning unit in own row

Put initial, unstructured thoughts in left column

Review division into meaning units and redo table

Review underlining of key phrases

Recreate table, checking that meaning units. Tie up with initial thoughts

Once "satisfied" start to code key points in right column

Count/review and group left-hand column

Complete all rows

Review comments

Revise comments Save table as file

Summarise comments as a text file linked to initial transcript

Use comments as output to further analysis Use underlined quotes as evidence

Any new ideas?

Any new ideas?

Any new ideas?

This is an iterative process! The "repeat analysis" adds value each time it repeats

Source: Authors' study.

To summarise the process in words, the interview transcriptions (typically 20-30 minutes), were converted into verbatim, accurate transcripts. These varied but were mostly 3000 to 4000 words. The complete text was then imported into the middle column of a 3 column table and scanned repeatedly for "meaning units"[33]. These were underlined. (see this chapter, section 3.3 for an extract). Figure 2 details this.

Each "meaning unit", with the phrase it is embedded in, (rarely complete sentences) has its own row. The table thus typically comprises well over 200 rows, each row containing typically 10-30 words but only 1 meaning unit. The criteria for identifying a "meaning unit are taken directly from Langridge's text: "When trying to determine the units of meaning, the analyst should be limited by two horizons to the meaning that they construe (...) to discern meaning units, it is necessary to do this with an eye for where the experience relates to issues appropriate (...). So one might notice motions (...) but not organisation dynamics, unless they impact directly (...) That is if one were researching the experience of acute illness, then that would be the focus (...)"[34].

"Initial thoughts" prompted by the meaning units were then noted in the left hand row. This process was iterative and often repeated 4 or more times. Additional rows were added where meaning units could be subdivided after this reflection. The process was informed by Langridge: "The third stage involves assessing the meaning units for their psychological significance (...). What is important at this stage is the move from idiosyncratic detail to more general meaning"[35]. In this study the authors chose "initial thoughts" to describe this. They were noted in the meaning unit row. The largest transcript analysis created over 400 "meaning units", the smallest around 50.

As a next stage the "initial thoughts" were marshalled into "emergent themes" or higher level ideas, in the right hand row. This again follows the methodology described by Langridge. He describes 4 stages, which the interpretative phenomenological analysis process used here follows closely. In stage 2 he states "Emerging themes are noted in the right hand margin (see table 1 for examples). Initial notes are transformed into more meaningful statements (…). These comments should reflect broader, perhaps more theoretically significant concerns"[36]. In this book they often take the form of "knowledge transfer, community of practice formation, situated learning etc. Finally, a textual summary was made below the table. This completed the actual interpretative phenomenological analysis for that interview. Each interview transcript was undertaken separately, where possible in different weeks, to minimise "habituation". Figure 3 details this process.

---

[33] Langridge, D., *Phenomological Psychology, Theory Research and Method*, Pearson Prentice Hall 2007, pp. 88 onwards.
[34] Ibidem, p. 89.
[35] Ibidem.
[36] Ibidem, p. 110-112.

Figure 3. From IPA output to final outcome. Stage 2.

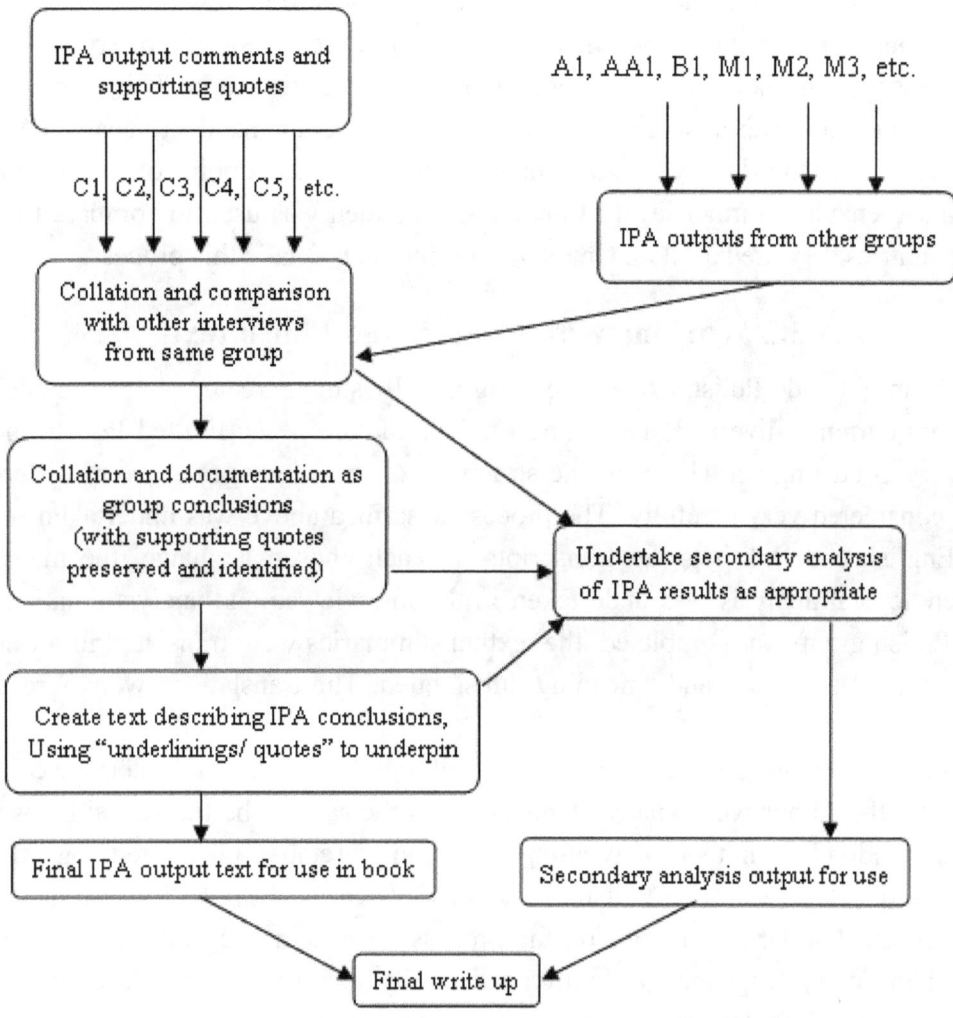

Source: Authors' study.

Thus 31 tables, were created, each from one person's interview transcript, containing the high level ideas, with the "meaning units" to evidence and support them. Once completed (after typically 10-20 hours work per transcript) the tables were stored in a sources document, with secondary data and other scanned sources. This comprised well over 400 pages.

When the analysis of a CoP group was completed (Interview transcripts L1-L5 etc.), the entire process was again reviewed, and a summary table created. These 10 summary tables make up Chapter 4 of this book. The original textual summary and supporting evidence for each group typically comprised at least 12 pages, giving well over 100 pages of output from the 10 groups. However, this has been reduced and heavily summarised. The 4 CoPs which provided multiple interviews are reported in more depth, in Chapter 4. The 6 groups which were sampled more lightly are reduced to typically 2-3 pages in Chapter 5. However, the full analysis is held, and being used elsewhere for papers. If requested, more detail can be given directly- subject to anonymity requirements.

The final stage, used as described by Langridge[37], was to review the textual summaries of all 10 groups to extract common meanings. This required extensive referrals back to the original transcripts in their tables, and occasionally a further iteration. This formed the final output used, but there was a clear need to simplify and label the results to enable conclusions to be shared. Thus the data was again mined, but from a standpoint of group rather than individual, to enable a further level of analysis. This then was used to compare the groups, and the countries they are based in. Chapter 6 outlines and details this process.

3.2 Working with English and Polish texts

The opportunity to add Polish CoPs to the original UK study, created a new dimension. The two authors currently live in Poland. The English author speaks limited Polish, the Polish author, very good English. However the structures of the languages are very different, and this was considered very carefully. The process described above was undertaken separately for the English and Polish group transcripts. In each chosen language, the interpretative phenomenological analysis was undertaken in the interviewee and analyst's native tongue. When a Polish group was completed, the textual summaries were translated into English, as were the "initial thoughts" and "meaning units" cited. The translations were agreed by the authors as representative.

To ensure rigour, the interviews were all conducted in the interviewee's native language, by the author whose native language was the same. The transcriptions were done by the same individual, in their native tongue. The interpretative phenomenological analysis was done in the same way. The Polish author was fully briefed on the English methodology and vice versa. Regular discussions on the process were held and both authors understand enough of the other language to identify and rectify inconsistencies. However, to ensure academic rigour a clear demarcation was made between text sources.

Thus there were tables of analysis in English, and in Polish. Each table contained the same headings, in the native language of the analyst. The processes for identification of „initial thoughts" and „emergent themes" were discussed and agreed in each case. A full analysis of example CoPs, in each language, is in Appendix 1.

Any translation process is always fraught with difficulty. Colleagues were consulted, in both languages, and an extensive literature search undertaken to ensure rigour. One consequence of this was that the translated extracts were often in „Polish English", because of differences in language structure and word usage. This style has been deliberately maintained. However, in every case the authors agreed that the original Polish meaning had been kept. Professional colleagues informally consulted (but not identified here) made comments such as:

---

[37] Langridge, D., *Phenomenological Psychology...*, op. cit., p. 110-112.

- „*My instinct would be to <u>deliver the best interpretation of meaning rather than translating literally</u>. Add a disclaimer that for reasons of understanding this is what you've done and everything is sweet*";
- „*<u>As long as you make your methodology clear and your reasons open to argument</u> and therefore your findings open to disproof*".

The literature search suggested several options, but overall the above suggestions were confirmed by most of the papers reviewed. Some are discussed in the literature chapter. Therefore the Polish material is represented by the authors best attempts at translating meaning rather than the literal words. Any oddities in language results from this. The authors take full responsibility. The matter is discussed further in the literature review chapter.

3.3 Interview Transcript Analysis Examples

Some very brief extracts appear here. The example from Poland has been translated into English by the authors. An original Polish transcript is also in Appendix 1. These extracts are cut from full transcripts for ease of reading (but not changed at all) and total less than a minute of speech taken from typically 20-45 minute interviews. The interpretative phenomenological analysis table is not included here, but an example follows these extracts.

This sample is asserted to be adequate to defend the subsequent chapter, which compiles the over 400 pages of IPA and its outcomes mentioned earlier, down to a reasonable level.. Including more detail would be unnecessary. The raw data is securely stored, will be used for other purposes, and can be discussed further if the authors are contacted personally (subject to ethical considerations). The CoPs are only identified as L, C, Y etc., members of the groups thus become L1, L2, C1, C5 etc. These extracts, whilst not reported here in full, or analysed, demonstrate the depth of data in these transcripts:

Example 1 - from **Group L** (5 interviews stored). L is a group supporting sufferers from a rare autoimmune wasting disease:

L1: *"And in my personal experience... my mother was a sufferer, and seeing my mother go through life in absolute agony, day after day, seven hours a day-er 7 days a week, 24 hours a day, is ...difficult, and you just wish you could turn to somebody and gain some knowledge of how to make that person's life a bit more liveable and help in any way you can. And therefore the L group was set up with that in mind, not as a charitable existence as regarding um...to get, you know funds. That was never its intention, it was there as a support and to help these people, you know, they do have good days and they have bad days. And the majority of the time its bad days, you know there is no pain relief whatsoever ... and asking, in my experience of the L group, coming on to that now(...) And um so the reason I got involved with this group, was purely through my mum, because I wanted to do something was to help my mother, and um, because I hated to see her suffering every l day, she was alone, she was in the house all day, she was housebound, she couldn't get out, she was you know restricted, and she couldn't talk to anyone about it and I was at work, my father was at work, she was alone but in constant pain all the time and she had no...nowhere to let that pain out, really basically, so we went to the first Yorkshire L group meeting... and we found, my mum enjoyed it, because it was a social event, it wasn't a meeting, it was held in a social capacity, in that, you know like was a coffee morning or you know it was a social event like for example making a social event as in people getting together, you know, like minded people getting together and talking, and so we got, we started getting involved, and the first thing I did for L was, I mean , because I wanted...had the determination and I wanted to help so much to get it pushed to the limelight that I helped in the first event which was that that, um I wanted to um... help make the public aware.*

Example 2 - from **Group C,** (6 interviews stored) from a group organizing a village festival.

C3: *I decided to run it, and...sort of...be the Chair, basically because the long standing Chair, C2??..., from the NT, umm, C2???. had been the Chair for 10 years or so, a very long time at least, and he err... he was ready to retire, and wanted to step down for personal reasons, and... I just thought, this would be a good thing to do you know, and I am capable, -I can do it, so, I decided I would do that then, umm, and that was fine, you know and yeah, I quite enjoyed it. I enjoyed the fact that as Chair I was sort of, able to meet more people, to get more people involved, umm, In terms of knowledge transfer I suppose I was keen to bring my knowledge to the committee, that was one of my own...desires, you know, err, I thought I knew something about err, Project Management, I err, I felt I knew something about, if you like the business environment, err, and so I was keen to bring that to the committee, to add value to the local community in that way.*

But I was also keen to get people on the committee to bring their own professional expertise with them. We were very lucky, in my last year as Chair , in that err, one of our new committee members, in that year 2011 was a local police officer, ... and he was very useful in helping us with liaising with the police obviously and...err. Umm..., err also knowing things we needed to know about safety and err... security for the public and so on... And that was the other thing I was keen for my time as Chair, was to bring more systems, to bring more procedures, so we brought in more and more defined Health and Safety, more err, more documented risk assessments, err, we invited St John's Ambulance, which was the first time we had done proper structured First Aid, although we had in the past we had had a couple of volunteers to tell us about Health and Safety, you know...(unclear words for 3 sec).

Example 3 – from **Group AA.** One interview representing an Air Ambulance supporting community of practice in Yorkshire (UK). AA1 is a volunteer for the Yorkshire Air Ambulance (Helicopter) service. The transcript is deliberately not fully anonymised at AA1's request:

AA1: *Its very, very organic in that way. You pick things up from each other, particularly ...the ways, of...putting things over in an effective way. Err, and obviously, people who are new to it are quite nervous. Maybe not quite sure of what they are doing, what they are saying, so yeah, but there is no (pause)... There is a err, actual formal training session for the actual, formal Power Point presentation, but when it comes to standing in a gazebo in the middle of a wet field it err, in a rainy July, then, there is only one way to learn. That is to get in there and do it.... Err, the reason that I prefer working for Yorkshire Air Ambulance is, ...I guess you would almost call it a selfish reason in that I can see exactly where the money is going. I can see where my efforts are making a difference. Cos, you see the yellow helicopter flying in and out of Leeds General Infirmary and other hospitals. And, because of what I do I get to meet people, that's picked up. And I have met people whose lives have been saved by... the efforts that I put in, and... you just can't buy that, can you?*

Example 4 – from **Group V.** Three interviews representing an group of vegan people from South Poland.

V1: *In fact, we came four years ago, but we worked for two years as an informal organisation in general...mmm... It was only in April last year, we have just formalized the form of the social organisation. The main motivation from the very beginning, the main goal, was really to prevent... not to prevent... to educate, inform consumers, how they can affect the fate of breeding animals, about the fate of these animals, because you cannot see, it is not advertised on shops windows...mmm...that it is really the alternative, it may be... in the form of a vegetarian or vegan diet, and tasting it, trying it...mmm...we are shaping the market already in some way. I think, that we reduce the demand for animal products... and... in the same way, we can impact on livestock production, and cause a decrease in the number of animals that are bred and eventually killed... We started the initiative on the basis of what has been in my mind: how to organize an event, how to write press releases, how to invite the media, how to talk to them.*

Example 5 – from **Group R.** Three interviews representing an group of parents, who started bringing up children with intellectual disabilities (PL).

R1: *I used to be a person who made parents come together, focus and work for the sake of their children, and in the future ensure them a worthy life when their parents are no longer there. That was the primary goal with the establishment of the association and we have proceeded in this direction for the whole period of time. All the time... hmm there has been the interest of our child, so as when we pass away he will not have to be left somewhere, among the people he does not know, where it is a shocking experience to acclimatize... And that has been the motivation and the goal. It is still ahead, isn't it? We have been going, going on for twenty years and here we are in this new building... At the very beginning it was said, if you work you do not pay the whole amount, you are released but you are obliged to work it off... A lot of parents have offered themselves, "O.K. I pay less but I will work it off". These are different actions...*

To introduce the interpretative phenomenological analysis process via an example, an analysis, from a short extract of the interview with L1 is reproduced in table 1 here. The "initial thoughts" demonstrate the process suggested by Langridge. Fuller examples are in

Appendix 1. The „first draft" emergent themes are also shown. This extract contains a few of the over 400 „meaning units" (underlined text) extracted from the L group[38].

This extract examples the interview transcript (middle column), with meaning units identified and underlined. It also shows the initial thoughts that arose and a first iteration of emergent theme classification.

Table 1. A small sample of interpretative phenomenological analysis from transcript L1

Initial Thoughts	Interview L1	Emergent Themes
Explanations/ Motivation	"And in my personal experience ....my mother was a sufferer, and <u>seeing my mother go through life in absolute agony, day after day, seven hours a day-er 7 days a week, 24 hours a day, is ...difficult</u>".	Motivation
Explanation/ Need for help	"<u>And you just wish you could turn to somebody and gain some knowledge of how to make that person's life a bit more liveable and help in any way you can</u>".	Motivation
Clarification of strategic direction/ Not fundraising	"And therefore <u>the L group was set up with that in mind</u>".	Rationale
	"Not as a charitable existence as regarding um...to get, you know funds. <u>That was never its intention</u>".	
Rationale /Driver	"<u>It was there as a support and to help these people</u>".	Rationale / driver
Explanation	"You know, they do have good days and they have bad days. And <u>the majority of the time its bad days, you know there is no pain relief whatsoever</u>".	Motivation
Memories	"...and asking, in my experience of the lxxx group, coming on to that now" (some transcript text not included here).	
Explanation and story Solitude/ Suffer alone	"And um, because <u>I hated to see her suffering every day she was alone, she was in the house all day, she was housebound, she couldn't get out, she was you know restricted</u>". "<u>And she couldn't talk to anyone about it and I was at work, my father was at work, she was alone</u> but in constant pain all the time and she had no... nowhere to let that pain out, really basically".	Motivation Lack of knowledge

---

[38] This extract is deliberately a „first draft". Several more iterations followed and the emergent theme labels changed considerably. Occasionally the initial thought labels also changed, but only slightly to aid clarity. This first draft is provided to example that an iterative process was used.

Initial Thoughts	Interview L1	Emergent Themes
Networking/ Enjoyment (of membership)/ Increasing public awareness	"So we went to the first Yorkshire L group meeting.... and we found, <u>my mum enjoyed it,</u> because <u>it was a social event, it wasn't a meeting</u>, it was held in a social capacity, in that, you know like was a coffee morning or you know it was a social event".	Networking and opportunity for situated learning
Increasing public awareness	"Like for example making a social event as in <u>people getting together, you know, like minded people getting together and talking</u>".	Networking CoP
Contributing	"And so we got, <u>we started getting involved</u>".	CoP formation
Contributing/ Motivation	"And the first thing I did for lxxx was, I mean , <u>because I wanted...had the determination</u> and I wanted to help so much".	Motivation
Public awareness	"<u>To get it pushed to the limelight</u> that I helped in the first event which was that that ,um <u>I wanted to um... help make the public aware</u>".	Marketing, Knowledge transfer

Source: Authors' study.

This chapter has outlined the rationale for the processes selected, with in depth examples of how it was used in practice. It takes the reader through the methodology usage, and how the authors mind-sets interpret its outcomes. It commences with a set of interview transcripts, produced in an unstructured way, and finishes with the Table above, which details initial IPA outcomes, exampling meaning units, the initial thoughts they created, and a first attempt to extract emergent themes from them. As a final point, the authors remind readers that the process is iterative, and that the examples above were the first outcome. Subsequent re-readings, and examples from other texts, create changes in emphasis, new emergent themes and classifications. Also, sometimes new meaning units are found, but rarely is there deselection of meaning units. The authors commend this very time consuming and intensive process to others.

The next 2 chapters reports the results of this process. Chapter 4 gives in-depth examples and details how they were analysed. It reports on the CoPs studied via multiple interviews and that gave the richest picture. Chapter 5 reports more briefly on CoPs that were studied via single or fewer interviews, but the authors wish to point out that the analysis process was the same, as rigorous and detailed, but reported more briefly as the processes did not change.

Chapter 4: Results of Interpretative Phenomenological Analyses, Multiple Interviews

4.1 General Introduction

The research for this book covers 4 CoPs in depth, possibly to a level of theoretical saturation. They are discussed in detail in this Chapter. 6 other CoPs were also researched via interviews with 1 or more members. These are discussed more briefly, although analysed in the same depth, in Chapter 5. All 10 were proven to be functioning community of practice's, as defined by the literature.

The 4 CoPs in this Chapter were mostly researched via 1 to 1 interviews, typically a single 30 minute interview with each of between 3 and 6 individuals per CoP, totalling 2-3 hours interview time. Although in each case 1 person was interviewed, sometimes others were present. The consequences of this have been considered. Occasionally repeat or follow-up interviews were held with the same individuals. Additional data from newsletters, Facebook pages, websites or other written material supplied, is also incorporated.

The 4 CoPs in this Chapter are discussed in depth. As already stated, an unexpected outcome was a clear division of strategy. „enterprises" focus on funds and fundraising for their technical good. „Organisations" focus on knowledge, either inward bound to help members, or outward bound as campaigns to change an aspect of society. All, however exhibited some characteristics of both roles.

They are disparate in technical purpose and stage of development: 2 are from the UK, a medical support organisation and a village festival enterprise. The other 2 are Polish, a vegan campaign organisation and a motorcycle enterprise which fundraises for an orphanage. This clear difference in type between enterprises and organisations is discussed here, and the rationale for this claim will become apparent.

4.2 The L Community of Practice (UK)

L Introduction

The UK (Yorkshire) L group formed over 30 years ago to identify and share information about a life-threatening disease. The members were sufferers from, or close to those who have the disease. The interviews revealed that the disease was not well known in the medical community, and sufferers reported many misdiagnoses in earlier years. They formed the group to share experiences, and also share their knowledge with the wider community and the medical profession. As such they clearly meet the need to study motivation in a community of practice and its knowledge transfer processes. Other regional groups were reported to exist, plus a loose „umbrella" organisation, which provided exemplars and some knowledge sharing, but not structural guidance.

The following quotes *(in italics)* are taken from the transcripts, and each contains one or more "meaning units", which are underlined. The quotes are long enough to demonstrate context. Words in brackets are the authors, to aid clarity or when a replacement was needed to aid anonymity. Interviewees are not identified, but were recorded as L1, L3 etc. Written material is identified but deliberately not referenced in the interests of anonymity:

- *We never knew (*a group*) existed until we found a bookmark lying in a car which we borrowed, advertising "if you suffer from L or know someone who does" pass this book mark on. ...* (L1 written note);
- *The group was specifically formed because the disease was relatively unknown and still is, even though there are public faces that try to bring it to the forefront of the public;*
- *(*The disease*) has also been brought up in the Houses of Parliament in order for sufferers to be recognised as sufferers of a lifelong deteriorating disease and be granted the benefits and recognition that other well-known organisations get i.e.: British Heart Foundation , Cancer Research etc.;*
- *Nothing more seems to have come out of this as L sufferers still pay for prescriptions whilst other sufferers of recognised life-threatening diseases are entitled to get free medication;*
- *X was a regular visitor at the local clinic...Her sister...also a regular feels that we all should be reminded of the symptoms which were then listed* (Obituary in L Spring 2009 newsletter);
- *Sufferer asked to write about experiences for newsletter " Remember how it all started* (lists symptoms*) ... After leaving school that afternoon didn't go back for months"* (Spring 2009 newsletter);
- *GP was totally confused, took months to even mention possible cause....then it all went over my head in a flurry of medical jargon.* (Spring 2009 newsletter*);*
- *"Think of being allergic to yourself" ..." Had whole world at my feet then swept off them by a crazy illness I had never heard of"....* (Spring 2009 newsletter);
- *"I (*now*) meet and talk to other people who have the same condition"* (Spring 2009 newsletter);
- *"AGM was a great success and provides a great opportunity to meet and chat with other sufferers and compare experiences"* (Spring 2009 newsletter);
- *"I run a drop in support session every month"* (Spring 2009 newsletter);
- *"implementing an advice line, setting up a service, and welcomes feedback on how the service can best be run"* (From a nurse funded by group, as reported 2009 newsletter);
- *It was first formed in order to give the chance for L sufferers to share their personal experiences and suffering of the disease. And to discuss about medicines and medical treatment which the sufferers had experienced and had heard about – a sort of exchange of information and discussion time.*

N.B.: All the information herein was extracted from interview transcripts with 5 people, identified here as L1 to L5, the supplied note and some of their published literature, also provided during interviews.

L Process

The community of practice members were initially identified by a „snowball" process. L1 was once a colleague of the UK author. Initially 5 members were interviewed, L1 then offered a second interview (4 years later), and also a written text. 3 of those interviewed were disease sufferers, 2 their supporters (a daughter and a husband). All became core community of practice members. Therefore 6 interviews with 5 individuals were transcribed. Other written material was also provided. A Facebook page now exists (2017).

These transcriptions and the written text were analysed in depth using the IPA technique documented earlier (additionally a brief "follow-up" was undertaken in 2 other cases). This created 6 transcripts totalling 2 hours of speech., plus written material. From this 11,000 words were transcribed. Over 400 "meaning units" were identified in the transcripts and underlined ,then placed in different rows of a table. Some are reproduced here below, in the phrases in which they occur, thus more than 1 "meaning unit" may be in a phrase. However they were clearly separated for the analysis. They <u>are underlined for clarity</u>.

Initial thoughts and higher level emergent themes were then added to each of the 5 tables. A short sample from 1 of the tables is shown earlier in the book. The "follow-up" discussions were not transcribed fully, but notes were made at the time and these are incorporated as addendums. Quotes reported here include all interviewees. The written material is identified as used, but nor referenced fully. However L1 agreed to be identified as the author of the written note, to aid clarity of reporting.

L Discussion of Interpretative Phenomenological Analysis

The "meaning units" and other outcomes demonstrate that the community of practice is real and meets all the desired criteria The group formed sometime in the 1980's to meet a technical need – help to disease sufferers. Although this book is not focused on such detail of their "technical" purpose, in this instance the need clearly influences and controls the behaviour, motivation and outcomes from the community of practice members. For this reason the rationale for the group features more heavily than would otherwise be appropriate. The need to acquire and share knowledge about the disease, here anonymised as L, clearly drove and motivated all interviewed. There is clear evidence that the L community of practice is firmly anchored in an early stage of the social enterprise evolution (for details see the social enterprise and organisation sub section in the Literature Review). There is very little desire to fund raise or otherwise form a business, although funding for specialist nurses is mentioned in passing. The overriding purpose is knowledge transfer, and the concept of a „not-for-profit" enterprise is hardly addressed, thus this is clearly an "organisation", not an "enterprise".

The subjects all reported a clear and evident lack of knowledge about their disease in the medical community, at least until the 21st century. In some earlier cases they were undiagnosed but exhibiting enough common features to enable them to seek out fellow sufferers, and formed a community of practice to help them cope with it. Furthermore, the medical community, especially GP's ("Family Doctors") were stated to be not familiar with the rare disease, so the organisation had to transfer knowledge they acquired personally, into the medical community, to help other future sufferers. Numerous quotes from all interviewed evidence this:

– *she actually started with it, when I was born* (around 1970), *but nobody knew about it, nobody could diagnose it, because nobody knew anything about it, the disease, the doctors didn't know anything;*

– *we felt the GP's didn't know anything about the disease, the consultant didn't know anything about the disease, we found that people had a lack of knowledge in the medical profession* (Discussing early 1980's);

– *I knew nothing, me mum knew nothing, my dad knew nothing about the disease at all;*

– *well, me and my family became a member of the group, solely because we happened to, funnily enough, um, my dad was loaned a car. And in that car was a bookmark ... you know, the ...general organisation, um...advertising about a L weekend;*

– *when I was first diagnosed I didn't know anything about L, whatsoever, um so it was a big shock;*

– *when I was diagnosed my consultant said things like "I know nothing whatsoever about L" My GP hadn't seen it in 40 years;*

– *the other one had had to go home and look it up in a textbook, as the vet and the dentist did;*

– *I was diagnosed in my very early 30's (c.1995) but I'm convinced I've had it since I was 16;*

– *got diagnosed after some years of having problems ... being fobbed off by (pause) um, medical people that she went to see, having been told it was her age, and various bits and pieces...;*

– *although it took me a long time, for diagnosis,...but for a while I'd had it at the back of my mind, that ...I had got a ...disease;*

– *So the information I got was ...um from a chap who lived in (Yorkshire town named), whose wife had ,who died of ...er um...L, and he sent me some quite useful information, and it was through the information that he sent that he'd got together.*

These quotes show the original technical problem and the resulting motivation and determination to face and manage their problem. The transcripts clearly demonstrate motivation for, and the presence of a community of practice set up to address the problem, meeting all the criteria discussed in the earlier chapter. Witness:

– *in my personal experience ...my mother was a sufferer, and seeing my mother go though life in absolute agony, day after day. And you just wish you could turn to somebody and gain some knowledge of how to make that person's life a bit more liveable and help in any way you can;*

– *....And therefore the L group was set up with that in mind;*

- *the L group is mainly social activities where sufferers were able to go and meet other sufferers who were in the same position, who were suffering of the same disease and same condition;*
- *...and also they could compare their, you know, their medical treatment, their hospital treatment;*
- *I felt well, there is only one thing I am going to have to do here, I am going to have to go to a meeting and talk to other people;*
- *....I thought, these are the only people, the only people, who I can talk to, who have a inkling of what is happening to me;*
- *And then I felt just like a piece of left luggage. I'd been picked up and I'd been dropped. And nobody kind of wanted to know;*
- *So that's how I got into the L Group. And we still try...try our best, to support;*
- *We started with, I think, 3 of us. and have gone on from there;*
- *and we found, um, among other things um, (long pause) L UK and the Yorkshire L Group, and we went along to a meeting, to meet up with other people and see if we could find a bit more about it;*
- *And I was shipped around from various doctors, and told to go away, that I didn't know what they were talking about;*
- *a lot of the time people just want to talk, be it somebody who's got L or somebody who's lost someone ...who's lost somebody, who's been diagnosed with L.*

This demonstrates that the overriding initial rationale was the lack of medical expertise shown to the sufferers in the last century and at the beginning of this. The disease was first recognised in 1981 (as stated by L1) but rare and not commonly known. All the transcripts evidence this. Thus, a community of practice organisation formed to discover knowledge, or situated learning acquired in their environment, and transfer it to its members, both mature members of the community of practice, and those on the edges undergoing legitimate peripheral participation in the group. This includes the external medical community who were involved.

The knowledge initially was mainly implicit, held personally by the members and shared, often 1-to-1. Explicit knowledge was rare, even in the medical profession, certainly until this century, and the ubiquity of the Internet. A quote evidences this well:
- *Doctors have no knowledge of it, no-one else has any knowledge about it,* (talking about the 1990's);
- *and I got to the stage where I was waiting for the doctor to tell me I needed some counselling. I didn't think I did, cos they kept telling me I was being emotional, and I didn't think I was;*
- *Well it was in the first place, when your doctor says like "I've been a GP for 40 years and I've never seen it.* (talking about the 1990's);
- *My personal recollection of one of these groups has been gained through being a family member of a L Sufferer who sadly lost her early life not through the disease itself but by*

the many effects of infections to the immunity system of the human body (L1 written account);

- *There are so few people diagnosed, out of the number of people who have got it, it doesn't seem to be something that's picked up normally, by every GP;*
- *you couldn't go into a library and say "have you got any textbooks on L, because they would look at you as though you'd dropped off the moon"* (talking about experiences back in 2000).

Therefore the individuals sought out others with similar problems (much harder to do before the Internet), and met or otherwise communicated: *The L group was set up in the South of England originally but later as it became a more known by the distribution of bookmarks, little area groups began to form and became a helpful resource for the sufferers as it provides them with the opportunity to speak to other sufferers about symptoms, medication and modern pain relief, recent research issues, possible cures and above all it provided sufferers with time to relax and have some short relieve from the suffering that they experience, which is often constant and without respite every single day. It offers a chance for sufferers and their carers to have a form of social life as well. This is all due to the setting up of social events arranged usually by suggestions from sufferers, the Social Secretary and the carers. These social events could be days out, meals out, fetes, even local and national conferences as well as talks from organisations, who offer ideas and suggestions that may provide a little bit of pain relief* (L1 written account 2012).

The outcome was the creation of a community of practice, grown without a clear desire for organisation, but with members determined to acquire, share and create their implicit knowledge, almost always gained via situated learning or other knowledge transfer:

- *talking to the various people in the group, listening about their experiences, you were able to, sort of, match what you were going through;*
- *what my mum was going through, what my dad went through, you know, that we were able to talk about it, we talked about it amongst ourselves;*
- *Its learning from other people;*
- *both other members and...;*
- *and outside specialists who come to give talks.*

An "umbrella" organisation (a national charity) also formed ,but did not influence local actions directly. It did not offer structure or control. but possibly did have a library of some explicit knowledge, as perceived by the individuals interviewed: *It also gave them the chance to discuss issues that had been printed in the National magazine which is sent to sufferers regularly by mail once the sufferer or relative becomes a member of L UK. This magazine often has articles about the latest research into all the different aspects of the disease, personal recollections of sufferers, notification of recent medical research and findings which may contribute to the possible alleviation of this disease. It also provides members with other contacts with organisations (which are a few) which may offer possible help. It offers a chance for members to see what other groups around the country are doing in order to raise funds to contribute to research* (L1 written account 2012).

This is one of the few references to fundraising and evidence of external support, in "later days" (probably after 2000), certainly well after the first recollections reported by the interviewees - the 1980's. Their fund raising (clearly a secondary role) also created some support staff:

- *at the group, we also, with the funds that we raised, we also, um we also, aided in a L nurse, paid by us, you know, by the funds that we raised. We, in xxx, we have been able to fund a, a L nurse, where and also, at one time, we also, had a L room, which I think we still have at xxx, where it was a place for L patients to go;*
- *It's a community type thing, I think we have also, as a group we have got funded a um .....a nurse... at xxx, ...at xxx and there is now one at I believe, and that's (from) money that's been raised by the Yorkshire Group.* (xxx= 3 towns in Yorkshire);
- *These social events usually are a way of promoting (recognition of -authors note) the disease and the raising of funds by means of raffles, selling of goods which have been donated by the members and even events such as runs walks and other activities have also been a good form of raising awareness and funds;*
- *These funds are collected and sent to the Head Office,* ... *to contribute to further research Unlike other well- recognised charities, L seems to have great difficulty in making itself known, it has also distributed leaflets and fact sheets in hospitals, clinics and Doctors waiting rooms.* (L1 written account 2012);
- *There are no lengths to which this charity will not go in order to make the public and its organisations aware of this incurable disease and its effects, at the same time being a resource, social and counselling service for its sufferers and the carers of these sufferers.* (L1 written account 2012).

There is also evidence in discussion of more recent times, of more generic help- for example with counselling: The transcripts are unclear as to the source of this but follow-up conversations (already mentioned, but not transcribed) showed that it came from external sources, not via the community of practice or its "umbrella" organisation. This is thus a source of external knowledge acquisition and transfer, sought by the community of practice members, then embedded as implicit knowledge and LPP offering opportunities to move to core, mature positions. However the role changed. Medical knowledge improved (reported here as happening in the very late 1990's, or early 21st century). For example:

- *and it was solely because we hit the right person, you know, who specialised in L, you know, L was one of his specialties. It just wasn't, you know, it just wasn't concentrated, on just knowing...you know...it wasn't something he had studied in a textbook, he'd specialised in it;*
- *...really, the way I found out about L was reading up about it, in sort of like, going to the library, trying to find out information there. Also, um... looking on websites, as well,*

.....and also, not only that, I subscribed to a monthly magazine called L UK, which is the main Organisation that takes care of L (discussing period after 2000);

- *My L nurse was, was act... was actually incubating at that time, a little group called L Link, which was...err a group attached to the main L um web of 12 Organisation , um and attached to the Yorkshire L group as well* (after 2000);
- *there is a programme on the radio called Medicine Now, and its got an article about L. So, I listened to it, and that was the first time that there was a little glimmer of hope, that I actually...perhaps...wasn't going to die, and there might be a bit of a future for me* (after 2000);
- *when she did get diagnosed, we looked on the Internet, to try and find a bit more about what it actually meant* (after 2000);

Thus the role of the community of practice changed, from straightforward knowledge acquisition, situated learning and implicit knowledge transfer amongst members, to a new role of counselling, interpreting and advising on the utility of internet and other explicit information:

- *and I don't think a lot of people realise that, if you talk to 100 people with L and they all vary;*
- *because a lot of the published information, was very gloom and doom and ....in some peoples cases it is gloom and doom and...;*
- *whereas in other cases it, some people are lucky enough to be able to cope with it and um (long pause), others go on to, a long time;*
- *I actually did a contact course, same as (L1), same as (L5), there was only ...one other husband there wasn't there and the others were all ladies who were suffering. And that was very interesting because it was about how to listen, again a little more about the disease, and...you're not a counsellor, of sorts, just someone who is there to listen, somebody is diagnosed, and wants somebody to talk to. We're down in the magazine as people for them to ring up. I'm a carers contact, I haven't actually got it.*

However the local nature of the community of practice has clearly declined in the last decade (since 12.2005), for reasons possibly associated with the formation of online community of practice's. A "follow-up" telephone call with 2 of the original interviewees (in late 2015) revealed that the group has now ceased to meet regularly, although the individual members still meet informally and exchange information. Online information has largely supplanted the need for the group. This change could be explored further with a new project.

N.B.: Most of these interviewees were unclear as to when and how the group started. The authors conclude that this is because it is a vehicle for situated learning and knowledge transfer, and is only valued for this, not in its own right. Change occurred around the turn of the century. This is evidenced many times, the increased availability of the Internet to most UK people seems to coincide with reports of increased medical awareness, ease of diagnosis and effective help. Finally, the dates are mostly "inspired guesses", taken from information elsewhere in the transcript - i.e.: "I was born in xxx but diagnosed when I was 30".

L Interpretative Phenomenological Analysis Outcomes

An examination of the analysis outcomes from this community of practice showed that, for over 2 hours of interview and over 11,000 words of transcript, plus a written note and several copies of old newsletters (2009), well over 400 "meaning units" were identified and underlined, then placed in different table rows. Some of these are used above to illustrate the results text.

As already stated, as a first stage of analysis of the "meaning units", the "initial thoughts" were noted. The commonest was "outward knowledge transfer", often to medical workers or other individuals outside the community of practice. This includes family and supporters who were not stated to be inside the core of the community of practice. It clearly includes LPP. It is followed by "situated learning". The following table lists their occurrence and frequency. The table below is indicative, it has no statistical value. The IPA process allowed "initial thoughts" but there is no obligation to place them against every "meaning unit", and to do so is repetitive, thus the only value is the list of topics, and that "at least 50 notes about motivation occurred.

Table 2. Community of practice L, frequencies of initial thoughts

Initial Thought	Frequency of use	Notes
Knowledge sharing/ transfer outward	90	Situated learning was acquired within then shared outside group.
Situated Learning	73	Examples of people learning, inward knowledge transfer (not common), situated learning and sharing knowledge within their community of practice (very common).
Lack of medical knowledge/help/ need for expertise	68	Clearly one of the leading comments! This is the reason why the "technical reason" for the community of practice features so heavily in this book. It clearly drove motivation, situated learning, knowledge transfer and the need for the community of practice itself!
Reflection/ Analysis/deep thought about issues	63	This suggests that the interviewee is thinking deeply about the community of practice and their experiences as part of it. It is associated with motivation and learning.
Motivation (to help others)	50	This was noted where a desire to help others was evident e.g. "I would hate, hate, hate others to go through this needlessly".
Need for Knowledge (inwards)/ Education/ Finding	50	Clear comment about external knowledge coming into community of practice. So, knowledge transfer from external source.

Initial Thought	Frequency of use	Notes
out		
Explanation/Storytelling/Clarification	33	This notes that the interviewee felt the need to explain/tell some part of the history or story behind their involvement. It possibly indicates motivation?
Networking/ Socialization	35	The ability to share experiences, make friends with people in similar situations and generally have contact with the world is clearly present.
Need for Group/ Community of Practice	23	This is noted where interviewee stated or discussed the need for sharing knowledge, experiences and ideas. Also where there might be "power in numbers". It is associated closely with situated learning and knowledge transfer, also with transitions from LPP to full, mature membership.
Marketing/ Public Awareness	20	This reflects the desire to raise awareness of the disease (and the group) and is often associated with motivation.
Solitude/ Lonely/ Alone	9	Comments like: "I felt abandoned. Dropped, so alone".
Fundraising	8	Provision of extra support not funded by UK NHS. Clearly not a priority for the group, but a secondary activity: "at the group, we also, with the funds that we raised, we also, um we also, aided in a L nurse, paid by us, you know, by the funds that we raised. We, in xxx, we have been able to fund a, a L nurse, where and also, at one time, we also, had a L room, which I think we still have at xxx, where it was a place for L patients to go" (L1).

Source: Authors' study.

L Interpretative Phenomenological Analysis Conclusions

The community of practice formed for technical reasons associated with personal issues. It has changed over the last 30 years, but the analysis shows clear evidence of knowledge transfer, both inwards and outwards, of situated learning, likewise, and the motivation for this. Therefore study of this community of practice, via 6 interviews with 5 mature community of practice members, a written note, published newsletters and 11,000 words of interview transcript, meets the objectives of the book: "What motivates individuals to join and take part in social enterprise, what behaviours do they exhibit, do they join or form groups that can be labelled as "communities of practice" and do they undertake and deliver situated learning, as part of a knowledge transfer process". (From Chapter 1, Introduction).

Motivation is clear, all 5 interviewees joined and participate in the community of practice because of a desperate need for knowledge. They recognised their personal need, and also their ability to share what they had. So, knowledge transfer, within the group and to external stakeholders including the medical profession, carers and new members, is demonstrated repeatedly. Most knowledge is acquired via situated learning, in the CoP and via their personal situation. Often it was transferred outwards, to their doctors, carers and other non-CoP members. Situated learning from outside but used in the L group was not often seen, until recently, possibly because it did not exist outside the group! The generic analysis below builds on these points.

The final stage was to analyse the "emergent themes". These are tabulated together at the end of this chapter. They were selected after extensive rereading of the transcripts and IPA tables. Immersion in the L transcripts made them stand out.

The strongest "emergent theme" in the L group was rationale, or motivation to help themselves and others. This was evidenced by a desire for knowledge transfer within and outwards, to others in the CoP organisation, and the supporting medical community. This theme was followed by situated learning -knowledge transferred to the interviewee within the CoP itself, often their careers, and created within the CoP by its members. Hegemony was almost never noted and structure and seniority, or official status, with its associated power factors was not stressed by anybody. Operationalization only related to knowledge, making it explicit to others. It was never about the operationalization of finance or structure -thus "fundraising" is not a significant emergent theme or "initial thought". Where fundraising is mentioned it is as a tool to assist in knowledge transfer, not a goal.

This is clearly an organisation built to share knowledge alone. Similarly recontextualization was only seen in the context of *"how can me knowing this help others.."*. Reflection and emergence were important, and in practice, indistinguishable from coaching and observation. This data was cautiously mined for the further analysis undertaken, especially the comparisons across groups and countries in Chapter 6.

L Organisation - Summary

There is clear evidence of knowledge transfer into and out of, plus situated learning occurring in this community of practice. There are clear knowledge management processes, as described by many, including Nonaka and Takeuchi[39]. The organisation members were desperate for external sources of knowledge, but, until the last decade felt let down by the medical profession. Such knowledge as existed, outside and via internal situated learning, was shared, then transferred into the group (internalization) and shared on to other members (socialization). After that the knowledge was usually combined with personal experiences and other tacit learning, and then externalized. There are many examples of aspects of learning occurring, as already described in the methodology of research. Examples of situated learning occurring include all the tabulated "labels", but the highest frequency goes to: motivation, and (specific forms of) operationalization. Less often seen are seen aspects of recontextualization and fading. Scaffolding and hegemony hardly exist. Fundraising was clearly not a priority, but some nurse provision was mentioned.

Community of practice "L" was formed in the 1980s, and developed to share knowledge, and help others. A very secondary role was to raise funds, but a L nurse is

[39] Nonaka, I., Takeuchi, H., *The Knowledge Creating Company*, Oxford University Press 1995.

mentioned. The organisation is local but changing. The emergence of the internet, together with wider recognition of the disease in the medical profession has moved them strategically. From desperately learning and sharing they have moved to a new support and interpretation role. Outsiders contact them with inexperienced evaluations of the internet and other data sources. The organisation tries to normalize their understanding and counsel them. Thus they are still helping people from beginner or LPP to maturity, but in a different context. This organisation meets all the criteria for a community of practice, functioning and managed as a social organisation, but probably will still remain in an early stage of development.

4.3 The C Community of Practice (UK)

C Introduction

This CoP strives to provide a village festival day. It offers a varied showcase of village life and activities, a fun day out and an opportunity to network and meet people. It gives local businesses the opportunity to promote themselves to a wider audience, and visitors an incentive to return. There are many broadly similar festivals in other local Pennine villages, organizing days and events including a straw bale carrying race and canal events.

The CoP was started about 1995, and consists of a group of very committed individuals supporting a "C village day". This is a village festival, and aims to promote a community spirit and shared experience. Fundraising is important and was stressed by the interviewees, and so it clearly qualifies as a social enterprise. The event is held in April each year and centres on a village tale - of admitted dubious provenance, that the villagers tried to keep a migratory bird walled up, as they believed that its continued presence would mean that Spring would remain all year.

It is run as a "break-even", not for profit event, although there is now (2016) some debate as to the possibility of turning it into a fund-raiser for community and village support activities. The event is funded by monies raised on the day, donations and also some grants. The National Trust (NT) - A UK charity, operating nationally, with over 4,000,000 members and that „(...) protects and open to the public over 350 historic houses, gardens and ancient monuments... also look after forests, woods, fens, beaches, farmland, downs, moorland, islands, archaeological remains, castles, nature reserves, villages - for ever, for everyone"[40]. The NT has a longstanding involvement with the village, as a result of a past gift of an adjacent grouse moor and land. There is also a parallel, but unconnected charity in the village, which operates a charity shop to raise funds for village activities. Some grants have been made available by this group, for specific activities, such as a visit from a Romanian band.

Music is a clear theme, the event is opened by the local junior band and closed by a silver band. There is a procession through the village which finishes at a local residential old people's home. There was considerable stress by interviewees on the need to involve all ages and sectors in the community. Activities cited included belly dancing, Morris Dancing,

---

[40] https://www.nationaltrust.org.uk/features/about-the-national-trust, Accessed 18 May 2017.

a karate club, walking groups, the canal society and gardening groups. A duck race, which sells tickets to raise funds is also a prominent feature. Local pubs and food outlets have been encouraged to provide a "special" on the day, and customers encouraged to vote for the best dish. This then results in a separate prize-giving later in the year.

C Process

The 4 interviewees were all formal committee members. They were identified and accessed via the chairperson, who was a colleague of the author, and lives in the same village as „B" - from the Victorian Heritage CoP. Snowball sampling then followed, as each interviewee suggested further contact, until 4 were reached. They stated that this was sufficient to evaluate their group.

The interviews were all held in the presence of the Chairperson, who was interviewed as C1. All interviewed stated without prompting that there were "no secrets", and that they had no problems with identification to each other or acknowledgment. The presence of C1 could potentially have led to some bias or skewing of data, but is a necessary consequence of the sampling process. She was very aware of this and deliberately took no part in proceedings other than inevitable introductions. All interviews were held in either members' homes or the local pub. Interviews C2 and C3 were held together, and C3 thus heard C2 speak. However the author asserts that the transcripts demonstrate that no adverse consequences ensued, although this factor was taken into account when the C3 transcript was analysed. These interviews were held in 2010, and C1 was re-interviewed in 2015 to update the information. The CoP have a website and a Facebook page, which has also been used. There are also numerous comments on other Pennine (local area, within 100Km) websites, which have also been reviewed. They are not referenced here to preserve anonymity of the interviewees. Also, identification of the technical purpose of the CoP would add no value to the aim of the analyses.

Thus, 4 main members of the group were interviewed -one was re-interviewed 5 years later (2015). They were all members of the organizing committee and longstanding members of this social enterprise. The results were transcribed and analysed in depth using exactly the same interpretative phenomenological analysis technique discussed earlier. The results were a total of over 90 minutes of speech and 11,500 words of transcription. A total of 430 "meaning units" were identified in the transcripts and underlined in a table, as was done for all groups. Similarly, the initial thoughts and higher level emergent themes were added to each of the interview tables. Where used written material is identified as such but anonymised.

C Discussion of Interpretative Phenomenological Analysis

From the interviews and supporting material provided, it is clear that "C" is a community of practice, and operates mainly as a social enterprise. The interviews recount that the festival day -now stretched to the weekend, began around the late 1980's as a village celebration administered by the village church. However, a UK national support organisation (the NT) became interested and the festival grew into a big event, with less church involvement.

Thus, what started as a little village fete has turned into a nationally recognised event. There is much commitment and local pride. Community feeling is strong:

- *the reason why I got involved was em because I am on err… another committee… as I was already the Chairperson of the after school club;*
- *one of the parents, who I knew through that committee … she was trying to encourage err… new people to join, … she actually got about 2 or 3 people, including myself;*
- *I went along to the meeting… it's the start of a new year, we want to keep C Day alive we want people with ideas, we want new things happening;*
- *I am a resident I mean, I have lived here for 17 years;*
- *enjoyed the event and I want to see it continue;*
- *it feels like quite a heavy responsibility, if you walk away and others walk away the whole Day dies;*
- *its hard work, and we would like a few more committee members;*
- *I am involved with the planning but I am not involved on the day, only at church.*

Analysis of the interview transcriptions demonstrate that the group is primarily an enterprise, but with significant organisation properties, as its priority is raising and managing funds to be used locally as a social good. It is a seasonal event, happening in Spring, so the commitment and involvement varies throughout the year, There is evidence of reflection, and feedback on past events. Situated learning, operationalization and coaching are clearly present:

- *we are generally active between September and the event itself (April);*
- *and then we have like just a quick post-mortem, going through the accounts usually about June;*
- *there was going to be pony rides, around the church, but it didn't materialise, the lady couldn't come and nobody else had a licence to do it. Health and Safety, got to be very careful now;*
- *Liability insurance… for the first year we had to pay that ourselves this year.*

Commercial organisations are also involved and benefit, mostly local businesses such as pubs and cafes. Knowledge transfer is important, and focused around the skills to manage the event. This includes financial management and legal skills. Fundraising is key but the "festival fun" is the primary technical purpose. This purpose and motivation unifies all the interviewees activity. Comments demonstrate this:

- *xx as a village has a high number of food outlets, lots of cafe's, lots of pubs and lots of takeaways, just lots of places that serve food;*
- *I want the village to be a prosperous one, and I want the businesses to do well;*
- *I could always see this broader context of the local region, the community I lived in, and keeping it vibrant and um, err …successful;*
- *This is part of what we are trying to do with C Day, get the publicity. Publicity is really, really important to us;*

– *everyone was impressed that I'd managed to do something, and I quite enjoyed it and that was great;*
– *And... its brought people to know (town) and its been good for the traders of (town) and its been good for the village, it's good for the people to look round;*
– *They come back and walk round, and go for walks, and experience things that they don't usually see.*

Community spirit shines throughout. Involving the villagers, especially the children, is a key activity:

– *we try where possible to involve the children, the schools, the floats. Over the years we have tried different types of encouragement for the children;*
– *they made their own banners, the 2 principal schools made massive banners which they themselves have carried;*
– *we more often than not have a presentation, the best banner or the best float or the best child, all this to create encouragement;*
– *The end of the procession was at xxx Court... The advantage of finishing in xxxx Court is that xxx Court is an old folks home. So all the old people that are in there, that aren't able to get round the village, see the final procession arriving at their front door if you like. And we entertain the people, the residents;*
– *like C2 said it is important to remember, that there is quite a lot of old people in (town) and in the sheltered accommodation in xxxx Courts, and it's a real treat for them cos people that are not good mobility wise can just look out of the window and feel part of the day;*
– *To try and encourage tourism, to try to bring people out of their shells, and to try to bring other interest;*
– *I think I came along about 2002-2003 I think, I work in the village, I spent all my life in the village and I have always felt it is important to give something back to the village;*
– *we appeal every year for various organisations to come along;*
– *it isn't about making money, it's about making friends;*
– *Once people take you into their hearts, they do care and it is quite a tight community;*
– *it is a community day, very much part of the community.*

Hegemony is important, as the need to openly manage considerable sums of money is one driver of it. Interviewees seem to take leading roles for a few years, then move on but remain involved:

– *I've been involved for, this is my 3rd year... - actually I have been involved with 2 C Days. The 2008 and the 2009 C Day, so I'm now involved with my 3rd cycle, working towards the 2010 Day;*
– *...was talking about wanting to pull back from the Chairperson role, because he'd been the chair for many years;*
– *We are not very formal. I try and to inject my own element of formality to it, I try and find roles, in a much more formal way than we used to. It used to be a lot more ad-hoc I think;*

- *I was persuaded to take on the Chair's role, but the condition I attached to that was give me a year to shadow, and understand what's involved;*
- *last year I took a bit more of an active role, chairing meetings and so on, but only as a sort of shadow Chair, a Vice-Chair;*
- *And at that time we introduced for the first time the idea of Vice positions;*
- *A Vice treasurer and a Vice Chair, as a sort of shadowing and as a support, for the main committee members;*
- *In terms of knowledge transfer I suppose I was keen to bring my knowledge to the committee, that was one of my own... desires, you know;*
- *One of the things about the committee at the moment its ...there are people like yourself (C4) who have been involved for years, (recollections of older participants);*
- *She did it for years... And P is giving up the craft fair this year, he is pulling back, he has given a lot to it over the years... That's one of our issues at the moment, finding someone, who is willing, because the Craft Fair is quite a big job, requires a lot of coordination, and finding someone to take it on, it's a big job.*

Fundraising is clearly important, with the money immediately recycled:
- *there are lots of tensions in the Committee though, over should we make a profit or not...Because the newer members, me included would like to see us making money;*
- *We almost broke even, which is our main goal in life, to break even;*
- *I think if we made money I think we could use that money for the community good, and we could literally donate chunks of that money to other associations in the area.*

Although leadership is evident, people also feel empowered and bring their own skills into the CoP. There is evidence of a move from LPP to maturity, coaching and, in some cases scaffolding, as people move on with their new skills, or create something similar in their own community (or country- the Romanian band). Tacit learning is more prevalent than explicit. There is lots of reflection and situated learning:
- *you find your own role, you come up with ideas, and go away and do it;*
- *I had to organize prizes for the prize draw, which were donated by local businesses, and mainly from the venues themselves;*
- *there has been a lot of learning involved on my part and its not been particularly easy;*
- *I was aware that as Chair I would ...end up having quite a bit of knowledge that is distributed amongst the committee, that no one person has it all together, which the Chair does. Usually it's the Chair that has that overview, and ...not many other people on the committee have the big picture in that way.* (2015 re-interview);
- *it's kind of been learning by asking what I need to ask, when I need to ask it. It's not been a very documented process;*
- *I've actually got a bag at home, of files. J gave me files, that had been at the office at the NT for years. P gave me his file when I took over the Chairperson role, and now I have P2's file;*

- *this year we had the wheelbarrow floats, we had them some years ago it didn't work quite as well as it did this year;*
- *we altered our timetable to fit in with the emergence of a boat coming from the other side of the canal tunnel ...But unfortunately we weren't able to engender sufficient people to go and look at the event, what was going on. Because people were too steeped in what was going on in the centre of (town);*
- *Romanian musicians came. They're wanting to do a Day there (in Romania).*

In summary therefore, the interviews demonstrate a clear motivation to provide altruistic help to their community.

C Interpretative Phenomenological Analysis Outcomes

An examination of the analysis from this community of practice showed that, for nearly 2 hours of interview and well over 11,000 words of transcript, plus a written note and use of their Facebook page, over several years, their website and other community websites, well over 400 "meaning units" were identified . Some are used above to illustrate the results text. When analysed "meaning units" were each in their own row but they are concatenated here to save space and add clarity.

As already stated, as a first stage of analysis of the "meaning units", the "initial thoughts" were noted. The commonest was "community", both in the context of creating a community of practice and in terms of supporting the village community. As part of this "internal knowledge transfer", was common, as people move on from key roles. It clearly includes LPP, and a transition to maturity via situated learning". The following table lists their occurrence and frequency. Because of the timescale of analysis, the terms are not always consistent between CoPs, but this is probably a benefit for IPA. The authors have used their judgement to group these terms as in the table below. The table 3 is indicative, it has no statistical value.

Table 3. Community of practice C, frequencies of initial thoughts

Initial Thought	Frequency of use	Notes
Community/ Community spirit	65	Clearly one of the leading comments! This is the reason why the "technical reason" for the community of practice features so heavily. It clearly drove motivation, situated learning, knowledge transfer and the need for the community of practice itself.
Motivation (to help others)	50	This was noted where a desire to help others was evident e.g. "To try and encourage tourism, to try to bring people out of their shells, and to try to bring other interest" (C2).
Reflection /Analysis/ Deep thought about	44	This suggests that the interviewee is thinking deeply about the community of practice and their experiences

Initial Thought	Frequency of use	Notes
issues		as part of it. It is associated with motivation and learning.
Situated Learning	43	Examples of people learning, inward knowledge transfer (not common), situated learning and sharing knowledge within their community of practice (very common).
Need for Group/ Community of Practice	23	This is noted where interviewee stated or discussed the need for sharing knowledge, experiences and ideas. Community spirit featured heavily. It is associated closely with situated learning and knowledge transfer, also with transitions from LPP to full, mature membership.
Knowledge sharing/ Transfer outward	20	Situated learning was acquired within then shared outside group.
Networking/ Socialization	12	The ability to share experiences, make friends with people in similar situations and generally have contact with the world is clearly present.
Need for Knowledge (inwards)/ Education/ Finding out	12	Clear comment about external knowledge coming into community of practice. So, knowledge transfer from external source.
Marketing/ Public Awareness	12	This reflects the desire to raise awareness of the festival and is often associated with motivation: "Publicity is really, really important to us".
Explanation/Storytelling/Clarification	11	This notes that the interviewee felt the need to explain/tell some part of the history or story behind their involvement. It possibly indicates motivation?
Reward	5	This was usually part of reflection.
Fundraising	8	Clearly a priority for the group: I think if we made money I think we could use that money for the community good.

Source: Authors' study.

C Interpretative Phenomenological Analysis Conclusions

The community of practice formed for technical reasons associated with community spirit. There is clear evidence of knowledge transfer, both inwards and outwards, of situated learning, likewise, and the motivation for this. Therefore study of this community of practice, via 5 interviews with 4 mature community of practice members, written notes, websites and 11,000 words of interview transcript, meets the objectives of the book: "What motivates individuals to join and take part in social enterprise, what behaviours do they exhibit, do they join or form groups that can be labelled as "communities of practice" and do they undertake and deliver situated learning, as part of a knowledge transfer process". (From Chapter 1, Introduction).

Motivation is clear, all interviewees joined and participate in the community of practice because of a desire to help the community. They demonstrated their ability to share what they had. So, knowledge transfer, within the group is demonstrated repeatedly. Most knowledge is aquired via situated learning, in the CoP and via their personal background. Situated learning from outside and used in the group was often seen. The generic analysis below builds on these points.

The next stage was to analyse the "emergent themes". They are tabulated at the end of this Chapter. The examples were very carefully selected, after extensive rereading of the transcripts and IPA tables. Immersion in the transcripts made them stand out.

The commonest "emergent theme" in the group was motivation to help others. This was evidenced by a desire to create a social good for others in the village community. This theme was followed by situated learning -knowledge transferred to the interviewee within the CoP itself, and created within it. Hegemony was noted fairly often and structure and seniority, or official status, with its associated power factors was stressed. Operationalization of knowledge was common, making it explicit to others as a transfer and coaching operation. It was sometimes about the operationalization of finance or structure -thus "fundraising" is a clear emergent theme and an "initial thought". However where fundraising is mentioned it is as a supporting tool, not a goal.

This is clearly an enterprise and an organisation. It was built to share knowledge but only raises and uses money to promote the festival. Recontextualization was often seen in the context of "how can this knowledge be used to help others create activities" Reflection and emergence were important, and in practice, indistinguishable from coaching and observation. The data was cautiously mined for the further analysis undertaken, especially the comparisons across groups and countries.

The key conclusion was stated by all, in different words: *"We are creating a village community for generations to come"*.

C Organisation - Summary

There is clear evidence of knowledge transfer into and out of, plus situated learning occurring in this community of practice. There are clear knowledge management processes. Knowledge of how the CoP works is shared, although often tacitly rather than explicitly. Knowledge was brought in from outside and via internal situated learning, was shared, then transferred into the group (internalization) and shared on to other members (socialization). After that the knowledge was usually combined with personal experiences and other tacit learning, and then externalized. There are many examples of aspects of learning occurring, as already described in the methodology of research. Examples of situated learning occurring include all the tabulated "labels", but the highest frequency goes to: motivation to create a village community, and as part of this, operationalization. Less often seen are seen aspects of recontextualization and only one of fading (the Romanian group). Scaffolding and hegemony exist, with clear recognition of a need to manage considerable sums of money.

This has to be done legally, and Health and Safety were also mentioned. Fundraising was clearly a priority, but only insofar as its requirement for funding the event.

4.4 The V Community of Practice (PL)

V Introduction

The V group was formed in 2010 to work for animals and draw consumers attention to their plight. The members are vegans, who actively promote public perception of animals rights and, consequently, a change to their fate. The main purposes of their activities are: to educate adults and children and young people to respect the rights of animals (especially livestock animals), to promote a plant-based (vegan) diet and a consciousness about meat consumption – so a re-shaping of this aspect of economic reality, with a particular focus on meat animals.

Their main activities include organizing street happenings, film screenings, and workshops for children and young adults. All these events seek to stimulate these younger audiences to gain respect for animals, and encourage them to try vegan food. The group organizes many regular activities, including amongst others: Empathic education at schools, circus days without animals, a week of veganism or a week of vegetarianism, a no fur day, and also actions popularizing the vegan diet in cafes and restaurants in Silesia. They also organize a campaign promoting a plant-based diet.

The group started formally in 2013 as an association (a Polish legal form of organisation), but the group had worked together informally from 2010. The founders have extensive experience in other charitable activities. They previously were (and still are) members of some other well-known associations. They formed the vegan group to share experiences, methods and knowledge with the wider community and nowadays the group has around 20 members. thus creating a typical community of practice. The focus of their activity is the Silesia region, in Southern Poland, (PL), where the interviews were conducted.

V Process

The community of practice was identified via the Internet, and chosen randomly from a list of local Polish organisations which fulfilled the conditions of the sampling criteria. Three main members of the group were interviewed. They were all members of the V board and founders of this social organisation. The results were transcribed and analysed in depth using the IPA technique discussed earlier. The results were a total of 54 minutes of speech and 6500 words of transcription. A total of 198 "meaning units" were identified in the 3 transcripts and underlined in a table, as was done for all groups. Similarly, the initial thoughts and higher level emergent themes were added to each of the 3 interview tables.

V Discussion of Interpretative Phenomenological Analysis

"V" is clearly a community of practice, initially formed in 2010, but formally registered as an "association" in 2013. Analysis of the interview transcriptions demonstrate that the group is an organisation, as its priority is campaigning and knowledge transfer. Fundraising is secondary. The technical purpose of this group is to educate local and regional society to respect the rights of all animals, to promote vegan diets and a vegan lifestyle. This purpose and motivation unifies all the interviewees activity. Translated comments[41] include:

- _The main motivation from the very beginning, the main goal really (...) was to educate,_
- _inform consumers about how they can affect the fate of the animals (V1);_
- _And that really is the alternative, that it may be in the form of a vegan or vegetarian diet (V1);_
- _The goal was a real change, really reduce the amount of consumers who depend solely only on these animal products (V1);_
- _Because of their (author's note: animals) location in the industry, positioning them as just such beings who we can abuse, we use only their particular characteristics, e.g.: milk productivity, or efficiency in terms of eggs, makes them just things. They become just products, and we just had to show everyone that we do not agree to it (V2);_
- _Later, from this area of disagreement, such a question began to appear: actually why do people, knowing for example, that such things happen, they are acting in such a particular way, that they are still using these products? (V2);_
- _And after, however, many such things we have come to the conclusion that people do not know or just do not want to know, they close their eyes, so it is necessary for us to talk about them. We try to talk about it (V2);_
- _There are different motivations that led us to this, to take action to start actively doing something for animals. For example, I have a different internal imperative, I later rejected meat, later the idea was born to join actions (V3);_
- _And I think really people who are inside the V, each of them has their specific reasons why he/she wanted to join the action... (V3);_
- _For me, for example, the imperative is a consensus on doing no harm, no exploitation of the weak. It also somehow is psychologically ingrained in me (V3);_
- _Therefore, as if, at the beginning of the formation of the V as an informal group, our specific reasons joined us together to create in us some sense, a sense of mission and our desire to transfer our point of view to a wider audience (V3)._

The 3 interviewed members of the organisation state that they created it from scratch, but two of them were active members of other organisations, thus "fading" may be present. These members transferred some knowledge from other organisations, but then adapted it to new conditions, changing it from tacit to explicit. There are thus examples of situated learning and knowledge transfer - numerous quotes from two interviewees evidence this:

- _I have a slightly different experience than, I think, most of the members of the association, because I worked previously for the Foundation xxx, so in another organisation, in which I really gained a lot of experience (V1);_

---

[41] See the brief note in the methodology chapter, and the extended section in the literature chapter for details of the translation process and its consequences.

- *Although the profile was different, it is really after the first year of work in the other foundation we started, the V initiatives, <u>on the basis of what was already in our head, that we knew how to more or less organize events, happenings, how to write press releases, invite the media, how to talk to them and we started to create from it</u> (V1);*
- *Actually <u>I'm connected with animals from childhood</u> and they were farm animals, horses. (V2);*
- *Due to the fact that most of these horses we rode and which were our companions, <u>in the moment they ceased to be usable horses, get older, however, they went to the slaughterhouse,</u> they have been sold to the slaughterhouse (V2);*
- *<u>I got into this because of the subject of horse protection</u> and how to work for them. These were the 90's (V2);*
- *<u>I think we certainly use these experiences from previous places of employment</u>, well we are not teenagers, we are just a little bit older... (V2);*
- *Personally, <u>I use some experience that I gained in the company, which I previously worked for</u> in the position of manager. So here <u>all these management training courses are useful at this point, so to say, actually to keep for using in actions later</u> (V2);*
- *The same, <u>I work in the organisation K ..., I confess to this, I actually draw knowledge from them. I draw a lot of knowledge from them - and such organisational methods</u> (V2).*

The knowledge in this vegan organisation was and still is both implicit and tacit. In the interviewees pronouncements it is clearly visible that they are searching for new knowledge (books, papers, films, meetings with other organisations etc.), undertaking active learning, and, again, transferring their knowledge and experience between people. It is clearly a manifestation of situated learning and knowledge transfer both between members and into them from outside:

- *While generally it seems to me all the time that there is a lot of work, such as our own, <u>on the basis that - we learn from our mistakes</u> (V1);*
- *The work of non-governmental organisation is not just that we have a mission in our heads and on this we rely, because <u>if we will not learn how to operate, how to speak to different audiences, and we will not be good at it, these actions may be not effective</u> (V1);*
- *So, <u>a nice phenomenon is also the fact that this movement educates itself</u> (V1);*
- *I am simply saying: <u>we read and we train ourselves</u> (V2);*
- *<u>It is necessary to look for inspiration in other people, because we really learn from each other</u> (V2);*
- *I guess there are not knowledge or scientific studies, of course, <u>there are some articles, you can observe other organisations, but the organisations, e.g. in Poland, acting on this area of activity, all more or less are on the same level</u> (V3);*
- *It looks at the moment so that <u>if an idea to spread our actions comes to our mind, the same idea appears elsewhere in Poland, and often simultaneously</u> (V3);*

– *I really think (...) that the persons acting (simultaneously - author's note) in other organisations operating on a larger scale derive to some publications in other fields, eg. business, in order to implement these findings (V3);*
– *Or they want, generally speaking, to enjoy the experience of others, from other sectors, in other fields, to implement them in the activities of our organisation (V3);*
– *So, organisations operating in Polish in the pro animal activity come together to exchange experiences (V3).*

The organisation's activity clearly evolved from a group of quite radical vegan people, to create a community of practice, which promotes a gradual change in eating habits. This is particularly evident in V1's statements. Initially they can accept other, less extreme forms of diet (vegetarian) and other forms of care for the animals' fate. It shows, how the organisation changes and adapts to the environment - so uses scaffolding ideas and arguments, and operationalization processes:

– *In fact, consumers - even those who go vegan or vegetarian, but who, for example, limit their intake of eggs, chicken, or even resign from these products actually reduce the demand and the production. It is simply logical (V1);*
– *We initially were also very, very radical, on the basis of only vegan, and how not to - there are no any conversation (V1);*
– *But at the time when (...) we want to achieve something, we have to speak to the whole society, not to a narrow audience that understands the message "go vegan", that is at once radically change. This (...) fraction that will change is really small in the relation to the whole society" (V1);*
– *We are already basically a year in this stage of modification and, so, the change. If something does not work, you have to simply change it and you need to do it differently, because perhaps some forms of action longer are simply no longer attractive, people need, the recipients need other things, so that we learn" (V1).*

Also, internal managerial aspects of the organisation are subject to processes of hegemonic change. The organisation was at first informal, then became formal, and the number of members is still changing, but they are open to co-operation with people from outside. They also started looking for volunteers and have divided up their work on projects. This is a "nimble organisation" and all these processes are clear evidence of situated learning having occurred, with aspects such as recontextualization and modeling. The quotes below demonstrate this:

– *We have a formal association, it is not that things aren't happening around the association, because there are a lot of people who, for example, come and go, it is rotational (V1);*
– *While we have a bunch of people, which are around the association, and it happens so often that those people, who are not formally members, are more active than those which are formal members (V1);*

- *(...) we have volunteers. Yeah we have some young people who are interested in such activities, but more on the basis of such an emergency, because it really so far ... err ... I think that it is associated with an excess of things that we do and responsibilities (V1);*
- *If we want to have more volunteers, then we need ... this is probably a psychological approach; that you have to immediately give them something to realize, at once exploit them, because if you don't do this, and that is what we know from experience, their enthusiasm cools and just ends (V1);*
- *we started with 18 people in the association, now we are ... twenty. These changes occur, they are smooth, there are usually really a dozen people working (V2);*
- *We also want to start a group of volunteers in order to join these people strictly to conduct action, somewhere outside, such ... happenings and other activities (V2);*
- *I think we formalized in a certain sense, therefore, to be able to act effectively as a formal group, however, it is more powerful than the informal group. Especially when it comes to the task of interventions, due to the fact that I like this type of activity (V2);*
- *When we are talking about direct contact and interventions, it gives me the room for manouver, to basically just writing a letter, writing an appeal, to interact with veterinary inspection, letters to the ministry. Formal organisations are treated quite differently (V2);*
- *That's why we were formalized, to have some more clout, to be an organisation that is considered more seriously (V3);*
- *We have a bit to adjust to the realities and when we are cool and do cool stuff, does not necessarily mean something for the official office, so as a formalized group we can more (V3).*

As a final point here, this community of practice has a clear leader. She has wide experience, gained in another organisation, and has completed training courses, which made it possible for her to effectively manage the organisation. The leader has a clear vision of the organisation, and uses a participative management style, which is quite democratic. It allowed her to form hegemonic relationships with co-workers and motivate them. These are typical features of co-operation in a community of practice through situated learning:

- *It is such a person, V1. She is the most involved and handles all the stuff, motivates people (V2);*
- *So in summing up I would say that being in a V... and our actions, or our motivating, leader .... In fact, we have a large autonomy, each of us doing so many as she/he can and as much as she/he wants (V2);*
- *Comparing those projects to vegan initiatives it can be seen that each group, however, needs a leader (V3);*
- *It is like the person managing a group, not a leader or president saying in a classic company or corporate sense of the word, just like hmmm ... charismatic leader (V3);*

– *There is a boundary to which, for example, the leader of the organisation is approaching and not being able to cross it, or rather do not want to cross it, the type of imposing the will by force on other members (V3);*
– *Ok, well, because it is, in some way, because the very idea of the first happenings came from me, from us, and then it somehow played. I think, due to the fact that I had an experience that I had gained in the previous organisation and why I wanted to somehow move them, but so that there are really a few people who actually are from the very beginning (V1);*
– *I think, managing an organisation... I have in mind something that if the element of coercion would come or mentally force methods - all the activities would came to nothing, or simply the organisation would fall apart. (V1).*

V Interpretative Phenomenological Analysis Outcomes

An examination of the interpretative phenomenological analysis from the "V" community of practice showed that, for 1.5 hours of interview and over 6,500 words of transcript, 198 "meaning units" were identified and transferred into table rows. Table 4 lists these meaning units' occurrence and frequency. It allows the authors the possibility to show how specific topics are prioritised and note conclusions. This is the process used throughout to obtain the preliminary results of IPA. The table demonstrates that the organisation is a community of practice and that situated learning takes place.

Table 4. Community of practice V, frequencies of initial thoughts

Initial Thought	Frequency of use	Notes
Motivation	36	This was noted, when interviewees demonstrated a strong willingness to act. Primary motivators are evident, affecting the interviewee from childhood: "It means to me just so I think from a child, I was more sensitive to the plight of animals" (V1) or "really I am connected with animals from a child. (…) I got to know the methods of dealing with horses (…) and then, I stopped to ride a horse"(V2). Secondary motivators are also evident, formed already during the activity in the organisation.
Knowledge/ Education	48	Clear information about looking for knowledge - inside and outside organisation (literature e.g. business books, other organisations, other sectors). Then knowledge transfer inside organisation (knowledge management) Clear comment about external knowledge coming into Community of Practice. So, Knowledge Transfer from external source.
Learning/ Organisational learning	9	This suggests that the interviewee is thinking deeply about the community of practice and their experiences

Initial Thought	Frequency of use	Notes
		as part of it. It is associated with motivation and learning.
Actions/ Activity	50	Frequently occurring word, which is a manifestation of the activity of members of the organisation, readiness to act fast. Reactivity to the needs and problems that arise in the environment.
Change	24	Change of people' awareness (consciousness), behaviour, animal treatment. Expected diametrical change since it affects the basic things - dietary habits. Also the Maslow hierarchy can be seen.
Effects of the action	8	Participants of interviews rarely mentioned effects or outcomes. Participants of interviews rarely talked about the effects, probably due to the difficult area of operation, small size of the organisation and short time of its functioning.

Source: Authors' study.

V Interpretative Phenomenological Analysis Conclusions

The V community of practice was formed for the promotion of a vegan and vegetarian style of life, and taking care of animals, especially farm animals. The organisation has existed since 2010 informally and from 2013 as a formal association. The interpretative phenomenological analysis shows clear evidence of knowledge transfer, both inwards and outwards, of situated learning and motivation. There is evidence that it is an organisation "in progress", growing and forming, undertaking organisational modeling, likewise "building scaffolding" - in terms of the concept, the scope of activity and organisational structure.

The CoP has a clear leader, who is well prepared to manage the organisation, has a wealth of experience necessary to perform such a function. Both the leader and other mature community of practice members constantly are developing the knowledge required for effective social activity. Then this knowledge becomes subject to the processes of transfer and dissemination. The emergent themes are tabulated at the end of this chapter.

V Organisation - Summary

There is clear evidence of situated learning occurring in this community of practice. There are clear knowledge management processes. The organisation members utilize external sources of knowledge, then transfer it into the group (internalization) and share it with other members (socialization). After that the knowledge is usually combined with personal experiences and other tacit learning, and then externalized. There are many examples of aspects of learning occurring, as already described in the methodology of research. Examples of situated learning occurring include all the tabulated "labels", but the highest frequency goes to: motivation, observation, coaching, modeling, scaffolding and hegemony.

Less often seen are seen aspects of recontextualization, operationalization, fading[42] and emergence. Fundraising, although clearly present, is not a key part of the activities of this organisation, but is subservient to its needs.

Community of practice "V" was formed and developed to campaign for a change of society, in respect to animal consumption for food and related eating habits such as dairy produce. They address their activities especially to young people, in schools, organizing tasting sessions of vegan food, promoting vegan food in restaurants and taking part in protests. Many restaurants in Silesia have placed such meals on the menu and received a special certificate from this organisation.

The organisation is local and wants to remain so. They try to gain funds from grants, but do not foresee this as a way to lead gainful activity. This organisation meets all criteria for a community of practice, functioning and managed as a social enterprise, but probably will still remain in this second stage of development, as there is no evidence that finance and employment will become important.

4.5 The M Community of Practice (PL)

The M group was formed in 2007 to conduct charitable activities for the benefit of pupils in an orphanage in Silesia. The group members are mostly motorcyclists, who actively promote their style of life. They chose one orphanage to make their assistance significant and comprehensive. The most characteristic manifestation of their activity is the collection of gifts on St. Nicholas's day (A significant Polish festival). So on 6th December each year, they organize a spectacular ride, on their motorcycles, dressed in Santa Claus outfits. They ride to the orphanage, where they hand out gifts. The Christmas gifts are not randomly chosen, earlier a campaign "letter to St. Nicholas" was organized, and so the gifts are carefully chosen as the answer to childhood dreams. Over time, their activities have evolved further, into year-round support for this children's home. Some other activities create better and more equal opportunities for the children who are fostered in this house.

Thus, the main purposes of their activities are all connected with helping children, they include: actions for the pupils orphanage in Silesia, activities for the protection of children's rights, supporting equal opportunities for foster children from educational - care facilities, and managing a charity for these objectives. However, in addition to these activities a second role in the organisation is also aimed at the dissemination of information and support for motorcycle use and tourism (especially among people with disabilities), promotion of automotive history, care and protection of historic vehicles, actions on public order and safety, (especially in traffic) and promoting knowledge among the public and automotive culture.

The main activities for children, are: fundraising, happenings connected to St. Nicolas Day, buying gifts for children and items needed to help self-empowerment of the people leaving the orphanage, and also supplying the orphanage with necessary items and utensils.

---

[42] Although the V association was a „fade" from another group

The organisation started formally in 2012 as an association (a Polish legal form), but the group had worked informally together from 2007, in cooperation with other associations. The founders of the group had not had other direct experiences in charitable activities. However the idea started via knowledge of similar organisations in Pomerania (PL), and the process of formalization was supported by another organisation, which focused on motorcyclists in Silesia. This limited acquired knowledge, however, was only the beginning of their own creativity, which allowed them to fit their activities to the specific needs of the local community. So, they formed the group to share experiences, methods and knowledge with the wider community.

Now (2017) the group has around 30 members and is a typical community of practice acting as a social enterprise and also as an organisation (using the definitions discussed earlier in this book). There are also around 30 other informal members who are active, but don't want be official members of the association. The board of the organisation has agreed to this form of participation. The main area of their activity is South Silesia and particularly the main city of this sub region, with a population of a little under 200,000.

M Process

The community of practice was chosen randomly from a list of organisations which fulfilled the sampling criteria. Initially they were identified as operating in a recreational area of Silesia, where they have their headquarters. Four main members of the group were interviewed, but at the express request of the respondents, the interview was conducted collectively. One interviewee (M1) is a president of the association, two persons are members from the beginning of the organisation (M2,M3) and M4 joined later. The main focus of the interview is M1's story, supported by the other participants of the conversation. However, they each also told some short stories, which demonstrated their motivation for undertaking these charitable activities, how they were involved in the work of the organisation, and how situated learning and knowledge transfer occurred.

The results of this group interview were transcribed and analysed in depth using the interpretative phenomenological analysis technique already covered. The outcome was 44 minutes of speech and 6050 words of transcription. 234 "meaning units" were identified in the collective transcript and these were underlined in the table. Then initial thoughts and higher level emergent themes were added to the IPA table. An untranslated IPA table is shown, in the appendix.

M Discussion of Interpretative Phenomenological Analysis

The transcription analysis demonstrates that the M organisation is a community of practice, initially formed in 2007, but formally registered in 2012. Analysis of the interview transcriptions demonstrate that the group is an enterprise, as defined earlier. The technical purpose of this group is support for foster children from an orphanage in Silesia. The co-operation is complex because, although they only support one orphanage, their actions include not only helping children, but also the institution itself. Membership fees and charity tributes are spent not only for St. Nicolas' gifts, but also goods essential for the functioning of the home and support for young people leaving home for self-empowerment. The purpose and motivation is clearly visible in numerous interviewees' statements[43]:

— *It started from our friendship, we have known each other for 10 years (hopefully soon to be 25 years, haha) and <u>really the desire to organize ourselves comes from the willingness of the meeting to help</u> (M1;)*

— *During this collection (for charity), because I am an outspoken person, you totally don't look at it in a way that you are engaging strangers, <u>for me personally it is sensational fun, where I can help, I meet people I like, I know</u> (M2);*

— *I have also another...* (motivation – author's note), *I was a volunteer for this orphanage years ago (...). Well, unfortunately... but mentally I did not get along with this too long... <u>For me as a woman it was a tragedy for these children</u> and at the time you wanted to have all these children and give them the home, and it is physically impossible to do (M2);*

— *I think there are two issues. One is selfishness, egoism on the principle that <u>I'm doing this for myself in a little bit some parts, knowing that I help someone I feel better</u> (M4);*

— *Just the idea appears: <u>we do something and we do it now</u>. Sometimes it comes out better, sometimes worse, but we do it, and the time to verify it is later. <u>So somehow I did not have to be specially encouraged to, to take part in it</u> (M4);*

— *I saw these children, I saw their smiles, some ....err crying and <u>it affected me so, it stated that, if I can help someone, why not</u>. It works in this way (M4);*

— *It cannot be forgotten and <u>you can't stop doing it, as you already have seen it</u>...(M2);*

— *<u>We became friends with these children</u> (M1);*

— *Well... <u>a noble aim, because it was at once, we were going to orphanages</u> (M3).*

There are also visible motivations related to the fact of being a motorcyclist, belonging to such a group and changing the stereotypes about motorcyclist:

— *<u>The idea that motorcyclists</u>... It started with just an idea that motorcyclists take out their motorcycles on December 6, which is already like a sensation, because normally the bikes are already "seasoned"* (authors note - put away for the winter), *yes?(M1);*

— *Such <u>an initiative of the motorists</u>, those with a little gasoline circulating in their veins - just for kids (M1);*

— *<u>The idea is that motorcyclists make up a social enclave,</u> you could compare it to a criminal organisation, maybe just in terms of comparison, but when it comes with some... err combination of this case (M4);*

— *<u>Motorcycles unite us</u> and it is generally recognized that in this environment there is no such thing that you have to motivate someone to do something (M4);*

— *We know what is the opinion of some riders. <u>That's all last till the opinion about motorcyclists thaws</u> (authors note "an icebreaker), that the motorcyclist is also a man (M1);*

---

[43] See the brief note in the methodology chapter, and the extended section in the literature chapter for details of the translation process and its consequences.

– We heard e.g. <u>they did not like motorcyclists, but when they hear what purpose we serve</u>... (M2).

The originator of the organisation and also the leader (M1), by her attitude motivates others to act. There is clear evidence of motivating, coaching and emergence. Quotes from all interviewed evidence this:

– In my case it began with <u>M1's call</u>...(M2);

– <u>I would have done a lot for her</u>, and actually it was a major impetus that pushed me to do this (M2);

– <u>Behind her you go in the "darkness"!</u> (M3);

– With me actually with my motivation it was ...err <u>M1 made the call</u>: "I need help – I need someone", it was the main impetus, when I can I do not wonder uh, there wasn't another motivation...(M3);

– <u>The second motivator was that M1 just called me</u>.... There was a spontaneous trip of the M people, but not in the winter, in the summer, we went there with pampers nappies and I simply did it...(M4);

– <u>M1 for us is a trusted person, she does not need to motivate us to</u>... (M4).

The M community of practice has undergone a full evolutionary cycle: from a spontaneous initiative of several motorcyclists, to a well-organized association. Their activity has become more purposeful. The growth of the organisation, however, was controlled to ensure that their actions were effective. These facts are clear evidence of LPP and situated learning occurring, with aspects such as recontextualization, operationalization, scaffolding and modeling present. The quotes below demonstrate this:

– <u>It began with a spontaneous meeting of 80 riders</u> with bags of sweets in their backpacks (M1) <u>Then it turned up in</u>... in a more organized structure, which created itself (M1);

– <u>Mainly desirability - more desirability of these gifts</u> (...), not just sweets (M2);

– <u>For 4 years we are practicing this form, we get along with the teachers</u> and they are asking the kids to write letters to Santa Claus and we collect those letters and prepare our 26-27 gifts (M1);

– <u>And those our gifts turned into such year-round assistance for this house</u> (...), the day of the child, help for children... (M1);

– <u>Then we came up with fund-raising</u>, so we had to legitimize it in the legal office (M1);

– <u>We wanted to do it on our account</u> , so we set up an association, and everything that came naturally (M1);

– We have in our statute this orphanage and the helping of children who as adults come out of it, and they want to become independent. Also, <u>they can take some help from us, so it went a step further</u> (M1);

– <u>So it is growing and I have hope that it will strongly evolve</u>, just... mmm due to the fact that the range of people associated with motorcycles expands, so new ideas... (M4);

– <u>It began with sweets in backpacks, and now they are already personal gifts for children</u>

*and vacuum cleaners, furniture, these are computers, detergents, diapers, money, so....
mmm it is like the snowball (M4);*

- *We cannot "catch all magpies by the tail"* (Authors' note - a Polish expression, similar to "a tiger by the tail"), *we have to look logically and evaluate our capabilities and options, so that later we will be able to fulfil this (M1);*
- *I have that consciousness of where are our boundaries, that hey, do not go too far, so that we can't do this (M1);*
- *It is also important for the children's home. Systematic and continuous acquaintance (M1).*
- *Certainly professionalization of action... (M4);*
- *Since we have created their own association and now we have already 6 years of experience - it's just we some things already learned and they just not go automatically, but we already know how to organize them without chaos (M1).*

This community of practise clearly operates as an open organisation. They are happy to co-operate with people from outside. This has created an increase in the number of active participants. The general idea is that not everybody have to become a member of the association, to function as a resource for it. These quotes evidence this well:

- *Membership fees about 30, but it isn't necessary be a member of the association to work (M1);*
- *Not everyone has to be a member of the association to act in our campaign, or go with us, I do not know - if they are there, for the children, on the occasion of Children's Day (M1);*
- *There are people who do not want to formally associate, I absolutely understand, we created the association in order to be legally easier(M1);*
- *We do not "close the road" to those who are not in our association, or do not have a motorcycle. Because it is absolutely not necessary, as long as they bother to help...(M1);*
- *Because it started with just the circle of those really tight friends and it has spread now with new friends (M2);*
- *Last year there were about 40, this year - I can confidently say - there are 60 people. Yes, there are people who simply I am able to call and go (M1);*
- *You know, the second thirty, it is not a group of close friends, but they are people, who I can count on, in this business. But the strict core was born out of a friendship, uh - that's true- from friendship (M1).*

This organisation co-operates with similar groups, and often it became a model for the formation of the next initiative. It also evidences the effectiveness of the their open strategy. Some of these other organisations were founded by them seceding from M, clear evidence for fading and operationalization. All these aspects are demonstrated in the following quotes:

- *Speaking honestly, <u>our group at some point broke into a few smaller ones</u>, because some motorcyclists, arrived there from C, Z, (Authors note - distant towns), and asked me, "and so many of us are here, why only one orphanage" And I say "selfishly", "I want to do this, and if you do not want this you can organize themselves in your own way - you have a free hand" (M1);*
- *<u>This action somewhat shattered us</u>, that e.g. there are friends from Z, who participate in our events and we are at their (...), <u>but we arrange different dates</u> (M1);*
- *<u>There is no competition between us</u> (M2);*
- *<u>Competition cannot exists in something that</u>, I do so I understand, absolutely, that <u>is the help to others</u> (M1);*
- *<u>I told them to give me their data when they go</u>, that we may not imposed (clash), to give us information on Facebook, when you do something and when we do (M1).*

The M community of practice largely bears the characteristics of a social enterprise, as defined for this book. The organisation is using a strategy of fundraising and subsequent action (as indicated above). The group is actively raising money and managing its budget. The funds are collected from association members' contributions, donations and sponsors. Then the funds are spent on ongoing support of the children's home, but they also keep a reserve for sudden needs of children. There is also clear evidence for scaffolding and operationalization:

- *<u>This year we collected over 20,000 PLN</u> (Authors note - 4,000 pounds in UK money - but it goes at least 3 times as far in Poland), and it is already an amount with which you can do something useful (M1);*
- *Since <u>we created the association we established a joining fee</u> of 60 PLN per year, but this contribution is like <u>for statutory purposes</u> (M1);*
- *<u>Really, we assume no cost of the organisation, because we all do it as non-profit</u>, so we need the consent of the (legal) office, for which we pay, a purchase of the tax stamp for things to do (legal) acknowledgments (M1);*
- *So, now as an association, <u>we can legitimately look for sponsors</u> ...(M1);*
- *Even t-shirts, which we need for fundraising (...), <u>I also found sponsors</u>, so now as an association we can legitimately seek sponsors...(M1);*
- *<u>Accountant also is non-profit, it is an accounting office, they also do it charitably</u> (M1);*
- *<u>During the year we do not have to spend all the money</u>. Because no one knows what will be extra necessary in a given year, because <u>there may be some unpleasant fortuitous incidents</u>, which will have to be realized. It will be something we need to buy for child, and <u>we need to have the money, purposeful</u> (M2);*
- *In an exceptional situations (author's note) <u>we are now the only donors currently...</u> (M1).*

M members promote their activity - they have created a logo, T-shirts, and a website. They use Facebook, smartphones for publicity and to contact each other. Most importantly, these methods are effective, because the number of active members and related persons is growing, through a "snowball effect". There are also proofs of knowledge transfer, scaffolding, modeling and operationalization:

- *(...) t-shirts, which we need for fundraising (...) <u>we want our image cool</u> and want people to join up to the fact that <u>we have a logo, that somehow we stand out</u> (M1);*
- *<u>This also that I found sponsors</u> (M1)* - advertised on T-shirts (authors' note);
- *Not without significance is the social networking, Facebook that it's <u>key important in informing people about our movements</u> (M1);*
- *All the time <u>there are plenty of people who are just using Facebook text messages, phones.</u> They are able to collect and just to visit the kids and we can take them to…(M1);*
- *But now <u>it's like… snowballing, it gained momentum and it is to such effect that people just write to me on Facebook, call and offer their help</u> (M1);*
- *There are also the <u>motorcycle forums, which also play a very big role, because you can toss information into topics</u> (...) on various events, technical things, about motorcycles…(M1);*
- *This is … <u>this marketing is released into the ether somewhere simply brings profits.</u> (M4);*
- *<u>Logo does not change, we always have the target, the same banner</u>, only the year is changing and people already remember it (M2);*
- *At the moment <u>it is on the Internet</u>, in the pictures how we are reaching… (authors note) the orphanage with gifts (M2);*
- *Organizing all this fundraising <u>requires promoting this and in the media, leaflets and these… banners</u>, requires us to grasp this in a hypermarket G…, which cooperates with us (M4);*
- *So it was evident, it was incredibly visible, because in the past, …4 or 5 years ago, we had to ask Radio B to come. Later, in the next year, <u>a journalist arrived by himself, and this year too. Actually, besides the press release, which was sent to various radio stations …we did not have to do anything</u> (M1).*

This organisation created a managerial structure based on functional divisions, which resulted in emergence of roles for leading members. Internally, managerial aspects of the organisation are subject to processes of change. This is also a "nimble organisation" and all these facts clearly evidence situated learning aspects: recontextualization, modeling and operationalization. It is clear that M1 is the undisputed leader. She started the activity, she focused their help on the one orphanage, to make it fully supported and comprehensive. However, it is a fully democratic style of management. M1 coordinates all activities in the organisation, cares about publicity and "determines strategic direction". It can be seen in the interview transcription: her statements are concrete and multi-thematic. These facts demonstrate other aspects of situated learning: emergence, hegemony, coaching and scaffolding:

- *Err, <u>I have to determine the direction</u> (M1);*
- *So, it's like <u>the track coordination and I play this role…</u> (M1);*

- _I'm more suited to spread the information_ or to send text messages by Facebook, email and to collect it all in the "pile" (M1);
- _I am for the interpersonal contacts and to join it physically_... (M1);
- _We also share ideas_, it is not that only M1 ... (M2);
- Of course, _this is not absolute authority_ (M1);
- _The division of responsibilities as in any organisation_ (M4);
- Well, _It must be one person, of course, who will manage all this_... (M3);
- I feel that _I'm more the person to spread information_. While the ideas, for aid, it is known, we share ideas, how to help the child's home (M1);
- _Everyone has the opportunity to submit a new idea_ (M1);
- _We see each other very often_ ...(M1);
- In this group of stable people, who have been cooperating for long time, _the tasks are divided_ (M2);
- R.W is _the most important person, who coordinates all official matters_, in the city council, important matters we need (M1).

M Interpretative Phenomenological Analysis Outcomes

An examination of the interpretative phenomenological analysis from the M community of practice showed that, for 44 minutes of interview and over 6000 words of transcript, 234 "meaning units" were identified in the table rows. Table 2 lists these meaning units' occurrence and frequency. It shows how some topics are repetitive and allows us to note conclusions and obtain preliminary results from the IPA. The aim herein is to evidence that the M organisation is a community of practice, its members are motivated, and that situated learning takes place.

Table 5. Community of practice M, frequencies of initial thoughts

Initial Thought	Frequency of use	Notes
Action, operation, activity	26	Frequently occurring words, which demonstrate the activity of members of the organisation, their readiness to act fast. Shows reactivity to the needs and problems that arise in the environment. For example: "Now these are already registered gifts for children: vacuum cleaners, furniture, computers (...)".
Fundraising/ Money	9	E.g.: "This year we collected over 20,000 PLN (...)".
Motivation	24	This was noted, when interviewees demonstrated a strong willingness to act. They often mentioned their motivation for grief, and sorrow caused by the children' situation: "We collect here to buy a gift for children, who have no parents".
Initiative, idea	15	Frequently occurred words, which demonstrate high activity and helpfulness: "Everyone has the opportunity to submit a new idea".

Initial Thought	Frequency of use	Notes
Relationship, cooperation	12	This is noted where interviewees stated or discussed the need for cooperation with other similar organisations: " I told them to give me the data when they go, that we may not imposed (…) "There is no competition between us".
Communi-cation, contact, media	11	Interviewees often referred to the aspects of communication, using Internet, Facebook, radio and outdoor marketing to contact inside and outside the community. Comments like: "This marketing is released into the ether somewhere simply brings profits".
Knowledge/ Knowledge transfer/	9	Clear pointers to looking for knowledge - inside and outside the organisation, and also processes of transferring it and learning: "Since we have created their own association and now we have already 6 years of the experience – it's just we some things already learned (…) we already know how to organize it without chaos". These aspects are reported in this organisation rarely, because the basis of the activity is comparatively simpler.
Organisatio-nal learning	5	"We some things already learned and (…) we know how to organize it without the chaos".
Enlargement / Develop-ment/ Evolution	9	The ability to develop, change and adapt: "And now it's working like a snowball, because it began to simply accelerate" "At some point we wanted to do it on our account , so we set up an association".
Leader	9	The organisation has a clear leader: "It must be one person, of course, who will manage all this". "I am for the interpersonal contacts and to join it physically..".
Innovation/ Creativity/ Invention	8	Statements related to these initiatives, which are novelty, innovation, as a results of creativity and invention: "I just came up with a children's home, I searched the Internet".
Coordination / Distribution of tasks	7	The leader carry out the management functions, typical for social enterprises: "I have to determine the direction, (…) the tasks are divided".
Purpose	6	Some statements accentuated the desirability of action: "this month, when we collect donations, I collect so I reject all other plans, at this time it is the determinant of my life".
Experience	6	Statements related to motivation through experience: "It's like going (to be) easy for us, because we know how to do it".
Relation/ Friendship/ Meeting	6	This was noted, when interviewees stated or discussed the need for meetings, sharing ideas. Friendship was the initial base of the organisation.
Solidity	5	The next attribute of activity, related to complexity and all year support: "Those, our gifts have now turned into such year-round assistance for this house".
Difficulty/ problem/	5	These words were noted, when interviewees indicates limitations to their activity. Comments like: "We know what

Initial Thought	Frequency of use	Notes
limitation		is the opinion of some riders. It takes place before the opinion is changing, motorcyclist also a man. So sometimes it is the witch-hunt".
Effects/ effectiveness	3	Participants of interviews rarely mentioned about effects and effectiveness. Probably due to the difficulty of this area of operation and the very intangibility and elusiveness of their activity.
Complex/ continuation	3	This notes that the offered help is complex. The continuity of help is particularly important, when children are the recipients: "Systematic and continuous connections" with the orphanage.
Open organisation	3	An important aspect of cooperation. The organisation is open for people who want cooperate and help, even temporarily: "We do not close the road for those who are not in our association or do not have a motorcycle".

Source: Authors' study.

M Interpretative Phenomenological Analysis Conclusions

The M community of practice was formed to conduct charitable activities for the benefit of an orphanage in Silesia. Fundraising is a key role in this enterprise. The organisation has existed since 2007 as an informal group of friends, but in 2013 was registered as a (Polish legal structure) association. The most characteristic action initially was the collection of gifts for children, undertaken only on the day of St. Nicholas (6th December), but their activity quickly changed into year-round support for this house. The interpretative phenomenological analysis shows clear evidence of strong motivating, scaffolding and modeling.

The organisation has undergone a process of evolution, both institutional and ideological. Knowledge Transfer is directly represented in this organisation quite rarely, probably because the basis of the activity is comparatively simple. (In some ways this CoP operates in a very similar way to AA, in the next Chapter). However this organisation exhibits the characteristics typical of a social enterprise. They act within a structure based on functional divisions and have a well specified strategy. There is a clear leader, who coordinates their activity, cares about publicity and manages the organisation. The organisation effectively promotes its activity, actively raises money and manages its resultant budget. The idea of the organisation, its operating arrangements and the visible management processes determine the presence of all situated learning aspects in a community of practice operating mainly as a social enterprise.

M Organisation - Summary

Altruistic motivation is clearly the key to this group. The leadership of M1 shines through the transcript, and the comments by M2, 3 and 4 reflect this hegemony. There is also clear evidence of situated learning occurring in this community of practice, usually combined with personal experiences and other tacit learning, and then externalized. Comments about fragmentation and subsequent formation of similar groups in other geographical centres evidence this fading. Thus tacit knowledge becomes explicit. LPP becomes maturity, and the cycle continues. Although not as pronounced as in other groups, there are many examples of aspects of learning occurring, as already described in the methodology of research. Examples of situated learning occurring include all the tabulated "labels", but the highest frequency goes to: motivation, and hegemony. Fundraising is a key component of motivation. Less often seen are seen aspects of recontextualization, operationalization, fading and emergence. This is a function of the "loose but strategically controlled" group focus.

Community of practice "M" was formed and developed with the technical aim to support an orphanage in the city, and is made up primarily of motorcyclists. Their hobby, or interest, underpins the groups function. Their main focus is fundraising, with a secondary dimension of promoting motorcycling as an acceptable interest. The organisation is local and wants to remain so -this is evidenced by the fragmentation already mentioned. There is no real evidence of trying to gain funds from grants, but sponsorship and donations are mentioned often. This organisation meets all criteria for a community of practice, functioning and managed as a social enterprise, but probably will still remain in the second stage of development (see the literature review).

4.6 Emergent Outcomes from the Multiple Interview CoPs

Table 6 lists the emergent themes identified via multiple interviews, and examples the „meaning units" which stimulated their creation. It is not quantitative, but only provided as a summary of the similarities and differences that led to the categorization. The authors do not claim that these are the only categorisations that could fit here, often multiple categories are possible and were considered. However the authors assert that this is not a failing. Whether a statement reflects hegemony, operationalization, situated learning, or all of them, is largely irrelevant. What is important is that the statement was made, and, in the authors opinion worth stressing.

The labels initially used to summarize the emergent themes were: Rationale, Situated Learning (creation), Situated Learning (usage), Motivation (for, participation), Community of Practice (initial) creation, Community of Practice joining, Reward, Legitimate Peripheral Participation (LPP), Observation, Coaching, Scaffolding, Modeling, Fading, Reflection, Emergence, Recontextualization, Hegemony and Operationalization. These are discussed in table 13 (page 125-127). The labels are used in the following table, which gives extensive detail about the analyses of these 4 groups. The same analyses were undertaken for the next groups, reported in chapter 5, but they are not shown in as much detail as that would just duplicate the earlier texts.

Table 6. The emergent themes from the group interviews

Label	L Organisation (UK)	C Enterprise (UK)	V Organisation (PL)	M Enterprise (PL)
Motivation for CoP (Rationale)	It was first formed in order to give the chance for L sufferers to share their personal experiences and suffering... and to discuss about medicines and medical treatment... a sort of exchange of information and discussion time. (L1 written account)	The C Day started I think in the late 80's,(C2) and it's been good for the traders of (town) and it's been good for the village, it's good for the people (C4). I want the village to be a prosperous one, and I want the businesses to do well (C1).	...the main motivation from the very beginning, the main goal really ....was to educate, inform consumers about how they can affect the fate of the animals ..., the goal was (to achieve) a real change, really reduce the amount of consumers who depend solely only on these animal products. (V1)	I saw these children, I saw their smiles, some ...err crying and it affected me so, ...if I can help someone, why not. ...and really the desire to organize ourselves comes from the willingness of the meeting to help. (M1)
Motivation (Individual) Reward	And you just wish you could turn to somebody and gain some knowledge of how to make that persons' life a bit more liveable and help in any way you can. (L1)	I work in the village, I spent all my life in the village and I have always felt it is important to give something back to the village.(C3)	...because of their (authors' note: animals) location in the industry, just such beings who we can abuse, we use only their particular characteristics, e.g. milk productivity or efficiency in terms of eggs, makes them just things. (V2)	With me actually with my motivation it was ...err M1 made the call: "I need help – I need someone", it was the main impetus. (M3)
Creation of SL	I had no idea what was going to happen to me, I had no idea about L and had to find out everything from the rest. (L2)	I think we have learned as we have gone on, we have made mistakes. (C3)	If something does not work, you have to... change it and... do it differently, because perhaps some forms of action... are simply no longer attractive. (V1)	It began with a spontaneous meeting of 80 riders with bags of sweets in their backpacks. Then it turned up in ... in a more organized structure, which created itself. (M1)
Use of SL and from LPP to Maturity	It was a place for the L sufferers to actually sort of talk to other L sufferers to find out how they feel, what they went through.(L1) I have certainly learnt as I have gone along, by talking to people. (L3)	And at that time we introduced for the first time the idea of Vice positions, A Vice treasurer and a Vice Chair, as a sort of shadowing and as a support, for the main committee members. (C1)	We have volunteers. (...) then we need ...this is probably a psychological approach, that you have to immediately give them something to realize, at once exploit them, because if you don't do this, and that is what we know from experience, their enthusiasm cools and just ends. (V1)	We some things already learned and they just not go automatically, but we already know how to organize them without chaos. (M1)

Label	L Organisation (UK)	C Enterprise (UK)	V Organisation (PL)	M Enterprise (PL)
Observation	Having been put into the situation I didn't want to see anybody else in it. a lot of it was gained from actually, physically, seeing it myself, seeing my mum deteriorate as time went by. (L1)	One of the things about the committee at the moment its ...there are people like yourself (C4) who have been involved for years. (C1)	The work of non-governmental organisation is not just that we have a mission in our heads and on this we rely, because if we will not learn how to operate, how to speak to different audiences, and we will not be good at it, these actions may be not effective. (V1)	NOT SEEN
Coaching	It's not the theoretical, its more the physical, its more you know, sort of touching ...and more being with that person, listening to that person and spending you know, 24 hours a day, 7 days a week, with a person who was constantly in pain, feeding her medication, you know, you learn. You begin to learn. (L1)	In terms of knowledge transfer I suppose I was keen to bring my knowledge to the committee, that was one of my own... desires, you know. (C1)	It is such a person (leader), V1. She is the most involved and handles all the stuff, motivates people... It is like the person managing a group, not a leader or president saying in a classic company or corporate sense of the word, just like hmmm... charismatic leader.(V2)	We cannot "catch all magpies by the tail" (Authors note -a Polish expression, similar to "a tiger by the tail"), we have to look logically and evaluate our capabilities and options, so that later we will be able to fulfil this. (M1)
Scaffolding	I thought, these are the only people, the only people, who I can talk to, who have an inkling of what is happening to me. (L2)	Once people take you into their hearts, they do care and it is quite a tight community. (C4)	I think we certainly use these experiences from previous places of employment, well we are not teenagers, we are just a little bit older... (V2)	NOT SEEN

Label	L Organisation (UK)	C Enterprise (UK)	V Organisation (PL)	M Enterprise (PL)
Modeling	Reading on the net, and talking to somebody who's has the illness for now, 46 years is a different, different matter. (L3) ...to meet up with other people and see if we could find a bit more about it. (L4)	In terms of knowledge transfer I suppose I was keen to bring my knowledge to the committee, that was one of my own... desires, you know (C1) So, actually doing this, I think it actually helped my people management skills, if you like, a different kind of relationship, a sort of, voluntary working relationship. (C1 re-interview)	...so, a nice phenomenon is also the fact that this movement educates itself. (V1) ...we have come to the conclusion that people do not know or just do not want to know, they close their eyes, so it is necessary for us to talk about them. We try to talk about it. (V2)	Because it started with just the circle of those really tight friends and it has spread now with new friends. (M2)
Fading	I then went on the contacts course, learn t quite a lot from that, and then, err I'm now a contact, for anybody that wants to join. (L5)	Romanian musicians came. They're wanting to do a (Festival) day there (In Romania).(C4) It was a super day and the Romanian people really enjoyed themselves. So they decided to have a go back in their country (C2)	...it looks at the moment so that if an idea to spread our actions comes to our mind, the same idea appears elsewhere in Poland, and often simultaneously. (V3)	(…) our group at some point broke into a few smaller ones, because some motorcyclists, arrived there from (Authors note - distant towns), and asked me, "and so many of us are here, why only one orphanage" And I say "selfishly", "I want to do this, and if you do not want this you can organize themselves in your own way – free hand" (M1)
Reflection	If I had been diagnosed earlier I wouldn't have done all the things I did do (L5) I think that when you are diagnosed with something like that you don't know quite how your life is going to turn out, and that just turned my life upside down. (L2)	there has been a lot of learning involved on my part and it's not been particularly easy (C2) But unfortunately we weren't able to engender sufficient people to go and look at the event, what was going on. Because people were too steeped in what was going on in the centre of (town). (C2)	….actually why do people, knowing for example, that such things happen, they are acting in such a particular way, that they are still using these products? (V2) We initially were also very, very radical, on the basis of only vegan, and how not to – there are no any conversation. (V1)	. Competition cannot exists in something that, I do so I understand, absolutely, that is the help to others. (M1)

Label	L Organisation (UK)	C Enterprise (UK)	V Organisation (PL)	M Enterprise (PL)
Emergence and Fund-raising	We have been able to fund a, a L nurse, where and also, at one time, we also, had a L room, which I think we still have at xxx, where it was a place for L patients to go. (L1)	I think if we made money I think we could use that money for the community good, ...(C1) I see (it) personally as a chance to unite the village, (C2)	If something does not work, you have to ... change it and you need to do it differently, because perhaps some forms of action longer are simply no longer attractive, people need, the recipients need other things, so that we learn". (V1)	Not without significance is the social networking, Facebook that it's key important in informing people about our movements (M1)
Recontextu-alization	We started with, I think, 3 of us. and have gone on from there. (L3) ...the Contact thing, knowing that they got the desperation stage, just knowing there was someone you could chat to. (L3)	...you find your own role, you come up with ideas, and go away and do it. (C1) It's kind of been learning by asking what I need to ask, when I need to ask it. It's not been a very documented process. (C1)	But at the time when... we want to achieve something, we have to speak to the whole society, not to a narrow audience that understands the message "go vegan" (V1)	NOT SEEN
Hegemony	NOT AN EMERGENT THEME	I was aware that as Chair I would ...end up having quite a bit of knowledge that is distributed amongst the committee, that no one person has it all together, which the Chair does. Usually it's the Chair that has that overview, (C1 re-interview)	It is such a person (leader), V1. She is the most involved and handles all the stuff, motivates people. (V2) ...I think we formalized in a certain sense, therefore, to be able to act effectively as a formal group, however, it is more powerful than the informal group. (V2)	In this group of stable people, who have been cooperating for long time, the tasks are divided. (M2) Well, It must be one person, of course, who will manage all this...I have to determine the direction. (M1)
Operatio-nalization	And in my personal experience ....my mother was a sufferer, and seeing (her) go through life in absolute agony, day after day, seven hours a day-er 7 days a week, 24 hours a day is ...difficult,(L1)	I could always see this broader context of the local region, the community I lived in, and keeping it vibrant and um, err ...successful (C1). And we try to keep prices down on everything, because we appreciate if you have a family. (C2)	... volunteers, then we need ... this is probably a psychological approach; that you have to immediately give them something to realize, at once exploit them, because if you don't do this, and that is what we know from experience, their enthusiasm cools and just ends. (V1)	It's like going (to be) easy for us, because we know how to do it. Those, our gifts have now turned into such year-round assistance for this house. M1

Source: Authors' study.

Table 6 summarises the outcomes of this very detailed analysis, made via iterative IPA and extensive re-readings. It examples extracts of text from each of the 4 CoPs studied in this depth, and how the meaning units embedded in these phrases were classified by the authors. In every case the process of: meaning units, initial thoughts, emergent themes classification, was followed.

Chapter 4 has reported on the IPA outcomes, exampling groups studied in great depth via interviews with more than 3 people, to gain variability and breadth of perspective. Additionally, in 2 examples single interviews were repeated after several years. One interviewee also supplied a written account. It also shows how websites and newsletters were mined for contextual information. The people studied, in the UK and in Poland, all volunteered their time, and were passionate about their cause. Most stressed the need for their work, the commitment they made, and the sense of community engendered.

Chapter 5: Analysis Outcomes from Further Communities of Practice Interviews

These 6 sections each also address 1 /community of practice, but represented by fewer people. Sometimes shorter interviews were held. This is the only way they differ from the groups above. The interviews, transcriptions and analyses follow the same processes and are reported in the same style, but, to save space, less depth of explanation is given here. Their value is in that they expand considerably the breadth of this book, taking it to 10 communities of practice, and 31 interviewed persons. The depth of analysis was the same, and is held by the authors, but here only a brief outline of the process is included, and the discussion is restricted to key points. However the conclusions chapter 8 draws on all the material, in the same way as the preceding chapter 4, with its in-depth descriptions.

5.1 HH Community of Practice (UK)

HH Introduction and Process

This community of practice is the „Yorkshire Hash House Harriers". Like the „Yorkshire Air Ambulance" group, identification was not an issue for the interviewees. The „Hash House Harriers" is an international organisation. Formed well over 70 years ago it has groups worldwide. The „Hash" was a club, where it all started[44], there is no other connection. Usually groups form when people move and bring their tradition with them. Although international in scope, each „Hash" is fiercely local and independent. There are no international or nationally set rules, although there are traditions. Therefore the group studied here meets the criteria of an independent community of practice, not controlled by outside influences.

This group was studied via several interviews, and also extensive use of websites, Facebook pages, and published literature including newsletters. It is best described by a quote from one of the websites: *The World Harrier organisation is a loose association of friendly groups or clubs who practice the sport of hare and hounds. In this sport, there are hare(s) (a runner or runners) who lay a trail (usually cross-country) with various trail marking materials (like the toilet paper used in the Orlando picture below). The hares are then followed by the pack of hounds (other runners), a few minutes after the hares are off. The eventual goal of the hounds is to catch a hare before the trail is completed. It is quite fun, with the side effect that you may accidentally get into shape doing the sport. Some participants may run fast, others just jog and some groups permit walkers to negotiate the trail. They are loosely kept together in ability packs through the use of false trails and ingenious trail design (hopefully)....Most groups finish their runs with some social activity, song, refreshment and snacks or food[45].*

---

[44]„Hashing began in Kuala Lumpur, Malaysia, in 1938, when a group of British colonial officials and expatriates founded a running club called the Hash House Harriers." http://onin.com/hhh/hhhexpl.html, Accessed 10.6.2017

[45] http://www.worldharrierorganization.com/, Accessed 3 June 2017.

Another website (the infamous Wikipedia) describes it equally well: *The Hash House Harriers (abbreviated to HHH or H3, or referred to simply as hashing) is an international group of non-competitive running social clubs. An event organized by a club is known as a hash or hash run, with participants calling themselves hashers or hares and hounds*[46].

A further quote illustrates the technical purpose of the group:

- *The offbeat group prides itself on eccentric costumes and social activities often involving alcohol. The next time you're out for a run and you notice flour or chalk on the ground, it probably means you're fresh off the tracks of the Hash House Harriers. But this running group isn't like your traditional track-runs-twice-a-week, non-competitive running club. The Hash House Harriers has become an international phenomenon, growing to nearly 2,000 chapters across the globe in 1,304 cities and 185 countries. However, the message is the same in all languages* [47].

- *Famously known as "a drinking club with a running problem," the Hash House Harriers only has one requirement for membership - a sense of humour - as the offbeat group prides itself on eccentric costumes and social activities often involving alcohol* [48].

The „Yorkshire Hash House Harriers" is a community of practice formed around 30 years ago. Its website states: *The Yorkshire branch of the "Drinking Club with a Running Problem"...For the uninitiated "hashing" is trail based running (a game called "Hare and Hounds" for the oldies). Runners follow a trail laid in flour, chalk etc. It is non-competitive and in most cases (including YH3) is suitable for all ages and abilities. Trails consist of false trails, checkpoints, waiting points, etc. which occupy fitter runners and allow slower runners and walkers to catch up. Everyone should start and finish roughly at the same time, with the fitter possibly having gone twice as far!...Runs almost invariably start and finish at a pub. Join us for a run and a few drinks. All are very welcome. Just turn up, no need to forewarn us...* [49].

Interviews were held with 3 members, but mostly this section focuses on one interview, sufficient to illustrate the nature of the CoP. HH1 is male. He was interviewed in 2014. He has been an active community of practice member since the 1990s (20+ years at time of interview). The interview duration was 25 minutes. Over 150 "meaning units" were identified in the 2560 word transcript. Some "follow-up" discussions were not transcribed but notes were made at the time and these are incorporated where appropriate. The Facebook pages were also reviewed and material from these are incorporated where appropriate.

Discussion of HH Interpretative Phenomenological Analysis

The interviews were clearly illustrative of the interviewee's motivations and desire to be involved in a social group, which has as its technical purpose „having fun", and possibly

---

[46] https://en.wikipedia.org/wiki/Hash_House_Harriers, Accessed 3 June 2017.
[47] http://www.worldharrierorganization.com/, Accessed 3 June 2017.
[48] Ibidem.
[49] http://www.yorkshirehash.net/about.php, Accessed 3 June 2017.

exercise, but also has an occasional, secondary more serious, fundraising side. As such it is primarily an organisation.

A clear, but occasional, usually only once a year, secondary role is, however to fundraise to help others. The "meaning units" identified and other IPA outcomes, together with the supporting material provided, demonstrate that the community of practice is real and meets all the desired criteria, despite the limitations of only using interview data from 1 primary source, plus some website and Facebook content.

He states that he was recruited, and motivated to join the organisation, because of a personal work contact:

- *I changed departments at work, and met up with a new bunch of people, in the firm where I worked. One of my new associates was a very clever woman, in a senior role. I was a „lunchtime runner", one of a group that went out into the nearby roads and fields. She joined us and recruited me to the Hash;*
- *I went to a Sunday run (we always met outside a pub at 11AM), and loved it. It was informal, and everyone was really friendly. Ability didn't matter, although I ran marathons and fell races then, I felt no pressure and often walked round. It was great!*

He enjoyed telling the story, and quickly gave some examples of how he used learning from other situations to support the community of practice he joined. There is much evidence of motivation for his continuing membership, both from him and the others he describes.

- *Not long after I joined I got roped in to organizing a fun weekend event. The club organized events with the excuse of some sort of anniversary. There was an anniversary weekend coming up. It would be the 777th run that our club had organized. We had to use some spare farm buildings as dormitories, a stage for some events, a bar and showers etc.;*
- *Because I was an engineer I sorted all the wiring, lighting and stuff. I used to be a roadie for bands so knew how.*

This evidences a move from LPP to core membership. Other interview material, not evidenced here, also demonstrates the rapid transition to maturity. So, it is clear that he is motivated to use his knowledge and skills for the benefit of his new CoP. As he states, his relevant skills and knowledge were mainly implicit, gained earlier and held by him personally. Thus, when he joined the CoP and volunteered to help them in this area, he gained knowledge of their needs, via situated learning. His initial motivation is apparent and he clearly gained personally from membership:

- *After that weekend I became heavily involved very quickly. I set trails...umm, that means organized the runs, and found pubs to host our after run rituals, that sort of thing;*
- *I suppose I became fairly central within a year or so, I was surprised it wasn't cliquey - not like a lot of other groups I joined. I was invited onto the... organizing group? Within a year or so. We were not formal but had officers and stuff, to meet the legal requirements;*

74

- *It was great, we met once a week, Sunday or Monday night, and it sort of took over my life. I made a lot of new friends, and we still meet up, though I don't run any more.*

He clearly enjoyed sharing the experiences and reflecting on how membership changed his life:

- *I suppose you need a bit of history. I joined in 94 -I think, and the Hash had been around for years. Umm, if it were 777 weekend, in the early 1990's, at a run a week that's 15 years I suppose, so around 1975. maybe 80. Dunno, but I think it came from some people in Cambridge, who moved to Leeds...;*
- *We did all sorts, not just the regular runs. We went to other Hash events, the initial one in Lancashire, and some in Sxxx (Other Northern UK towns). We also went to national events. It was always a good time;*
- *Oh yeas, I must tell you about RED Dress runs -err, that's capital letters. Apparently a woman turned up to a run in America in a red cocktail dress, thought it were a party or something. She ran anyway, got covered in mud, swim a river or whatever, as we do... It has turned into a worldwide tradition, once a year, usually Christmas, we all go to a city centre in red dresses, men too, and collect money for a charity. Made thousands for a hospice, I think, one year in York. Loved it!;*
- *Going back to what I said earlier, it's not about money. There is a joining fee, but ts only a tenner or so, and we have raffles and stuff, but that's just for expenses. It's all self-funded. It's just for fun, unless we do a red dress run for charity;*
- *It's about having fun. By organizing things we all enjoy ourselves. Better than a pub crawl, and better than a running club- been in them too!*

Thus altruistic motivation and personal reward for effort form the basis of his involvement. These extracts, and their "meaning units" demonstrate that the community of practice is real and meets all the desired criteria. It was formed around 15 years before the interviewee joined, and he was active for over 20 years. The overriding rationale for his joining was the original community of practice members recognition that their charity needed and always welcomed more members, and help organizing events.

An examination of the interpretative phenomenological analysis showed that, for this single 25 minute interview and over 2600 words of transcript, over 150 "meaning units" were identified and underlined ,then placed in different table rows. Some of these are used above to illustrate the results text.

The commonest were identified as "reflection and storytelling. "Motivation" featured heavily too, as did unspecific „friendship" or community spirit.

Table 7. Community of practice HH, frequencies of initial thoughts

Initial Thought	Frequency of use	Notes
Reflection /Analysis/ Deep thought about issues	31	This suggests that the interviewee is thinking deeply about the community of practice and his experiences as part of it. It is associated with his motivation and learning.
Explanation/Storytelling/ Clarification	24	This notes that the interviewee felt the need to explain/tell some part of the history or story behind their involvement. It possibly indicates motivation?
Motivation to have fun and share it	13	This was noted often.
Knowledge transfer into social organisation from outside.	12	Examples of people learning, inward knowledge transfer, situated learning and sharing knowledge within their community of practice.
Hegemony	6	Not stressed, but evidence of mature members helping others become mature.
Situated learning	5	Within community of practice between members.
Fundraising	3	Provision of income for nominated charities.

Source: Authors' study.

The community of practice was formed for one key technical reason -to have fun. Thus it is a social organisation, under the definitions used here. A secondary, but important role is to raise funds for a nominated charity though 1 or 2 annual events.

Although only one interview is featured here, because the others largely duplicated the story closely, there is evidence of knowledge transfer inwards from previous experiences, or situated learning elsewhere, and also of knowledge transfer within the CoP. Motivation is also very clear, and appears altruistic, although reward can be seen „we have fun" etc. The key driver for activity is enjoyment, exercise and socializing.

Therefore study of this community of practice, via mainly 1 interview with a mature community of practice member, and extracts from websites, meets the objectives of the book: "What motivates individuals to join and take part in social CoPs, what behaviours do they exhibit, do they join or form groups that can be labelled as "communities of practice" and do they undertake and deliver situated learning, as part of a knowledge transfer process" (From Chapter 1, Introduction).

The next stage was to analyse the "emergent themes". They are not fully documented here but were produced in exactly the same way as the groups in Chapter 4. The outcomes are used in the next chapter. Not all the "standard" emergent themes were seen, however this was mostly only 1 person's view.

The most stressed "emergent theme" was the need for sharing out the duties that allowed all to have fun, usually organizing weekly events, so „trail setting and finding new pubs", clearly the key role of the group. Motivation was the key underpinning theme for this. Altruistic reward was noted „ it were great". Situated learning and knowledge transfer were less important but evident.

After extensive study of the literature these authors can confidently assert that their noted frequency is related to, but not necessarily a direct function of their importance. However this data was cautiously mined for the further analysis undertaken, especially the comparisons across groups and countries. Therefore, the examples here, with those in the "initial thoughts" table earlier, form the basis for the comparisons and overall conclusions in Chapters 5 and 6.

HH Summary

The community of practice was formed for a key technical reason socialization. Thus it is a social organisation, under the definitions used here. Therefore study of this community of practice, mostly reported via only 1 interview with a mature member, meets the objectives of the book, because it adds a slightly different perspective to the other community of practice's studied, whilst meeting the objectives. The interviewee's situated learning or background from his earlier life was purposively used for, but possibly not explicitly transferred to, the community of practice. He stated though that he experienced situated learning himself, discovering how to analyse, identify and propose solutions to the problems he found. In this time he moved from his initial status of only undertaking legitimate peripheral participation, as a newcomer, on the periphery, to mature membership of the community of practice.

5.2 The Air Ambulance Support Community of Practice (UK)

AA Introduction and Process

The Yorkshire Air Ambulance support group is independent, not part of a larger body, and is run only as a not-for-profit social enterprise. It does, however have knowledge of, and contact with, other parallel groups in different geographical areas. Its technical purpose is to raise funds and create awareness for the Yorkshire Air Ambulance Service. This is a charity, funded solely by donations - a fact not widely known and repeatedly stressed by the interviewee. The group clearly meets the community of practice definitions stated in this book. It is included as an example of a different social enterprise, unlike some of the others used here, but that still meets the criteria required.

A1 is male. He was interviewed in 2014. He has been an active community of practice member since 2003 (11 years at time of interview). The interview duration was 15 minutes. Over 100 "meaning units" were identified in the 1450 word transcript. Some "follow-up" discussions were not transcribed but notes were made at the time and these are incorporated as addendum's where appropriate. The Facebook pages were also reviewed and material from these are incorporated as addendum's where appropriate.

AA Discussion and Conclusions

This interview was clearly illustrative of the interviewee's motivations and desire to help others. There is evidence that its origins were altruistic, but that personal satisfaction also occurs. The "meaning units" identified and other IPA outcomes, together with the supporting material provided, demonstrate that the community of practice is real and meets all the desired criteria, despite the limitations of only using interview data from one source, plus some AA website and Facebook content.

He states that he was recruited, and motivated to join the enterprise, because of a personal tragedy:

- *Way, way back in...2003 I think it was, Chris, A friend of mine was on his motorbike and come off. And, err, he and his bike became separated, at high speed. Err, He was picked up by the Cornish Air Ambulance, but unfortunately didn't survive...;*
- *So I ...took the money to Truro ...and I got chatting to the folks there. And then I was told all about it and that's where I thought, well, I can find out what goes on back at home. And that is how I came to find out about the Yorkshire Air Ambulance.*

The following quote, from the Yorkshire Air Ambulance website, names the interviewee „AA", and supports the interview transcript: *"Like many people, I first became aware of the charitable status of the UK Air Ambulance services when they had a significant impact on my own life. A number of years ago my best friend was picked up by the Air Ambulance in Cornwall after he was involved in a motor cycle accident. At his funeral, a collection was held for the Air Ambulance and his parents asked if I would ensure the money got to the charity. After meeting the people involved, I decided that I would like to get involved in helping this vital service keep going and so approached Yorkshire Air Ambulance offering to help in any way I could... In my career I spend a lot of time in different parts of the world, dealing with issues that at the end of the day don't really matter that much. But, by volunteering for the Yorkshire Air Ambulance I know that for that small amount of time I am making a difference"* - Ian Andrews, YAA Volunteer[50].

There was a lot of storytelling, and some examples of how he used situated learning from his previous life, to support the community of practice he joined. There is much evidence of motivation for his continuing membership, both from him and the others he describes:

- *You have known me long enough. I am not backwards at coming forwards, when it comes to talking to people;*
- *Because of what I do I get to meet people, ... I have met people whose lives have been saved by... the efforts that I put in, and ... you just can't buy that, can you?*
- *If I am available I will do anything that is needed, Yeah, But I am very conscious that we need to get some new blood in, I keep banging on about it, and maybe one day something will get done.*

---

[50] http://www.yorkshireairambulance.org.uk/info/volunteers, Accessed 1 April 2017.

So, it is clear that he is motivated to use his knowledge and skills to fundraise, and the enterprise was motivated to receive and pass the funds on to the totally volunteer funded Air Ambulance Service: *there is still a lot of people out there who just don't realise the need to raise 10,000 pounds every day of the year.*

The above quote from the transcript is supported by an extract from the Annual Report for 2014: *In my report for the year ending March 2013, I concluded with the following key comments: The key to our lifesaving Charity operation is the continuation of funds being donated to enable the operation of our two helicopters, and we are still totally reliant on financial donations that have now increased to £9,990 per day, to keep both helicopters operational*[51].

As described by AA1, his relevant skills and knowledge was mainly implicit, gained earlier and held by him personally. Thus, when he joined the enterprise to help them in this area, he gained knowledge of their exact needs, via situated learning, during his initial membership. He thus clearly moved from legitimate peripheral participation to maturity fairly quickly, with limited support from his peers:

- *And that is how I came to find out about the Yorkshire Air Ambulance. So I err, I approached them, and said, y'know, is there anything I can to to help;*
- *You pick things up from each other, particularly ...the ways, of...putting things over in an effective way;*
- *Err, and obviously, people who are new to it are quite nervous. Maybe not quite sure of what they are doing, what they are saying;*
- *When it comes to standing in a gazebo in the middle of a wet field ...., in a rainy July, then, there is only one way to learn. That is to get in there and do it...*

His initial motivation is apparent and the altruism clear:

- *Err, the reason that I prefer working for Yorkshire Air Ambulance is, ... I guess you would almost call it a selfish reason in that I can see exactly where the money is going;*
- *I can see where my efforts are making a difference. Cos, you see the yellow helicopter flying in and out of Leeds General Infirmary and other hospitals;*
- *And, because of what I do I get to meet people, that's picked up. And I have met people whose lives have been saved by.... the efforts that I put in, and ... you just can't buy that, can you?*

A second factor is obvious, in that he receives personal satisfaction from the activities:

- *And on more than 1 occasion I have picked up a huge "comedy cheque" and had a photograph taken and, err say a few words. Have a small sherry and a vol-u-vent, its great;*

---

[51] http://www.yorkshireairambulance.org.uk/files/file/content/YAA-annual-report-accounts-13-14.pdf, Accessed 1 April 2017.

– *I go to events that normally I wouldn't even think about going to. ...I went to a wrestling match in Castleford. Previously I would never have even thought of going to something like that... we had a right old time. It were grand!;*
– *We regularly now go to the Bramham Horse Trials, not something I would go to. (These names describe places, events and occasions in Yorkshire, UK).*

Thus motivation and reward form the basis of his involvement.

These extracts, and their "meaning units" demonstrate that the community of practice is real and meets all the desired criteria. It was formed some years before the interviewee joined, and he has been active for over 13 years (A telephonic update on his membership was made in late 2015). The overriding rationale for his joining was the original community of practice members recognition that their charity needed and always welcomed more help.

An examination of the interpretative phenomenological analysis showed that, for this single 15 minute interview and over 1400 words of transcript, over 80 "meaning units" were identified and underlined, then placed in different table rows. Some of these are used above to illustrate the results text. The commonest were identified as "Reflection and Storytelling".

Table 8. Community of practice AA, frequencies of initial thoughts

Initial Thought	Frequency of use	Notes
Reflection /Analysis/ Deep thought about issues	20	This suggests that the interviewee is thinking deeply about the community of practice and their experiences as part of it. It is associated with his motivation and learning.
Explanation/Storytelling/ Clarification	15	This notes that the interviewee felt the need to explain/tell some part of the history or story behind their involvement. It possibly indicates motivation?
Fundraising	12	Provision of income for AA.
Motivation to create change	3	This was noted where a desire to find other volunteers.
Knowledge Transfer into SE/ From Outside/ Situated Learning in SE	3	Examples of people learning, inward knowledge transfer, situated learning in community of practice, and sharing knowledge within their community of practice.
Situated Learning	2	Within community of practice between members

Source: Authors' study.

The community of practice was formed for one key technical reason -to raise funds. Thus it is a social enterprise, under the definitions used here. A secondary, but important role is to raise awareness of the AIR Ambulance having charity status, without government funding.

Although only one interview was held, there is evidence of knowledge transfer, inwards to the enterprise, from previous experiences, or situated learning elsewhere, and also of knowledge transfer within the CoP „picking it up as I went along". Motivation is also very clear, and appears altruistic, although reward can be seen „I get to go to places" etc. The key driver for activity is fundraising.

Therefore study of this community of practice, via 1 interview with a mature community of practice member, 1400 words of interview transcript, and extracts from Facebook, meets the objectives of the book.

The next stage was to analyse the "emergent themes". They are not fully documented here but were produced in exactly the same way as the groups in Chapter 4. The outcomes are used in the next chapter. Not all the "standard" emergent themes were seen, however this was only 1 person's view. An important point was the Air Ambulance management's choice of the interviewee, with almost the same quote, used as their website leader.

The most stressed "emergent theme" in the Air Ambulance social enterprise was the need for fundraising, clearly the key role of the group. Motivation was the key underpinning theme for this. Altruistic reward was noted „ it were grand". Situated learning and knowledge transfer were less important but evident. The interviewee was very self-reliant and, other than a few comments, not deeply involved in educating others in the enterprise. His focus was more on raising public awareness. Operationalization entered into this, with comments about training others and the need for new blood.

After extensive study of the literature these authors can confidently assert that their noted frequency is related to, but not necessarily a direct function of their importance. However this data was cautiously mined for the further analysis undertaken, especially the comparisons across groups and countries. Therefore, the examples here, with those in the "initial thoughts" table earlier, form the basis for the comparisons and overall conclusions in chapter 6.

AA Summary

The Community of Practice was formed for one key technical reason -to raise funds. Thus it is a social enterprise, under the definitions used here. A secondary, but important role is to raise awareness.

Therefore study of this community of practice, via only 1 interview with a mature member, meets the objectives of the book, because it adds a slightly different perspective to the other community of practice's studied, whilst meeting the objectives. The interviewee's situated learning or background from his earlier life was purposively used for, but possibly not explicitly transferred to, the community of practice. He stated though that he experienced situated learning himself, discovering how to analyse, identify and propose solutions to the problems he found. In this time he moved from his initial status of only undertaking legitimate peripheral participation, as a newcomer, on the periphery, to mature membership of the community of practice.

5.3 The Victorian Heritage Campaign Community of Practice (UK)

B Introduction and Process

This social organisation formed in 2012 to protest against a plan to extensively modify a Victorian Heritage site - its "technical purpose". It is, as reported by the interviewee, totally uninterested in raising funds except as a side issue. This identifies that it is an organisation, not an enterprise,. It is included as an example of a quite different social organisation, unlike some of the others used here, but that still meets the criteria required. The organisation has a website and a Facebook page, quoted herein but lightly anonymised.

The social organisation was identified via personal contact. The sole interviewee was a resident in the village that holds the village festival, analysed earlier. She was suggested by C1. The first interview clearly covered more than enough to evaluate the organisation, thus only 1 interview was held (in 2014). B1 is female. The interview duration was 21 minutes. Over 140 "meaning units" were identified in the 2,000 word transcript. There were "follow-up" discussions, which were not transcribed but notes were made at the time. The Facebook pages were also reviewed and material from these are incorporated as anonymized addendum's where appropriate.

B Discussion and Conclusions

B1 went to a public meeting held in the village in 2012. The meeting was called by the owners to present their plans to improve safety by rebuilding a Victorian Heritage site. She went to find out more after friends reported that the owners didn't seem to understand the heritage aspect. Because she works in planning her professional skills were very relevant to the problem she and others identified. This knowledge and subsequent use of her professional skills is evident throughout:

– _The way I got involved, emm, I am a planning consultant by profession and ... the owners wrote to local residents and said they were going to do work on the... (heritage);_

– _So I went along to find out more. ...I had spoken to the engineer beforehand, ...and found out a lot about the scheme..., so I just went along to find out more really._

This implicit knowledge from her background, and subsequent use of it, via her professional skills, is evident throughout. Thus knowledge transfer and application of situated learning from elsewhere has been used in this organisation. She is used to working for developers, so there is clear evidence of wry reflection, that she is now "on the other side":

– _Thinking (the owners) were going to have a hard time here. If there turns up a lot of whingers...- I went to the meeting because I thought (the owners) were going to have a hard time and was sympathetic,(to them), so wanted to know more;_

– _But when I was at the meeting, ...I felt that what they were proposing to do wasn't the best thing we could be doing... They didn't understand the Heritage aspects at all._

These "meaning units" demonstrate how the meeting and potential consequences for the village, created the motivation to form a community of practice. B1 works in planning, so her professional skills were very relevant to the problems she and others identified:

- *(The) process, or lack of process (they) had gone through, and which was really apparent;*
- *quite a few of the people at the meeting, umm, didn't seem to like the plans either;*
- *I came out of the meeting, I got chatting to a guy, and (I) said a lot of people don't seem to know what they are planning to do here;*
- *It became more and more apparent that what they were doing was...we were against what they were doing;*
- *So we decided we would set up a Facebook group, just try to let more people know what was going on;*
- *Mainly, just to start with for information purposes, and so people could make their own mind up... But it soon kind of, sort of sort of escalated.*

As a direct result of the Heritage owner's presentations in the village (in 2012), a community of practice formed to study the proposal and raise awareness of the planned changes. The group used Facebook as its communication medium, quickly gained 800 "followers" and a core of around 10 activists (information from interviewee and Facebook page). These make up the community of practice. The group has a website. A quote is copied here, but lightly redacted to preserve anonymity, as the interviewee did not wish to be identified[*]:

- *...is located in the Pennine moorland village of ... The ... is crafted exclusively in natural stone masonry and designed by the country's foremost ... engineer of his time, (It) is the largest, most impressive, architecturally-detailed, Victorian ... in the country. It is the only... to be listed in its own right and is in a near original condition. (From the organisation website);*
- *Save ... is a group that is campaigning to preserve the ... In doing so we seek to ensure that (the owners) employ best practice and transparency in its design and consultation processes to achieve the best possible heritage and environmental outcome. **If you are proud of and love ... then please help us to save it!**;*
- *When this heritage is lost it will be gone forever... (From Facebook, 2014)*

And finally (in 2016): *Very sad but inevitable news. At least we can be proud that our collective efforts resulted in a significantly improved scheme; we saved more of it than the original plans, if not all of it!*[52].

When interviewed in 2014 the group had been active for 2 years and had an active core of 70 members, who keep in touch on Facebook. There are 10 really active members -the community of practice. The interviewee was a core founder member:

---

[*]The authors recognize that the anonymity of the group could easily be breached via a search engine. They request that the wishes of the interviewee be respected and that the site is not named in any public reviews or correspondence.

[52] All the above taken from the group website and Facebook site, Accessed 1.4.2017.

– *(We needed to) give the village a voice really... so friends of friends started spreading the word and we put posters up and things;*
– *And it just escalated and now we have got about 800 supporters online;*
– *People have come forward and given an awful lot of time to help with the cause and people got together... the skills that they have got ...and really good and all really complementary and quite a strong group together.*

The interviewee was new to campaigning. She had been involved for 2 years when interviewed in 2014. She reflected extensively on the networking and other marketing that emerged from the community of practice:

– *Haven't been in any campaign group, pause... no not at all. I haven't done anything like this before;*
– *I am normally the one who kind of...hates this kind of thing... I can't quite believe that I am on the other side of the fence now, completely;*
– *It was one of those things, we started off, you know... And umm, it's been going 2 years now;*
– *It was in all the national newspapers, and (TV) covered it, for the local news, and it was on the BBC website and ...and the (unclear website) (Yorkshire Newspapers) all covered it;*
– *That's when it went national, ... and even international, because we have got quite a lot of people following us abroad as well;*
– *And then on the back of the Victorian Society, backing us in our campaign, the Council for British Archaeology got in touch and they spent a lot of time helping us as well and ...*

Networking publicity and marketing are clearly key to the technical purpose of the group, and considerable effort and expertise is evident. Thus implicit knowledge, situated learning and knowledge transfer are all evident:

– *I think that can help people understand what kind of an asset that is, and how important it is to the village;*
– *We also did an exhibition in one of the local cafes , an art exhibition, which one of the guys in the village organized, because he was a photographer... we got loads of people to volunteer photographs;*
– *We have been thinking about kind of,...local history leaflets, if we pulled all this together.*

As part of her involvement she is now researching the site's history and talking to the descendants and families of the Heritage's original designers and workers- this is a new interest for her and clearly a factor in her motivation and reward:

– *As a consequence of that we started researching the history, a lot, and that is what I did... When I researched the history we discovered the guy who designed the (Heritage Site) was a really famous Victorian and a famous engineer and a prominent ... engineer of the day;*
– *And so I did loads of historical research ...I really enjoyed researching all that.*

Thus rewards have clearly emerged, for the interviewee, the village and the community of practice. situated learning has occurred, and a move from legitimate peripheral participation to maturity for many.

The group is not finance based, so is a social organisation, clearly not an enterprise. The activists are almost entirely self-funded but gained a financial windfall as a result of the owners mistake. The Heritage owners used photos without copyright permission and made a payout to avoid legal action. Background knowledge in the community of practice enabled her to recognize this and capitalize on it: *(The owner put up)* _a display in the village and_ _used some of my photographs I put on Facebook, without my consent...- I took legal advice_ _on it_, because they shouldn't have used them -..._that knowledge, that they had used my_ _photographs without authorization, against copyright_.

This money was donated by her, to the group and, at the time of interview was all their funds. This was being used for campaigning, purchasing leaflets and posters mainly:

− *We bought a couple of ?? units, we bought some historical maps, for research, and some* *old photographs and things ...* _we had a push on trying to encourage people to write in_ _and object;_
− *We did a leaflet drop around the whole of the village. Which, that paid for the printing* *costs. And we printed the posters and things as well. It's been useful;*
− _We ran some workshops actually as well_.

B1 stated that she wished the issue hadn't escalated and caused her to become so committed, but that she had learned a lot! There is clear evidence of her motivation, and the rewards she gained:

− _It's been very rewarding,... It's been really hard work and sometimes I wished that it_ _hadn't escalated so much as it has... I don't know how many hours I have spent doing_ _it...;_
− _I wrote the group's objection letter which was 13 pages long just before I went on_ _holiday and I was up until about 3 o'clock in the morning 3 nights in a row_.

In summary, this interview, held in 2014, was clearly illustrative of the interviewee's motivations and desire to help others. B1 states that she was instrumental in forming the organisation in 2012 and has been an active community of practice member since. (Just over 2 years at the time of interview). There is evidence that the origins of the group, and her involvement were altruistic, and that the campaign was very time consuming and tiring. „*I have a very understanding husband*", was her final comment, but that personal satisfaction also occurs often. The "meaning units" identified and other outcomes, together with the supporting material provided, demonstrate that the community of practice is real and meets all the desired criteria, despite the limitations of using interview data from one source.

The commonest emergent theme was motivation, followed by campaigning as a form of knowledge transfer - via terms such as raising awareness and PR at a similar level. Fundraising is clearly not required by or important to the group. Situated learning and knowledge transfer between members were not very evident from this interview. The interviewee was very self-reliant and motivated, thus hegemony is apparent. She clearly drew on her past life in undertaking this new challenge. Her, and the community of practice focus was on raising public awareness by campaigning.

A final comment from Facebook. Lightly anonymised but evidence of emergence and maybe fading: *Given the commencement of the work... Save (the Victorian Heritage) has changed its name to "Supporters of xxx". The group aims to carry on in its work to promote the heritage of xxx, as well as that of the wider xxx valley and felt that this name was more appropriate going forwards. Despite our differing views on how the work ... should have been undertaken, the Group always has and continues to work well with (the owner) for the greater good of our shared heritage. We hope to share more news with you as regards our further work in the near future...*[53].

Table 9. Community of practice B, frequencies of initial thoughts

Initial Thought	Frequency of use	Notes
Motivation to create change	14	This was noted where a desire to help others was seen and is separate from motivation to join the CoP. It includes maturity and thus links to hegemony.
Networking/PR	12	The ability to share experiences, find skills and generally have contact with the world is clearly present.
Motivation to become involved	12	The drive to work on the technical purpose.
Operationalization/ Need for Knowledge Transfer between members to educate and transfer skills/ Ownership	11	This is noted where interviewee stated or discussed the need for sharing knowledge, experiences and ideas. Also where there might be "power in numbers". It is associated closely with situated learning and knowledge transfer, also with transitions from LPP to full, mature membership.
Reflection /Analysis/ Deep thought about issues/evaluation	9	This suggests that the interviewee is thinking deeply about the community of practice and their experiences as part of it. It is associated with motivation and learning.
Explanation/Storytelling/ Clarification	8	This notes that the interviewee felt the need to explain/tell some part of the history or story behind their involvement. It possibly indicates motivation?
Technical purpose	8	This was clearly about community spirit and protecting the heritage.

---

[53] From Facebook, Accessed 4.5.2017.

Initial Thought	Frequency of use	Notes
Situated Learning	6	Within community of practice between members. Teaching others and making tacit knowledge explicit
Knowledge Transfer into SE/ From outside	5	Examples of people learning , inward knowledge transfer which led to situated learning in the CoP, and sharing external knowledge within their CoP to make it explicit.
Leadership and roles	4	This includes hegemony and control.
Fundraising	2	Provision of income for technical purpose. Not really seen here, but mentioned in passing.

Source: Authors' study

B Summary

The community of practice was formed for one key technical reason -campaign for a better outcome to the Heritage restoration. A secondary, important role is to raise awareness. Money is a very distant third.

Therefore study of this community of practice, via only 1 interview of a mature member, meets the objectives of the book, because it adds a slightly different perspective to the other community of practice's studied, whilst meeting the objectives. The interviewee's situated learning or background from her earlier life was purposively used for, and expressly transferred to, the community of practice. She stated though, that she experienced situated learning herself, discovering how to analyse, identify and propose solutions to the problems she found. In this time she moved from her initial status of legitimate peripheral participation, as a newcomer to a new group she co-founded, on the periphery because she was new to campaigning, on to mature membership of the community of practice.

5.4 The A Theatre Arts Community of Practice (UK)

A Introduction and Process

The Theatre Arts community of practice is independent, not part of a larger body, and is run only as a not-for-profit social enterprise. Its technical purpose was to organize theatre performances, with associated training for new actors, in a Yorkshire city. This role is evidenced by voluminous supporting written material supplied at the time of the interview. The material is not referenced here to preserve anonymity, but was used and is held by the authors. The group clearly meets the community of practice definitions stated in this book. It is included as an example of a Social Enterprise, unlike some of the others used here, but that still meets the criteria required.

A1 is male. He was interviewed in 2010. A1 joined the theatre arts group 3 years prior to this interview, as a non-executive Director. A1was recruited specifically to bring business skills to the management team, after a successful career in industry. Thus, his role in the enterprise community of practice, and therefore the interview focus, is key to the social enterprise's success. However, he clearly was not involved in, and did not really discuss, its core technical purpose:

- *I am not involved in A because I am interested in art (the technical purpose of the social enterprise).* _I am in there because it's an opportunity to apply business practice and learn new stuff_;
- *1 or 2 of us, _me included, who didn't even have an arts background. And this is fundamentally a creative arts company_.*

The social enterprise was identified via personal contact. The interview clearly covered enough to evaluate the business focus of the enterprise, although not its technical purpose. The value of this interview for analysis of knowledge transfer and situated learning were clearly evident however. The interview duration was 37 minutes. Over 140 "meaning units" were identified in the 4400 word transcript.

A Discussion and Conclusions

This interview, held in late 2010, was clearly very reflective and also illustrative. The "meaning units" identified and other IPA outcomes, together with the supporting material provided, demonstrate that the CoP is real and meets all the desired criteria, despite the limitations of using interview data from one source.

There was a lot of storytelling, and many examples of how A1 used situated learning from his previous jobs and life, to undertake a massive transfer of knowledge from him, into the failing community of practice he joined. He states that he was recruited, and motivated to join the enterprise, specifically to bring business and financial expertise to a failing group. It demonstrates much knowledge transfer from him, but also demonstrates his situated learning, of the new enterprise and how it operated. This then enabled him to apply his previous experience, gained via situated learning in his prior career, and then transferred inwards to his new community of practice. There is much evidence of his motivation for this: _It would be interesting to learn how to apply this stuff that I've got in my tool kit, in a non-profit environment,_ *in the 3rd sector, rather than in XX,* _which where I learnt most of it_.

He was thus motivated to share his knowledge and skills, and the Enterprise was motivated to receive and apply it. Although only 1 interview from this group has been used here, it matches well the other enterprises analysed in this respect.

He was clearly recruited specifically for his business knowledge and skills, and the visible community of practice weaknesses he describes, motivated him to find out what was lacking. He found out, via legitimate peripheral participation in his new community of practice, then was able to share his expertise:

- _Talked to one or two members of staff as well and spent time in the office, um, so picked it up that way_;
- So, _technically you might describe that as a level of unconscious competence of what you do_;

– *But stakeholder management...* <u>*Because they weren't conscious of the need for*</u> <u>*Stakeholder Management*</u>*. I mean,* <u>*different people were doing different bits of it*</u> <u>*incidentally, but we've never got it. It's still not good enough;*</u>

– *So* <u>*you've got to deliver whatever they need, no matter how poorly they might specify*</u> <u>*what they need*</u>*.*

From the other side, the enterprise was motivated to receive and apply it. He was recruited for this purpose, and known to be available to help the community of practice gain new knowledge in an essential, but not core technical area:

– <u>*I'm not sure who I want ...yet, but we will get somebody;*</u>

– *But Z came onto the Board and* <u>*what he brought was accountancy skills at high level;*</u>

– <u>*Strategic accountancy skills although he is a tactical accountant*</u>*. And we get Profit and Loss forecasts, we get balance sheets, we get a cash flow forecast.*

These extracts, and the "meaning units" extracted and attributed, demonstrate that the enterprise community of practice is real and meets all the desired criteria for inclusion. It was formed 5 years before the interviewee joined, specifically to meet a technical need, to foster theatre arts, but the founders were not aware of the need for financial business skills, and so was failing in its technical purpose, because of a lack of this key knowledge. The overriding rationale for his recruitment and joining was the original members recognition that their charity needed help: <u>*"Oh crikey, what's a cash flow forecast"? Seriously, they*</u> <u>*didn't know, a, what one was and b, why it was important*</u>*.*

Thus, there is a lot of storytelling, and many examples of how A1 used the learning that he had acquired from his previous jobs and life, to undertake a massive transfer of knowledge into the failing community he joined. So, talking about his previous career: *I suppose in this parallel career, for a lot of the time I was sort of doing the day job, which was science, for about half the time and* <u>*the other half to do this leader development,*</u> <u>*manager development, facilitation and this other interesting stuff*</u>*.*

Although it is only the story of 1 individual from his social enterprise, and thus may not be truly representative of the actual enterprise and its technical need, it certainly outlined his motivation, knowledge acquisition and transfer, plus the learning from his previous situation that he had acquired and also transferred to others:

– <u>*The basic, boring stuff, research that you might do on any company you want to get*</u> <u>*involved*</u> *with, a company that you might want to do some work for. You get the Annual Reports out, you have a look on the website. You get hold of one or two case studies that they've done;*

– <u>*If you get the chance you talk to one or two clients. I was able to talk to one or two*</u> <u>*people that worked with them;*</u>

– <u>*I talked to the then Chief Exec, quite a lot about what do you do;*</u>

- *Then the induction process would say, OK, new Director, spend a day with the Chief Exec, then spend half a day, maybe with 3 or 4 key members of staff. Go and talk to, err 1 or 2 key customers;*
- *Flexing an existing tool, but it's like I've got this massive great tool kit. That keeps growing all the time.*

As described by A1, his relevant business knowledge was mainly implicit, gained earlier and held by him personally. Thus, when he joined the enterprise with a brief to help them in this area, he gained knowledge of their exact needs, via situated learning, during his initial membership. He thus clearly moved from legitimate peripheral participation, during the period whilst "learning the ropes" about the problems the social enterprise faced: *it would be interesting to learn how to apply this stuff that I've got in my tool kit, in a non-profit environment, in the 3rd sector, rather than in XX, which where I learned most of it.*

He then applied his expertise to the problems, and transferred potential solutions, either directly, or by suggesting the recruitment of others:

- *Yes I agree with Team Briefing... A brilliant idea that is often implemented very badly, but what its reminded me of, is that whenever we have a Board Meeting we have a 20 minute presentation from some member of staff about some aspect of the company's work. So we learned something that way;*
- *We are going to be doing, we haven't fully done it yet, we are going to attach individual directors to stakeholders, so that Directors start to build high level relationships with key stakeholders.*

Although it is only the story of 1 individual from his social enterprise, and thus may not be truly representative of the actual community of practice and its technical need, it certainly outlined his motivation, knowledge acquisition and transfer, plus the situated learning he acquired and also transferred to others:

- *Then the induction process would say, ok, new Director, spend a day with the Chief exec, then spend half a day, maybe with 3 or 4 key members of staff. Go and talk to, err 1 or 2 key customers;*
- *Flexing an existing tool, but it's like I've got this massive great tool kit. That keeps growing all the time.*

An examination of the interpretative phenomenological analysis showed that, for this single 37 minute interview and over 4400 words of transcript, over 140 "meaning units" were identified. Some of these are used above to illustrate the results text.

Table 10. Community of practice A, frequencies of initial thoughts

Initial Thought	Frequency of use	Notes
Reflection/ Analysis/ Deep thought about issues	27	This suggests that the interviewee is thinking deeply about the community of practice and their experiences as part of it. It is associated with his motivation and learning.
Situated Learning	22	Within CoP between members.
Knowledge Transfer into SE/ from Outside	15	Examples of people learning, inward knowledge transfer, situated learning in Community of Practice, and sharing knowledge within their community of practice.
Explanation/ Storytelling/ Clarification	14	This notes that the interviewee felt the need to explain/tell some part of the history or story behind their involvement. It possibly indicates motivation?
Networking	12	The ability to share experiences, find skills and generally have contact with the world is clearly present.
Need for Knowledge (inwards)/ Education/ Finding out	11	Clear comment about external knowledge coming into community of practice. So, knowledge transfer from external source.
Operationalization/ Need for Knowledge Transfer inwards to educate and transfer skills/ownership	11	This is noted where interviewee stated or discussed the need for sharing knowledge, experiences and ideas. Also where there might be "power in numbers". It is associated closely with situated learning and knowledge transfer, also with transitions from LPP to full, mature membership.
Motivation to create change	6	This was noted where a desire to help others with his business skills was evident .
Technical purpose	2	Clearly not A1 motivator! He states that he wants to apply his business expertise, technical purpose is almost irrelevant to him.
Fundraising	4	Provision of income for technical purpose extremely important.

Source: Authors' study.

The commonest "emergent theme" was "reflection", followed by "situated learning" and "knowledge transfer inwards". Storytelling was similarly evident. Further analysis of these outcomes is undertaken in the next chapter.

A CoP Summary

The community of practice formed for technical reasons - to foster theatre arts. It soon struggled to meet its objectives because of a lack of business skills, which it recognised. The interviewee was recruited specifically to transfer these to the Community of Practice membership (the role of a "non-exec" director is not operational, it is to advise and provide opinions). His role is to manage and raise funds, but this is not the only view, 1 interview does not make this just an enterprise.

Therefore study of this community of practice, via only 1 interview of a mature member, meets the objectives of the book, because it adds a slightly different perspective to the other CoPs studied, whilst meeting the objectives. The interviewee's situated learning from his earlier life was purposively transferred to the community of practice. During this knowledge transfer he undertook situated learning himself, discovering how to analyse, identify and propose solutions to the problems he found. In this time he moved from his initial status of legitimate peripheral participation, as a newcomer, on the periphery, to mature membership of the CoP.

It addresses: "What motivates individuals to join and take part in social enterprise, what behaviours do they exhibit, do they join or form groups that can be labelled as "communities of practice" and do they undertake and deliver situated learning, as part of a knowledge transfer process" (From Chapter 1, Introduction).

5.5 R Community of Practice (PL)

R Introduction and Process

The R enterprise was formed in 1994 by several parents, who were bringing up children with intellectual disabilities. The association brings together parents, caregivers and friends of people with disabilities. At the moment, the enterprise contains about 70 families. The area of their activity is in Southern Silesia, geographical coverage is very narrow, but their help is very comprehensive.

From the beginning, they have tried to allow disabled people to have active and dignified participation in society. They aim to create the most favourable conditions for their physical and personal development. This purpose is realised through the provision of social assistance for people with disabilities, and their carers (care takers): transport of disabled youth to therapeutic activities, conducting various types of therapeutic activities (arts, education and sports), the organisation of visits, trips, camps, sports, cultural and integration events. The association also conducts training for parents and carers of people with disabilities.

The main objective of their activity, from the beginning, was to build a residential house with workshops for complex therapy. They want to provide the opportunity for participation in such activities, to all those people who still do not have such capabilities. By this provision it allows a place for people with disabilities to live a decent life. These people would otherwise become alone, after the death of their parents. The house is already finished and has an area of over 950 square metres including single and two-bed rooms, a kitchen, halls for art classes, therapy and rehabilitation. Places for 22 disabled people provide opportunities to stay in this house.

The main active processes are charity fundraising for building the house, equipping it and carrying out aid to the disabled. The enterprise members have found many sponsors, conducted long-term fundraising for the entire project, provided the house with specialized equipment and offers programmes for the mentees. The enterprise operates many business activities including the offer of paid services in the field of: physiotherapy, rehabilitation, physiotherapy exercises and other services. They organize workshops and therapeutic classes under the framework of tasks or projects co-financed by public bodies (Ministry of Labour and Social Policy), as well as private companies.

They formed the group to share experiences, methods and knowledge inside and outside, with the wider community of mentally disabled people and their families. Their growing experience, and the knowledge gained over time has been made available in the local community, and in the wider area. Their cause, and methods of operation have been repeatedly published in the media, both locally and nationally.

The community of practice was chosen randomly from a list of organisations which fulfilled the sampling criteria. Members of the enterprise were identified to be operating in a newly opened home for the disabled. Two main members of the group were interviewed (R1,R2) and one member (R3), who joined the enterprise shortly before the interview. The first interviewee (R1) is the President of the association, the second person (R2), is a long serving member, who is one of the main fundraisers. R3, although quite a new member, knew of this enterprise some time ago and began to participate in its events before joining. All interviewees are parents of disabled people and their protégés ultimately will dwell in the new built house.

The results were transcribed and analysed in depth using the interpretative phenomenological analysis technique. The outcome was 54 minutes of speech and 5670 words of transcription. 143 "meaning units" were identified in the 3 transcripts and underlined in the table.

R Discussion and Conclusions

The analysis of interviews' transcriptions demonstrate that the Rxxx enterprise is a community of practice, formed in 1994, as an association (Polish legal form of operation). The main goal of the enterprise is to guarantee a safe future for disabled people - the relatives of members of the enterprise. Motivation among respondents is clearly noticeable. The members are afraid of the future for their disabled children, especially when they are left alone. The motif is distinctly noticeable in the following comments, taken from the three interviews (Translated from the original Polish):

– *I used to be a person who made parents come together, focus and work for the sake of their children, and in the future ensure them a worthy life when their parents are no longer there. That was the primary goal with the establishment of the association and we have proceeded in this direction for the whole period of time (R1);*

– *All the time ... hmm there has been the interest of our child, so as when we pass away he will not have to be left somewhere, among the people he does not know, where it is a shocking experience to acclimatize ... (R1)*;

– *How was it possible not to act, when a man realized that something must be done for them (the disabled - author's footnote), for their future (R2)*;

– *Actually there has been a gnawing thought , what is going to happen with them when they miss their beloved parents? (R2)*;

– *Who is going to take them in one's arms? And that has been the driving force behind the idea to do something (R2)*;

– *I have never been a member of the association. However... my past family problems in a year (...). I began to think about my son's future, I began to think what is going to happen? (R3)*;

– *Thus, the persistent thoughts are the main reason. What is going to happen next? What shall I do not to leave him... (R3)*.

The above-mentioned motives have been realised in the form of the key goal, which has been chosen by founder members of the organisation: a construction of the house for the disabled. The actions were reinforced by strong motivation and determination:

– *That was the primary goal with the establishment of the association and for many years we have proceeded in that direction. (...) We have been constantly going ahead (R1)*;

– *And that has been the motivation and the goal. It is still ahead, isn't it? We have been going, going on for twenty years and here we are in this new building (R1)*;

– *We have been thinking about the place for them, where they would live. Where they could be when we pass away (R 2)*.

Co-operation, co-ordination and distribution of tasks are undertaken at this time. R1 is the Chairman of the enterprise, who is responsible for management and co-ordination. Her husband was the builder. R2 normally deals with enlisting sponsors' help and the other members run the house and its surroundings:

– *Many a psychologist, who has had meetings here, remarked: "Oh it is you to hold parents in your iron fist" (R1)*;

– *They don't like me because I run the association finances ... I do not accept everything they want ...(R1)*;

– *My husband built it all. If he hadn't been here what would it be, because I don't know a lot about it (R1)*;

– *A carcass of the house was made by a construction company, but painting, laying tiles, floor, lamps, all sorts of things have been done by parents. Parents have worked a lot (R1)*;

– *The whole construction was done by the chairwoman's husband (R 1). He built his house on his own. He had experience... (R2)*;

– *I was looking for relations, to find people somewhere and means of payment (R2)*;

- *It has been normally my responsibility...(R2);*
- *We have a lot to show and say, that it has been done with our bare hands. We have been labourers and we have done intellectual work here to achieve our goal, whenever it has been possible (R2);*
- *I phoned, I wrote... There is no other way: to look for, look for and look for (R2).*

The new members of the organisation are employed to work for the joint property. Also the new people bring their experience and share it with others based on the transfer of knowledge and experience:
- *We have new people, especially the ones who know, when they can see, that we have the building, that there will be new rooms for people, that they will be able to live here. These are the parents who follow this direction, who look at it from the perspective that it would be good for their child to live here, wouldn't it? (R1);*
- *We arrange meetings, a parent arrives, stays here, can chat with others... As you can see, mothers are sitting round the table, they are doing something. They share their experiences, they can gossip a bit. They have a nice time (R1);*
- *We try to employ them kindly, We show them the way (R2);*
- *Well, if my wife goes there and does something, or any other mother, automatically the new one, who wants to learn something, follows the same way (R2);*
- *At the very beginning it was hard because of new environment... I wasn't able to find myself but after a couple of meetings I began to talk, to show the interest. I began to take an active part in cleaning. I happened to pop into classes for teenagers, to have a look what was going on there (R3);*
- *(...) of course I give someone a hint, I have my experience which I can share (R 3).*

There is also a mechanism in the enterprise that excuses some people from payment in exchange for their labour. Employing new members also means overcoming different barriers, which is generally mentioned by the R1, that clearly refers to managing functions of the person:
- *At the very beginning it was said, if you work you do not pay the whole amount, you are released but you are obliged to work it off... A lot of parents have offered themselves: "O.K. I pay less but I will work it off". These are different actions (R1);*
- *Honestly speaking, it is not easy. It is not simple. A lot of parents among 140 members come here eagerly, take an active part... (R1);*
- *However, if it is necessary to mow the lawn, we have an enormous garden, to prune branches, to weed... It is more difficult... It is necessary... Or when we finish classes, we do not have a cleaner, we have to tidy up. We have to wash up. Those are usually the same people (R1);*
- *A person is forced to do that: "perhaps you will stay and help us today in the kitchen? (R1).*

The organisation has many distinctive features of social enterprise. It runs its business which funds the statutory tasks, takes an active part in collecting financial resources and searches for sponsors. Media activity and information management are a distinctive feature of the enterprise. These are aspects of the resourceful features of the enterprise:

– *A collection of money in front of a church. They are significant, not only from the financial point of view, but we can also tell the people who go to church that there is something like this (R2)*;
– *We did our best to become known in TV programmes... It somehow bears a good fruit, because when we arrive with a request it appears that..."I have heard about you" (R2)*.

The construction is a long-standing project and goal, a complex one, employing many sponsors and donors. The publicity gave rise to other financial and material resources for the house, with help from famous politicians and artists. The activities were inspired by the R2:

– *Mrs. M.K. had a donation to the house, she gave a concert in a P. Theatre to celebrate her 85th anniversary, the whole income of the concert was devoted to the house (R2)*;
– *An M.P. arranged the first congress. There she collected sponsors who gave over 30 000 zlotys as a donation to the construction of the house (R2)*;
– *A former member of the European Parliament talked to us, she arranged a performance in a Polish Theatre, the whole income was transferred to our house (R2)*;
– *We met Mrs. A.G. She organized an awesome concert in a P. Theatre, she and her friends sang in the carol concert. (R2)*;
– *Wall papers made of glass fibre, by warehouses in G., floors made by a company K... (R2)*.

An examination of the interpretative phenomenological analysis showed that, for this 54 minute interview and over 4800 words of transcript, over 145 "meaning units" were identified and underlined, then placed in different table rows. Some of these are used above to illustrate the results text.

Table 11. Community of practice R, frequencies of initial thoughts

Initial Thought	Frequency of use	Notes
Activity/ Organizing, methods	25	Frequently occurring words, which are a manifestation of the activity of members of the organisation, their readiness to act, organize the activity and use sophisticated methods. Finally, high reactivity to the needs and problems.
Motivation	23	Frequently occurring word, which is a manifestation of the strong focused activity from the members of the organisation. It is associated with the readiness to solve problems and help children.
Initiative/ Invention/ Idea	20	Many times actions were novel and innovative ideas. The area of operation was new and required new solutions,

Initial Thought	Frequency of use	Notes
		another way of thinking.
Co-operation	19	This is noted where interviewees stated or discussed existing cooperation between members and outside the organisation. The number of stakeholders in the case of this organisation is large.
Problems/ Solving problems	17	Problems were identified, especially in the M1 interview - the leader of the organisation. The problems resulted from a highly complex purpose, innovative activity and the lack of known "good practices" in this area of activity.
Raising funds/ Seeking sponsors	15	The high cost of building a house for disabled children and broad support for them, needs an incessant search for sources of funding and support.
Knowledge/ Knowledge transfer/ Organisational learning	13	Clear information about looking for knowledge - inside and outside the organisation and the processes of transferring it and learning. The organisation because of its extensive experience, also transfers knowledge to the outside.
Reflection	8	Extensive parts of the interviews have "the nature" of reflection, which resulted from the difficult situation arising from the care of a disabled child.
Purpose	7	Statements accentuated the desirability of action and also solving problems. There are often answers demonstrating motivation.
Change	7	This is noted when interviewees (M1 and M3) pointed the need of change. It is symptomatic for M3, the new member of the organisation. She would like to bring her own experiences into group M.
Leader/ Management	3	The organisation has a clear leader – M1. Respondents rarely mentioned this fact but it is clearly visible from the context and researcher's observation at the headquarters of the organisation.

Source: Authors' study.

R Summary

Community of practice R was set up by parents and families of the disabled, out of concern for their future. The creation of a house where they could live permanently, was the key objective of their activity. The house has been already constructed with a tremendous effort from the members of the association. At present the place offers a stay for the disabled, including the future inhabitants, as well as therapy, psychological help, educational classes, housework and gardening etc.

An intensive initiative, raising financial resources and winning sponsors, applying methods of promotion and establishing co-operation with the area, learning and sharing knowledge, solving numerous problems and facing adversities, has developed among the members during the course of the house construction. The members of the organisation also plan chargeable services for residents, in order to provide income to cover the expenses of the house. The CoP has a leader - his statements reveal the managerial skills, for example the ability to make decisions, solving of problems and motivating other members. There is strong evidence that the CoP meets the fundamental conditions to be treated as a social enterprise. The idea of the organisation, its operating arrangements and the visible management processes, demonstrates all the aspects of Situated Learning.

5.6 T Community of Practice (PL)

T Introduction and Process

The group T was established in 1999 as an initiative by a group of enthusiasts: artists and educators. An educational and therapeutic effect, to be achieved by means of theatre and artistic activity, was the main purpose of the organisation. The association runs educational and artistic programs for children and young people in difficult social situations, disabled people, addicts, elderly people and other groups that need support. They arrange performances with children, young people and the disabled in conjunction with schools, pre-schools and therapeutic communities. The members of the association organize training for teachers, trainers and therapists, and they also publish books, films and magazines. The subject matter of their publications is therapy by means of art, social education and amateur theatre.

The organisation, in an active way, shares its knowledge with other operators within social business incubators. The performances with children, young people and the disabled as actors and audiences are among many other activities arranged in conjunction with schools, pre-schools, centres for disabled people and therapeutic communities. Working against discrimination, searching for proper ways of interpersonal communication, and pointing out methods of coping with everyday problems, are the core subject matter that is talked about in the performances.

Running the volunteering centre, which is a part of the Polish network of volunteering centres, is an important issue as far as the activity of the association is concerned. The organisation also runs a workshop for occupational therapy which teaches and prepares disabled people for their future life, operating in 6 rooms. There are approximately 15 people who take an active part in the association, and approx. 60 disabled people are employed. The organisation T has features identical with social corporations.

The association runs two work places for professional activity - a printing house and a holiday home, where the disabled people get ready to enter the labour market. They also rent a conference room. Its income enables them to spread and develop the offer of the organisation. It allows the particular initiatives within the projects, to be subsidised by means of local, national and international competitions. The association actively searches for sponsors and donors. The organisation activities are actively promoted in the media by its own marketing department. The promotional activities and other PR made the organisation well known in the country and it is often a matter for concern for media coverage.

The interview results were transcribed and analysed in depth using the interpretative phenomenological analysis technique. The outcome was 28 minutes of speech and 3160 words of transcription. 94 "meaning units" were identified in the 2 transcripts and underlined in the table.

Discussion of T Interpretative Phenomenological Analysis

Making disabled people fully active is the main concern of the organisation, however the goal is achieved comprehensively: from the artistic activity of the disabled people, to the professional stimulation into activity in companies run by the association. The T shares its knowledge and experience with other organisations of public benefit and people who want to support the disabled people by means of volunteering and incubators (Translated from the original Polish):

- *The heart of volunteering is (...) in this room (...). Conversations with certain individuals who became volunteers (T1);*
- *Overall we deal with the activity for other organisations, for example the incubators, we run two or even three incubators in this room (T1);*
- *We run the centre of social assistantship (...), we run external actions (T1);*
- *I have the separate place for my association, apart from projects I deal with the surrounding, in other words with council estates, clubs, particular senior's houses (T1);*
- *And this is called the social projects department ... oh yes it is next to the artistic projects department and they are both more connected with the first activity of the association, the actors, creative minds ... because we are more technical and social ones (T1);*
- *At that time I had a call (...) with information that they were going to open the work places of professional activities and employ the disabled people (T2);*
- *(...) I found my place in the department of professional technology. The work place employs the disabled people (T2);*
- *Since the beginning of our activity we have employed 40 disabled people, mainly the handicapped ones (T2);*
- *In fact, from the very beginning I have dealt with (...) recruitment of the disabled people (...) (T2);*
- *(...) We have managed to change the attitude of the disabled people, to specify the target. For what reason there was created the work place of the professional activity (...) to prepare the disabled people for work on the open labour market (T2).*

The respondents are motivated to deal with the disabled people and other organisations in the field. It is noticeable especially in the statements of T1:

- *But it is my passion indeed and... you know my fate was involved in non-governmental organisations in such a way that I have worked in the third sector for over 10 years;*
- *I started as a volunteer and this is natural order of things;*
- *It is based on self-motivation , a deep conviction about your own worthiness, about its integrity.*

The organisation T has all the features of a community of practice. Its members cooperate on projects, share their experience, also outside the organisation:

– *I have the feeling that , the same way as the natural family and the extended one, we teach each other (T1);*

– *We normally make contacts, thus through conversations, meetings, exchange of services on the basis: you share your experience and I share mine (T1);*

– *(...) in general I share the experience (T1);*

– *Here indeed, at least in our organisation there is a healthy level of competition, because we inspire and encourage each other - this is the competition (T1);*

– *Or on the other hand we share our failures, we share our experiences (...) on a daily basis we comment on real life, we simply share our experiences (T1);*

– *I have gained knowledge from my previous experiences, from my previous work and passed it to, to our work place (T2);*

– *(...) Here I have had a very great deal of experience, and I have had knowledge and I have shared some things. However, as a matter of fact I have learnt (T2);*

– *(...) We already have a good team, it is ... we have already acted for 10 years, some people have joined in, but the team has worked properly (T2);*

– *Each person has contributed to something new, a self-professional experience - especially in their own activity (T2).*

The organisation raises funds, taking part in competitions and projects and it runs its own business. The professional activity of the disabled people is the main purpose of the enterprise, but it also helps to achieve profit that is devoted to support the association:

– *I meet different people and generally I am in touch with the outside world, er ... or providing the organisation with 1 % because it is also important, applying for co-financed aid (T1);*

– *For example by means of union project, or other sources of financing, we are familiar with it, we know where we should go so as to achieve the goal (T1);*

– *This is the way we work, there are five of us and there are seven or eight projects in the implementation, different people are related to varying degrees (T1);*

– *We are glad we have been given a grant from the Norwegian fund (T1);*

– *The disabled people are employed as a bookbinder assistant, a printer assistant and a graphic designer assistant (T2);*

– *It is a work place of professional activity, the majority of the instructors come from companies, where they gained some experience (T2);*

– *The work place of professional activity has to prepare the disabled people for a work on the open labour market (T2).*

Table 12. Community of practice R, frequencies of initial thoughts

Initial Thought	Frequency of use	Notes
Co-operation/ Working in group	24	This is noted where interviewees stated or discussed the cooperation within the group and with other organisations and enterprises
Action/ Invention/Initiative	19	Frequently occurring words, which demonstrate the activity of members of the organisation, their readiness to act fast. Some actions were novel and there are treated as invention.
Learning, Situated learning	12	Within the organisation from other people and in some situation outside the community of practice.
Motivation/ Self-motivation	10	Frequently occurring word, which is a manifestation of the strong focused activity from the members of the organisation (self-motivation) and motivating other people (other members and disabled people).
Knowledge transfer/ Knowledge sharing	8	Examples of people sharing knowledge within the community of practice and transferring knowledge and experiences from outside.
Fundraising	3	Raising funds from public and EU, EEA grants. Achieving income from business activity
Empowerment/ Approach changing	3	This was noted in T2 statements, connected with disabled persons' empowerment and changing their lives.

Source: Authors' study.

An examination of the interpretative phenomenological analysis showed that, for 28 minutes of interviews and over 3100 words of transcript, 94 "meaning units" were identified and underlined, then placed in different table rows. Some of these are used above to illustrate the results text.

T Summary

The association T was established to support disabled people who were "touched by fate". The organisation has worked since 1999 and has the features of a social business. The people who took part in the research proved that they made a positive contribution to the organisation with their previous experience and knowledge. There are visible processes of learning, knowledge acquisition and its transfer, in the organisation and particular project groups. It gives rise to new innovative ideas and projects. The organisation T runs its business, by raising funds through participation in projects and searching for sponsors. The processes of management are clearly visible in the activities, they have a clearly defined strategy of action, and their activity is actively promoted in the environment.

Chapter 6: Results

6.1 Moving from IPA Outcomes

The 31 transcripts each produced a long table of „Initial Thoughts" and subsequent „emergent themes". These are exampled in the preceding chapters. Thus over 400 pages of transcripts and „meaning units" were reduced to around 100 when discussion and clarification were included. The next stage was to summarise this. The outcome is chapters 4 and 5.

To move on, it was necessary to understand and categorise the generic forms of community of practice membership occurring across the 10 groups, and the common situated learning and other forms of knowledge acquisition and transfer that occurs within them.

Collins, Brown, & Newman identified 6 features of a "cognitive apprenticeship" that included <u>observation, coaching, scaffolding, modeling, fading, and reflection</u>[54].

A second tool to assist in evaluation of the community of practice stories was taken from the work of Fairclough and co-authors. This distinguishes four "research objects": <u>emergence, hegemony, recontextualization and operationalization</u>[55], used in discourse analysis and in part related to strategic critique. This work informs, among others, knowledge transfer, community of practice formation, motivation and reward, so was ideal to apply here.

Thus, the 10 labels described above, plus the broader knowledge transfer and situated learning concepts, were mapped onto the thoughts, themes and relationships that emerged from the IPA stages - they are just identified as "labels", so as not to differentiate the status of their origin unwisely. Thus, and with modifications by these authors they are adopted for this further analysis of "common themes". The literature expansion covers their sourcing in depth.

The figure below outlines the overall process used henceforth. It was used to compare, contrast and otherwise analyse the IPA outcomes, into a form which could be reported as conclusions. Thus comparisons between groups which evidenced their financial focus and utilization, and thus could be called "enterprises", and those that didn't, thus were "organisations", became possible. Similarly, comparisons between countries were feasible (fig. 4).

---

[54] Collins, A, Brown, J.S., Newman, S.E., *Cognitive apprenticeship: Teaching the crafts of reading, writing, and mathematics.* In: Resnick, L. B. (ed.), *Knowing, learning, and instruction: Essays in honor of Robert Glaser* Hillsdale, NJ: Lawrence Erlbaum Associates, 1989, pp. 453-494.

[55] Fairclough, N., *Analyzing Discourse and Text: Textual Analysis for Social Research.* London: Routledge, 2003; Fairclough, N. *Critical discourse analysis.* „Marges Linguistiques" 2005, No. 9, pp.76-94; Fairclough, N. Jessop, R., Sayer, A., *Critical realism and semiosis.* In: Joseph. J., Roberts. J. (eds.), *Realism discourse and Deconstruction*, Routledge, London 2004; Fairclough, N., Wodak, R., *Critical discourse analysis.* In: van Dijk, T., *Discourse as Social Interaction*, Sage, London 1997, p. 12.

Figure 4. The high level analysis process

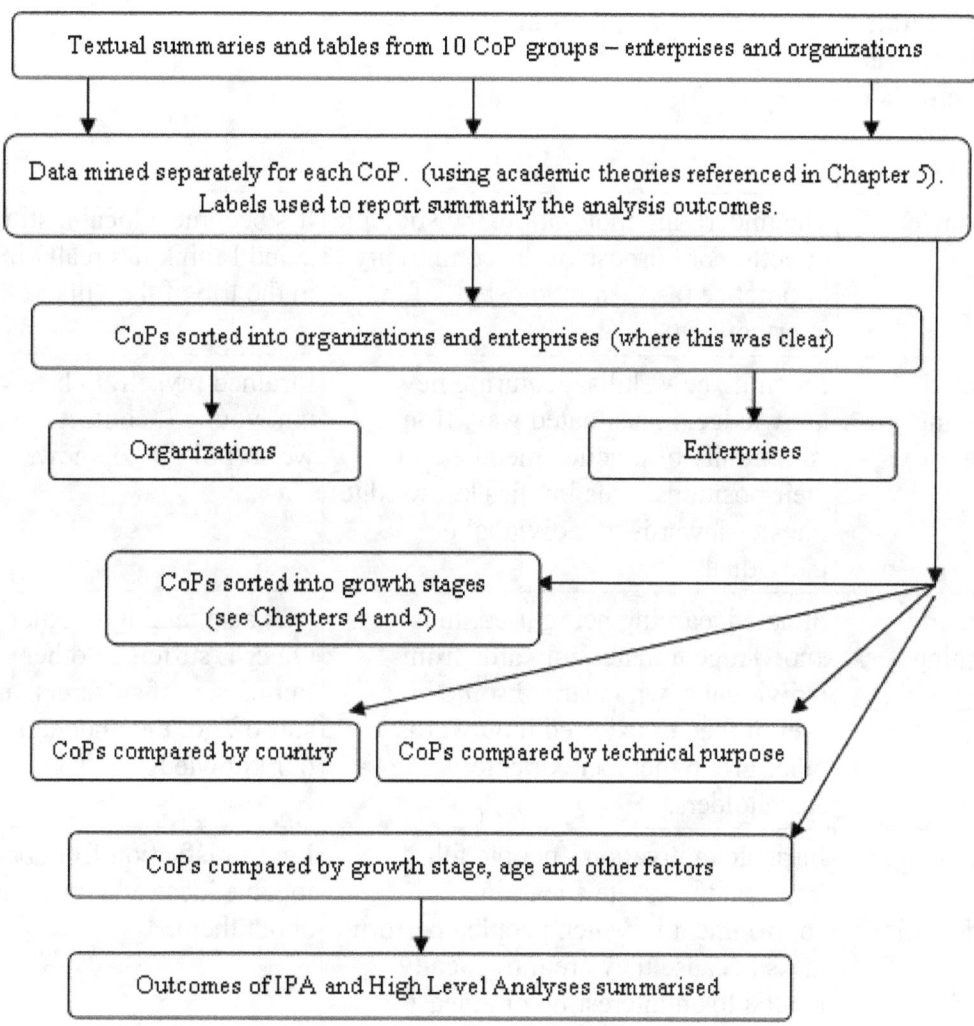

Source: Authors' study.

Table 13 is provided as a brief summary of the labels and how they are used. To reiterate: observation, coaching, scaffolding, modeling, fading, and reflection plus emergence, hegemony, recontextualization and operationalization, together with terminology from community of practice and situated learning literature itself, are used in the text below as exemplifying "common themes" and are briefly introduced here.

Table 13. Example of the application of the theories

„High level" label usually from "initial thought" or "emergent theme"	Explanation and description of its application	Example meaning unit
Rationale	The underlying motivation, the strategic direction or purpose of the community of practice (as seen by most/all of the interviewees).	It's become a local institution, ...and I think it's really important in the life of the village.
Situated Learning (creation)	Learning new skills, acquiring new knowledge, in a situated way, from community of practice members or their positions. This implies knowledge transfer inwards to individual or individuals.	I trained myself, to be a young, um, young L contact... that's how we sort of got to know.
Situated Learning (usage)	Situated learning being used, thus knowledge transfer outwards from individual/s, who learned something useful, then transferred it outwards to other group members or external stakeholders.	(...) also talking to other people. Other L sufferers, other families... of sufferers, and we all sort of, got together and shared our knowledge.
Motivation (for participation)	Intrinsic motivation - people felt it important to create a learning environment in which people "perform tasks because they are intrinsically related to an interesting or at least coherent goal"[56].	I get satisfaction from being able to have ideas and do something about them.
Community of Practice (initial) creation	The original motivation to find others and share knowledge. "Communities of practice are groups of people who share a concern or a passion for something they do and learn how to do it better as they interact regularly"[57].	Generally speaking the new members have all been parents err..., with children the same age as mine.
Community of Practice joining	Producing activities/ events in situated ways, but using social structures and social practices to do so.	I was involved, err, as a committee member I have been involved for Cxxx Day 2007, 2008...

---

[56] Collins, A., Brawn J. S., Holum A., *Cognitive apprenticeship: Making thinking visible*, „American Educator" 1991, No. 15, pp. 6-11.
[57] Wenger-Trayner, B., *Introduction to communities of practice...*, op. cit.

„High level" label usually from "initial thought" or "emergent theme"	Explanation and description of its application	Example meaning unit
Reward	The „return on investment", that came from community of practice membership. The creator of motivation.	Everyone was impressed that I'd managed to do something, and I quite enjoyed it and that was great.
Legitimate Peripheral Participation (LPP)	When the CoP provides an underpinning framework for new individuals to become active, in a community of learners. Often leads to mature membership. In being engaged in reproducing itself, the community gives newcomers access to the knowledge of that community[58]. However, LPP is more than simply learning situated in a practice, it is learning as an integral part of a practice that give meaning to the world: learning as "(...) generative social practice in the lived in world"[59].	See if there is any way, any avenue, where I can help, um newly diagnosed people... I then went on the contacts course, learnt quite a lot from that.
Observation	Degrees of skill encourages new members to view learning as achievable. It also helps people to developing a mental or conceptual model before they have a go at attempting to execute it.	X was conscious that the business was changing, it was growing, it was getting mature.
Coaching	Situated learning and subsequent knowledge transfer. Mentally embedding skills and knowledge in a social and functional context, reinforcing what is done well, encourages observation of new ideas etc.	I was also keen to get people on the committee to bring their own professional expertise with them.

[58] Hougaard, G.. R., *Legitimate Peripheral Participation as a Framework for Conversation Analytic Work in Second Language Learning*, „Forum: Qualitative Social Research" 2009, No. 10(2), Art.4., http://www.qualitative-research.net/index.php/fqs/article/view/1280/2750, Accessed 25 May 2017.
[59] Lave, J., Wenger, E., *Situated learning...*, op. cit., p. 35.

„High level" label usually from "initial thought" or "emergent theme"	Explanation and description of its application	Example meaning unit
Scaffolding	Co-operative learning and problem solving provides a source of support (scaffolding), through knowledge and processes distributed throughout the group.	It was the first time we had really done it in, what I regarded as in a proper, systematic way, …so I was keen to bring that to the committee and again, I think it was something that stuck…
Modeling	Creating access to models of expertise, against which to refine their understanding of complex skills[60].	We were asked for a team of volunteers from the National Trust to take it on board. And have a go with it.
Fading	The gradual removal of support (deliberately or not), to allow independence and maturity- a move to maturity from LPP	Our Hash running group was started by people from another...
Reflection	Allowing people to match their own skills against those of experts and consider how others solve problems, and how they learned to do it[61].	Formal training? Very little to be honest mate. Training is there if you need it, but to be honest, I have had enough experience of life, in talking to people.
Emergence	The emerging into mainstream knowledge and awareness of peripheral members, of new newly emerging discourses, of how the CoP acts, behaves and expresses its values. So, emergence of explicit and tacit knowledge, Situated Learning (SL).	Knowing there is somebody there, if you need to, …and it's very useful, to have other people in a similar sort of position.
Re-contextualisation	Dialogue, discussion and debate between stakeholders as to the utility, application, value and realities of the new SL that is occurring, and its usage in the field (Knowledge Transfer).	(…) having been put into the situation I didn't want to see anybody else in it. were able to go and meet other sufferers who were in the same position.

---

[60] Parscal, T., Hencmann, M., Cognitive Apprecenships in Online Learning, @4th Annual Conference on Distance Teaching & Learning, University of Wisconsin, 2008, http://www.uwex.edu/disted/conference/resource_library/proceedings/08_12686.pdf, Accessed 5 June 2017.
[61] Collins, A., Brown, J. S., & Newman, S. E., *Cognitive apprenticeship: Teaching the crafts of reading, writing, and mathematics*, op. cit., pp. 453-494.

„High level" label usually from "initial thought" or "emergent theme"	Explanation and description of its application	Example meaning unit
Hegemony	Power and leadership relationships in the CoP formed and working to operationalise the new skills. Also core competencies that need to be transferred, at least in part to the other parties (so knowledge transfer). Both parties can exert hegemonic power in different situations[62].	I enjoyed the fact that as Chair I was sort of, able to meet more people, to get more people involved, umm, So last year I took a bit more of an active role, chairing meetings and so on, but only as a sort of shadow Chair, a Vice-Chair.
Operationaliz ation	Move of a situated learner into a mature CoP member. May also relate to the change in attitude and behaviour of the group, the realisation of visions implemented by their later actions.	And I learned an awful lot, about, if you like, policy and procedure, you know, …like I never realised, I felt that, I felt I benefited personally from some of the relationships that I developed

Source: Authors compilation of existing sources and own study.

6.2 Generic Analysis

As already stated the interpretative phenomenological analysis process itself was totally fluid, open and unconstrained, but the subsequent summation here ties the "Common Themes" from it back to published literature. The conclusions the authors draw are their own, but there is an academic base for their second level interpretations here. The tables below contain the higher level „labels" that apply from the "emergent themes", with samples of the initial thoughts and transcript that created them. As a first stage, a table is provided for each community of practice studied, which draws out the "common themes" from the individual interviews. A further series of tables and commentaries then compare the common themes across community of practice's, by purpose and country.

This section takes that data, and uses it to compare the CoPs by purpose and country. As stated above, it is firmly based on the IPA itself and grounded in the initial work. It takes the data, at levels ranging from initial thought and emergent theme down to „meaning unit" and subjects it to a cross-CoP, in depth probing.

6.3 The Tools Used

Two tools assisted in this. First, using keywords to attempt a quantification of Initial Thoughts (other ways were tried but discarded). The keywords came from the initial thoughts. A simple word search of each transcript produced table 14. It is not claimed to offer value itself, it is only included because it was part of the process that created the

---

[62] Fairclough, N. *Critical discourse analysis*, „Marges Linguistiques" 2005, No. 9, pp.76-94

conclusions presented. The value lies in the actual textual presentations that it pointed to (in chapters 4 and 5).

The „initial thoughts" overlap, so (as an example) „activity", „participate" and „help/support" may be counted twice. Some of the counts relate to interviewee numbers and length, so should be treated with care. Also, some groups focused on technical issues only relevant to their group. These "initial thoughts" have not been placed in the above table, but examples are noted here for completeness. e.g. in the "L" group disease (40), pain (7) and diagnosis (42) were key comments, but for obvious reasons not present in the other group. Similarly in the "C" group community was stressed heavily (but as the other groups mentioned it to a lesser extent it is included in the table). We would argue that, if anywhere, they contribute to the "motivation" emergent theme. Profitable economic activity was only present in a few groups.

Table 14 . The 10 groups IPA emergent theme frequency

Initial Thoughts	L	C	V	M	A	AA	B	HH	R	T
Fundraise/Fundraising	5	9	0	5	12	1	3	3	15	3
Cash/money	1	15	1	3	5	7	3	2	9	4
Profitable economic activity*	1	1	0	0	3	0	1	0	2	6
Management aspects	5	21	4	6	11	1	7	3	4	5
Activity/ Action	31	43	48	26	7	22	33	17	21	15
Idea/ Invention/ Change	0	0	21	23	0	0	0	5	20	4
Support	8	11	2	4	0	1	2	4	17	0
Help/Helping	33	12	3	5	5	4	7	7	2	3
Reward/Results/Solidity	1	0	4	8	0	1	1	2	5	3
Chair/person/man	2	43	1	3	2	0	0	0	2	0
Transfer	3	6	3	4	1	0	2	3	4	0
Member/Membership	15	18	4	5	6	2	3	15	3	4
Know/Knowledge	208	61	41	9	30	12	10	8	11	8
Community	3	24	4	6	4	1	1	11	2	24
Motive/Motivation	6	1	25	24	1	0	3	9	23	10
Learn/Learning	17	11	5	6	21	4	1	5	3	12
Participate/Participation	1	4	2	3	0	0	1	7	5	4
Lead/Leader/Leadership	0	5	9	12	6	0	0	0	4	0
Interviews	5	4	3	4	1	1	1	1	3	2
Total words	11000	11000	6500	6000	4400	1700	2100	2600	5670	3160

Source: Authors' study.

* All are not-for-profit so „profitable EA" means raising funds via paid work, not donations.

One finding was that IPA is such a good tool to extract meaning. Almost every interviewee used different words (cash/money/fund/fundraise etc.) so quantitative data from searches is innately limited, even if informed by a good knowledge of the text it derives from. It is only included as an indication of the authors views about the relative frequency with which the interviewees raised topics. The process is fraught with difficulty and has a potential for error. Its main value is its innate weakness.

However, it did reinforce some IPA findings. Knowledge appeared in all the CoPs. Transfer did not. Community was strong in the Village Festival, but not really in the other CoPs. Leadership mattered in C, A, M and V, but not at all in the others, thus the stress on the role of hegemony in a CoP is supported.

Table 15. The 10 groups IPA emergent theme scale

„High Level" Label	L	C	V	M	AA	A	B	HH	R	T
Rationale and Motivation for group existence	5	5	5	5	5	3	4	3	5	3
Motivation for participation/-ing CoP joining	5	5	5	5	4	5	4	2	4	3
Reward (personal)	**2**	**4**	**3**	**4**	**4**	**5**	**3**	**4**	**4**	**2**
Fundraising *	**1**	**5**	**1**	**4**	**5**	**5**	**1**	**1**	**5**	**3**
Community of Practice (initial) creation	5	4	5	5	2	2	4	3	4	2
Situated Learning (creation)	5	4	3	3	2	3	4	2	2	4
Situated Learning (usage) (Change to) Maturity	4	5	4	4	3	5	4	4	3	4
Legitimate Peripheral Participation (LPP)	4	4	4	3	1	3	4	4	3	2
Observation	3	3	4	2	0	4	1	2	4	2
Coaching	3	4	4	3	2	4	1	2	4	3
Scaffolding	1	4	3	4	0	3	1	2	3	4
Modeling	1	4	4	4	3	4	2	3	4	3
Fading	1	3	2	4	0	3	0	2	1	0
Reflection	3	3	2	2	3	4	1	2	4	1
Emergence	3	3	2	2	4	3	1	2	3	2
Re-contextualisation	2	4	4	4	3	5	2	3	4	2
Hegemony/Leadership	**1**	**4**	**4**	**5**	**3**	**4**	**0**	**3**	**3**	**1**
Operationalization	3	4	4	4	3	4	3	3	3	5

Note: The ranking is as follows: 5 = Very Important, 4 = Important, 3 = Stressed slightly, 2 = Mentioned more than once, 1= Mentioned in passing, 0 = Not seen

* "fundraising", was a prevalent "initial thought"- in the enterprises. In the organisations it was almost never mentioned. It is included here as an "emergent theme" because of this.

Source: Authors' study.

Moving on, table 15, above, summarises the emergent themes. It is used to provide comparisons between groups. It ranks, empirically, the stress placed by the interviewees on each emergent theme. The values were created following an in depth review of the transcripts, plus the summary text produced. Other supplied material, including websites etc., also informed the choice. The rankings are the authors opinions, and can only be supported by their intimate knowledge of the transcripts. The emergent themes in bold are discussed briefly, and presented graphically later. Where no significant differences were seen they are not detailed here, but are discussed in the conclusions. Knowledge, its type, transfer and position, matters to all, so will be discussed later.

6.4 Comparison Between Groups

Comparison by "Technical Purpose" or "Role"
One finding was quickly evident. Some of the CoPs were focused on fundraising or otherwise providing money to achieve their technical purpose of creating a social good. Others were focused on knowledge acquisition or dissemination, with fundraising taking a very secondary part.

This division is described earlier, and underpinned by the literature reviewed. The authors here chose to use the terms „organisation" and „enterprise". Organisations exist to share knowledge, whether for internal use or for dissemination. Money is clearly a secondary issue. Campaigning for a social good comes into that category.

Chapter 4 and 5 evidences this and it is unnecessary to repeat the detail. Statements extracted as meaning units, and the emergent themes provide the justification to class the L, V, H and B groups herein. L exists to create, collect and disseminate knowledge on the disease they share, also how to manage it. V exists to collect and share knowledge about our treatment of food, animals, and campaign for change. H exists to share knowledge and thus opportunities to enjoy a healthy lifestyle which includes running, walking and socialising, often with beer. B exists to share knowledge of a historic structure which is under threat, by campaigning and awareness raising. None of these focus on fundraising.

Chapter 4 and 5 evidences that the enterprises raise funds, then direct them towards the social good. M, AA and possibly C, A, R, T fit in here. M exists to support a local orphanage. Their main role is fundraising and awareness promotion for this. Knowledge is created and shared by the needs of the beneficiary, and the processes of fundraising. Awareness of the community lifestyle they share -motorcycling, is a secondary benefit. AA exists to raise large sums of money to support the Air Ambulance. Knowledge of how to achieve this is mentioned but not stressed. Campaigning to raise awareness of the need for funding is however, a significant knowledge transfer role. The figure 5 illustrates this.

Figure 5. Fundraising and profitable economic activity, compared between CoPs

FUNDRAISING/ PROFITABLE ECONOMIC ACTIVITY		TYPE OF COMMUNITY OF PRACTICE								
		Organisation ← → Enterprise								
	High						R	A	AA	
									M	
	Relative Importance							C		
										T
	Low	L	V	HH	B					

Source: Authors' study.

In between, but clearly mainly enterprises, are C and A. C exists to collect and share knowledge on how to run a village festival. Fundraising is a key part of this and knowledge about fundraising and cash management were stressed. Knowledge about the events in the festival was not stressed, and tacit rather than explicit. A is only represented by one interview, and the interviewee repeatedly stressed that his role was relatively new and not totally representative. His story was clearly about fundraising and cash management, very similar to that discussed by the C interviewees. Thus the authors regard them as mainly enterprises.

Comparison by "Leadership Behaviour" and "Personal Reward"
Some of the CoPs talked about leadership and hegemony. The figure 6 illustrates this. Others either did not stress it or ignored it totally. Chapter 4 evidences that M exists to support a local orphanage. Leadership and hegemony are clearly evident and respected. In CoP R both leadership and hegemony is seen clearly – this CoP has a leader with managerial, coaching skills. She created the organisation, she sets the direction of its development and can solve problems. Also organisation V has a clear leader „with vision". She is a member of other nationwide organisations, takes part in many training events and this knowledge gives her an advantage.

Figure 6. Hegemony and leadership, compared between CoPs

HEGEMONY/LEADERSHIP		TYPE OF COMMUNITY OF PRACTICE										
		Organisation ⟵⟶ Enterprise										
	High								A		M	
			V		B		R	C				
	Relative Importance			HH								
											AA	
												T
	Low											
		L										

Source: Authors' study.

Conversely, AA exists to raise large sums of money to support the Air Ambulance. Knowledge of how to achieve this is mentioned but not stressed. Leadership also is mentioned „in passing". C exists to collect and share knowledge on how to run a village festival. Knowledge about fundraising and cash management were stressed, as was the need for effective leadership and hegemony. T is divided by functions, so has many leaders, who cooperate. A is only represented by one interview, and the interviewee repreatedly stressed that his role was relatively new and not totally representative. However, the story was clearly about fundraising and cash management, very similar to that discussed by the C interviewees. Leadership was stressed in this context.

Personal reward attributed to membership of the CoP was a significantly different stress point. The vegan group, the motorcycle fundraisers, the Air Ambulance and the individual recruited to manage funds for the theatre arts group all stressed the need. High personal reward is also characteristic for CoP R. The background of their activity is connected with help for disabled children and consequently their empowerment. It creates strong motivation and its effects resonate. For the others this was of less value. The figure 7 shows it.

Figure 7. Personal reward and motivation, compared between CoPs

		TYPE OF COMMUNITY OF PRACTICE										
		Organisation ⟷ Enterprise										
PERSONAL REWARD/MOTIVATION	High								A		M	
			V					R			AA	
	Relative Importance								C			
												T
				B								
	Low			HH								
		L										

Source: Authors' study.

Motivation is always one of the key factors in charitable activity, especially internal motivation or drive, so personal motivation. On the other hand, the ability to motivate others is an important managerial feature. This approach to motivating is associated with leadership, as discussed above. A strong ability to motivate is visible especially in group M and R. The AA, HH and L groups did not really address motivation to lead, only motivation to participate and "change the world". Conversely the C, B and A CoPs all stressed a need to lead and influence members.

6.5 Comparison by Country

Poland and the UK have quite different cultures, as seen by the authors. However, in social organisations people behave quite similarly. Leadership was important to some, not others. It appears to be more a function of technical purpose, and possibly who chose to join, and less about national character. Reward was also quite similar, as reported by the interviewees. Knowledge transfer though, was stressed very differently. The Polish interviewees seemed to feel a need to educate and campaign much more strongly than the UK groups. The reasons for this are outside the scope of this book and may well relate to national character and history.

The importance of situated learning and support seemed more "grouped in the middle" in Poland, but there was more variation in the UK. This is possibly related to technical purpose rather than national character. Finally community spirit was slightly more evident in

Poland, but its importance varied more. The English author recognises this to be true, at least in his new community, seen clearly from his 7 years as a Polish resident.

Leadership was stressed by 2 groups, and mentioned by 4 others, but with less stress (fig. 8). The village festival (C) valued it, but possibly because there was a lot of money and other legal issues involved. Health and Safety was stressed, and the need to lead on it. The M group stressed it "After her we go in darkness", and clearly valued the leader. 4 groups almost totally ignored it, possibly because of their values, but possibly because money was less important, so structure mattered less. The other groups were in between. For instance group T is divided into a few subgroups, all at the same level of importance with no overall control or person who is a strong leader: "And this is called the department of social projects and... well, the next is the department of artistic projects, and they are more related to the primary activity of the association, so they are the actors, the more creative minds, more... whereas we are so technological and social". So, decisions are taken in small groups, totally democratically, although there is knowledge transfer between groups.

Figure 8. Leadership, compared between CoPs and countries

	UK			CoP behaviour- LEADERSHIP		Poland		
High	C					M		
	A					V		
	B					R		
Relative Importance								
	H	AA						
Low	L					T		

Source: Authors' study.

Reward was stressed by nearly all, the Air Ambulance interviewee said: "It were great to see the yellow helicopter fly to the hospital", The medical support CoP L said many things such as: "Em, ...what have I got out of the group - I don't really know, apart from the satisfaction that I'm... possibly helping somebody." (L5), and "Because you do think that you are isolated. And you do think, you don't realise that other people are having... exactly the same (problems) as you", etc. So, reward is implicit in most of what these CoPs chose to stress. Knowledge acquisition is valued because of the reward it creates (fig. 9).

Figure 9. Reward, compared between CoPs and countries

	UK			CoP behaviour-REWARD			Poland		
High	L	AA							
	C	A					V	R	
	B						M		
Relative Importance	H								
							T		
Low									

Source: Authors' study.

In CoPs M and R from Poland reward is quite strongly visible. The interviewees from group R showed it emotionally in their statements: "Well, first of all, I must stress that the son wants to go there very much. (…) Here he has their workshops, something else… I think he found himself in this environment here". In group M similar statements show it: "I saw these children, I saw their smiles, some err they were crying and it affected me so…". Most of the other groups valued the return they gained on their time investment, but H and T possibly not as much.

Figure 10. Knowledge transfer and coaching, compared between CoPs and countries

	UK			CoP behaviour-KT/Coaching/LPP			Poland		
High	L								
	C	A					V	M	
							R		
Relative Importance							T		
	H	B							
Low	AA								

Source: Authors' study.

Knowledge transfer and coaching (fig. 10) were stressed by the medical CoP L, probably for similar reasons. For example "and in my personal experience ….my mother was a sufferer, and seeing my mother go through life in absolute agony, day after day, seven hours a day-er 7 days a week, 24 hours a day, is ...difficult. And you just wish you could turn to somebody and gain some knowledge of how to make that person's life a bit more liveable and help in any way you can". Also " ... in the L group is mainly social activities where L sufferers were able to go and meet other sufferers who were in the same position who were suffering of the same disease and same condition, and also they could compare their, you know, their medical treatment, their hospital treatment "(L1) .

Polish groups, especially R and V, valued it. Especially organisation R, who started pioneering work in '90 and still need more knowledge for effective activity. As a mature group they also transfer knowledge to others. Group V is looking for information in other, larger and experienced environmental organisations. The fact that the main members belonged, or still belong to other organisations help them with it. Also group M stressed knowledge transfer, although their activity is more repeatable and cyclical. On the other hand, coaching is the most visible in this group . Conversely the Hash House Harriers, the Air Ambulance and the Victorian heritage group did not stress it. This is possibly because the tasks were simpler or the members interviewed were more experienced.

Figure 11. Situated learning and support, compared between CoPs and countries

	UK			CoP behaviour-SL and support		Poland		
High	L	C						
		A				T		
	B					R	M	
Relative Importance						V		
	H	AA						
Low								

Source: Authors' study.

Surprisingly, situated learning and support (fig. 11) were valued quite differently to knowledge transfer by some groups. The Victorian heritage (group B) interviewee valued it, but this could be attributed to "never done anything like this before". The Polish CoPs were more "middle of the road" in their valuation. It was stressed a lot in group T, where volunteers and LPP members are involved in activities to become mature members. Also in group R there is a visible system of new members involving themselves into organisational life.

Figure 12. Community spirit, compared between CoPs and countries

		UK		CoP behaviour-Community spirit		Poland			
High	C	L				M			
						V			
	H								
Relative Importance	B	AA				R			
						T			
Low	A								

Source: Authors' study.

Community spirit (fig. 12) was repeatedly stressed by the L medical group, the village festival and the motorcyclists. It was also valued by the vegans, running club, the Heritage group and others. All were clearly motivated to help their community, and wanted to tell the world why. The low valuation in the UK theatre group may be an artefact created by his specialist position.

Altruistic motivation is evident in every transcript. Everybody wants to make the world a better place. So, they join with others and create a community of practice. They share knowledge and find it, from others, sometimes it comes from their previous activities or just by sharing.

The medical group formed and exists because dissatisfied with the support availability. The village festival group formed to improve their village life. The motorcycle group formed to help disadvantaged children. In these and all the other cases considered people wanted to change society. Every group exists to help others. Community, although not a word often used emerges from every transcript.

All interviewed were active because of a perceived failure in society. Vegan food was seen as less damaging to animals. The Air Ambulance fills a gap where the UK state fails. The Victorian heritage tried to save a feature but the commercial owners wanted to upgrade inappropriately. The other groups were similarly motivated. There was evidence of personal reward. Several interviews stated that they gained personally from new opportunities to apply their knowledge in new situations. However, that was never their priority.

Chapter 7: Conclusions

This book was designed to be a report about motivation and knowledge transfer. To keep the scope manageable it was constrained to be only a study of knowledge transfer in communities of practice working in a not-for profit environment. The concept of an "social enterprise" versus an "social organisation" was one of the first clear emergent themes that arose from the study. Originally only the loose term "group" was expected. When the authors started this work, they too were under the impression that income was a key need. However, the general impression, first gained during interview and transcription, that there were 2 different things happening, was quickly confirmed.

All groups were formed to meet the same need. A social good needed to happen, and the individuals who were sufficiently motivated to "right the wrong", or provide the service, gathered people into a group to change the world. Quickly, 2 strategies to achieve this, emerged. Some groups focused on fundraising to do this - the UK Yorkshire Air Ambulance is a prime example, the M and R Polish groups too. Others chose awareness raising, and other forms of knowledge transfer. The L medical help group and B heritage protection group sit at this end of the spectrum. For these, fundraising was clearly secondary and just a "means to an end".

The authors here struggled to classify this divide, some of their research is presented in the literature chapter. They decided to use two terms, often used by others. enterprises focus on obtaining funds, and organisations on sharing knowledge. Thus, communities of practice operating in differing ways, as social organisations and enterprises were identified from the analyses.

Most academic literature in this field assumes that only groups exist only to raise and use finance, and that groups operating without structured income from donations, work or sale of product or services are "beginners", as addressed in the research underpinnings chapter. This book illustrates that it's not true. Only half the cases considered are focused as fundraisers.

Therefore, a key finding is that social organisations can exist in the long term, with almost no hegemony, structure or income stream. As already stated, the UK L and B communities of practice illustrate this well. The next subsection applies some of the "labels" used earlier in overall conclusions.

Motivation and Reward

Human motivation was a clear factor in the planning of the book. Why do people undertake these activities, and what rewards them, was clearly key to a study of what they do and how they do it. Thus, these factors are addressed in the early chapters of introduction, design and processes. The scope was designed in this way, to include as many technical purposes as possible, without losing depth of study. The final choice of 4 groups, reported in depth, plus 6 with smaller samples meets this criteria.

So, motivation clearly drives knowledge acquisition and transfer in all of the cases studied here. The overriding, clearly evident and dominant conclusion is that each community of practice is trying to create a social good, and cultivate a community ethos. They all want to "change the world for the better". Their efforts are focused on this technical purpose, whether it be better medical or social care, a vegan lifestyle or a better village community. All the individuals stated things that tie well into Maslow's "self-actualisation", although some have a secondary goal, of personal development or even survival.

It was easy to conclude that all the CoPs are driven purely by a technical purpose, and that their motivation was to achieve this: For example: organisations such as the L (UK) CoP, trying to find out and share knowledge about a rare medical condition; The B (UK) Heritage CoP campaigning to raise awareness of a potential loss of a social good; the (Polish) V CoP, trying to change behaviour towards animals. These groups are therefore, all communities of practice working in an organisation, trying to share knowledge and raise awareness, with money very much a secondary consideration.

Conversely, the Air Ambulance and M CoPs are primarily fundraisers, thus enterprises (as defined for this book). Awareness raising is important, but a secondary purpose, sitting well behind the primary aim of "helping by fundraising".

Finally, some groups studied, have components of both. The Village Festival group (C) is clearly financially aware and motivated to create funds to promote the festival. The interviewees core motivation was to "help the village". The interview with A, suggests that the Theatre Group knew it needed financial management to continue achieving its technical purpose of providing theatre arts. Although M is an "enterprise", and devoted to fundraising for the children's home, promoting motorcycling is clearly a secondary but important role. The R group, whose prime motivation is raising funds for a new house for the disabled, is clearly an enterprise, managing resources to build and maintain the house. However it is also heavily involved in awareness raising and knowledge transfer.

Reward is clearly part of motivation, but can be separated where interviewees stressed what they got out of their involvement. Their "return on investment", is mentioned often. For example, their acquisition and subsequent sharing of knowledge, via situated learning in the environment of their CoP. A further, altruistic reward is mentioned, and is the cause of their subsequent knowledge transfer within and out of these communities. An important and distinct part of this is their reuse of learning from their prior life situations, and how the implicit knowledge resulting from this is transferred into their community of practice. This was repeatedly stressed by A, mentioned several times by AA, B, and by the C interviewees.

All the groups, as evidenced by all the interviews, are driven primarily by motivation, or "self-actualization", as Maslow discussed. Its form varies, but altruistic motivation shines throughout.

Knowledge Transfer, Coaching and Observation

The need for explicit focused knowledge runs through all the transcripts. Whether medical, financial or legal knowledge, there is considerable evidence of searches for it, and processes to make tacit knowledge explicit enough to share. People need knowledge that is not biased by commercial or other pressures, and the CoP acts as a repository for this. In some cases it is transferred face-to-face, by meetings or presentations, or via phone calls and newsletters. The degree of formality varies greatly between groups, but the outcome is the same, an increase in explicit knowledge that can be shared. People are coached and helped, they observe others and create models of their situation.

The organisations express this best, as their primary purpose is awareness raising, but the enterprises need it too. Whether their role is to transfer knowledge on how to fundraise, „by sitting in a muddy field with a stand" (the Air Ambulance), or riding motorcycles dressed as Father Christmas (the M group), or gaining and acting as a knowledge repository (the L medical group), all exhibit characteristics of knowledge transfer, sharing, coaching and moving from legitimate peripheral participation to maturity.

Situated Learning and Scaffolding

Two forms of situated learning were seen. Firstly the move from the fringes, or "legitimate peripheral participation" (LPP), to maturity, as a result of new learning becoming embedded in the situation or context. Secondly, the application of prior learning to a new situation.

The first type is well evidenced in the L group. Members were desperate for help, for themselves or their loved ones. They could not get effective help from their medical professionals (doctors, nurses and dentists were cited), so they turned to each other and shared what they had. This enabled them to move to maturity, and counsel others. The B CoP interview also evidences this, as does the M interview.

The second form is best evidenced by A.... He stated that he was recruited specifically for his financial skills. He transferred them into the CoP, and moved from the edge to a key role. The V CoP also discussed this, using skills from animal husbandry and other prior experiences, to back up their campaign for a new way of living.

Both these types of SL create "scaffolding" and models, from which people gain support. Co-operation is inherent in a CoP.

Hegemony and Leadership

This was a variable function. Hardly mentioned in the L and AA CoPs, stressed repeatedly in the V and M CoPs. Evident in the A, C and B transcripts, but possibly because the interviewees had leading roles. This usage of the IPA technique revealed insights but it is difficult to draw firm conclusions. This area needs further study, but possibly via new interviews with a different focus.

Fundraising and Money

A key activity in half the CoPs studied. Clearly evidenced enough to divide them into organisations and enterprises. So, a reflection of the original technical purpose, and the strategic choices as to how it was to be achieved. The mechanisms were not often discussed, suggesting that the interviewees did not rate them as of key importance. The interviews were open ended, with very little direction by interviewers, so, when they were raised by interviewees, for example in the C enterprise, and the Air Ambulance, they were only alluded to in passing. Explanation of processes was clearly not considered relevant. Again, this area needs further study, but possibly via new interviews with a different focus.

Community and CoP

A major factor in all the groups. Although not always explicitly stated (this can be evidenced by the keyword searches), it was important to all. The "community" made up the CoP, but the CoP served the wider community. The Air Ambulance serves the community of Yorkshire, with a few dedicated individuals raising money to keep it extant. The C village festival CoP had features of both enterprise and organisation but was there to promote the village community and draw in a wider audience to use the village facilities. The B organisation campaigned to keep the Victorian Heritage available to the village community and wider population. The V group exists to help its members and campaign more widely, and the M enterprise serves a similar function, as does the R enterprise.

All interviewees expressed their pleasure at being "in a community", without prompting. This again possible comes back to psychological drivers, as a motivation to perform and find friends.

Operationalization

This exists in all the CoPs studied. They all exist because of their motivation to learn, share knowledge and operationalize it. Whether by fundraising (and learning how to do this), using the funds raised, or just learning and sharing the knowledge gained, every CoP exists just to operationalize their activity. How they do it is the most interesting feature, and IPA revealed this well. As already stated, enterprises operationalise knowledge about fundraising and usage of the funds, plus a secondary operationalization of their understanding of awareness raising. Organisations gather knowledge, of medical conditions, social needs, or community actions, and have learned how to share it, transfer it and otherwise make it explicit.

Fading is related to operationalization, in this context. Once people reach maturity, they often move on, personally, geographically or socially. When they do they often start or join a similar group in their new environment. Whether they use the knowledge gained, in their own transitions from LPP to maturity, or knowledge from an earlier role (as in the case aof the A group), to create new groups, utilising the learning they gained in new places, as in the case of the M CoP, or reacting to new sources of information, as in the L CoP. In both cases the models changed, and the knowledge gained was refocused.

Summary

Finally, as already stated, every CoP exists to plug a gap. State and commercial interests fail to provide for these passions. Whether vegan food availability, village life. arts or medical support, all are perceived to be lacking and the CoP tries to fill the gap. No real differences between the UK and Poland were noted, although cultural, social and legal differences influenced processes.

The authors conclude and assert that this analysis provides an original contribution to learning, especially as it is considered against the context of published literature on communities of practice, situated learning and other concepts. Analysis of over 20 hours of transcripts, in English and Polish, allowed the authors, and will allow others to consider whether the common knowledge transfer activities and behaviours, inherent in the education and learning the social enterprise community of practice members undertook, may be of value and potentially transferable to other social enterprise situations.

Chapter 8: Discussion of Research Underpinnings

This chapter inevitably expands and amplifies in part the material in the main text, mostly chapters 2 and 3. The main text is intended as a linear read. Thus, it introduces key concepts as it progresses. Brief summaries of what is to be used, why and how they are there. They are reproduced and expanded here, adequately to "tell the story", the section is intended to act as a reference work, and also to stand alone. Thus, this chapter is intended to comprise an in depth introduction to all the concepts used in this book, sometimes with the rationale for its use by the authors, but without the distraction of the actual examples in chapters 2 and 3. It is structured "by concept". It begins by introducing quantitative analysis, why and how it is used in this book, from methodologies to outcome analysis. It continues by re-introducing the concepts that underlie the research, such as motivation theory, the CoP, situated learning and other forms of knowledge transfer, and other ideas used herein.

8.1 Methodology and Analysis

8.1.1 Qualitative Analysis

The research hypothesis behind this book, was that qualitative tools can be used to reveal the motivations and knowledge transfer techniques operating in voluntary groups, or non-governmental organisations (NGOs). After „reading around" it was realised that there was a difference in processes between large, centrally managed charities and small, usually locally managed groups. To study both would be too large a challenge here, however an interesting one.

The authors were surprised how little directly relevant academic research they could find. There is much on business analysis, and much on the voluntary sector. However, there is little on use in communities of practice, especially the motivation and knowledge transfer in the small, independent, not-for profit, voluntary, NGO field.

One interesting quote, from the Guardian (UK) newspaper in March 2015, illustrates the point about small and independent: „Two weeks after launching my small charity, I was invited to meet the chief executive of the largest and oldest charity in my space. <<You're doing the wrong thing>>, I was told, <<you're fragmenting the charitable space. You should just raise money for us as we know best how to spend it. You don't know what you're doing.>> ...My response? <<If I truly thought you were doing a good enough job, I wouldn't be doing this.>>...Many small charities are born out of a desire to have some element of control over a situation with little hope. In my case, my young son has an incurable disease that will get progressively worse. When I set up my charity, I needed to take control of our lives and help to focus research that could potentially save his life and the lives of so many children like him. For me, small charities can operate and access places that the larger ones can't. They are often more effective. Many bigger charities are bogged down in their own organisation. They are often slow and bureaucratic, and hold a belief that because they are big they need to control the message. They are not fleet of foot and they are not entrepreneurs but – in my opinion - professional politicians. As a small organisation, we are beholden to history. We are not scared for our jobs. We're neither worried about our major donors nor bothered by politics"[63]. This sums up many views heard during primary research for this book.

A second example, from the website ukfundraising.co.uk, entitled "Why charities should make a big deal of being small", lists positive attributes including flexibility, local knowledge and ties with the community[64]. Academic sources were found, but these two internet sites summed up the author's ontological positions well, so are reported here.

Thus, the authors chose only communities of practice (CoPs) to limit the scope of study. In these, there was a clear need to draw out and evaluate motivation, its rationale, the forms of knowledge transfer and other knowledge management processes in use because, as stated above, existing research is sparse. Qualitative inquiry was in this instant, the chosen approach. The concept of CoPs is discussed later but was chosen because members have to find, create and transfer knowledge on the issues they study. The authors therefore considered ways to establish why and how members joined their groups and communities, their motivations for doing so, and their subsequent situated, social and cognitive learning. So, how to identify when and how this occurs between group members and/or is acquired from outside, in this specific social enterprise context. As described by Cresswell it represents "a legitimate mode of social and human science exploration (...). Good models of qualitative inquiry demonstrate the rigour, difficulty and time-consuming nature of this approach". The intention is that the researcher "gathers words, analyses them inductively, focused on the meaning of participants, (to) describe a process (...)"[65].

From the authors' prior experience they recognize the "multiple dimensions of the problem or issue, and wishes to display it in all its complexity"[66]. Thus they take the ontological position that human reality is subjective and that "variables cannot be easily identified, theories are not available to explain behaviour of participants (...)"[67]. This approach, using concepts discussed by Cresswell above, predicates a general approach to research design, with detailed research design emergent from the initial research outcomes. It is necessary to experience the perceptions of the participants under study, and look for meaning- from their viewpoint.

Phenomenology is appropriate for this study because it allows the use of an "orienting framework", a perspective rather than a theory, but a perspective that informs the study and gives it some rigour. However, from the literature review the authors undertook, it is clear that there is no single, commonly accepted methodology for this type of qualitative study and analysis of attitudes, behaviours and paradigms. The process required is an inductive, phenomenological process of observations "enabling a thorough understanding of the

---

[63] http://www.theguardian.com/voluntary-sector-network/2015/mar/15/why-i-believe-small-charities-are-better-than-big-ones, Accessed 27 May 2017.
[64] http://fundraising.co.uk/2015/09/10/why-charities-should-make-a-big-deal-of-being-small/#.V0gt2vn9lph, Accessed 27 May 2017.
[65] Cresswell, J. *Qualitative Inquiry and Research Design: Choosing among Five Traditions*, Sage 1998, p. 14.
[66] Ibidem, p. 15.
[67] Ibidem, p. 18.

research sample and context" but not allowing "the meaning of events to individuals to be ignored"[68]. This quote led to the approach of phenomenological data capture, leading to analysis of the captured narrative and a final process of integration.

The authors note that this qualitative, interpretative approach, albeit with considerable variation in detail, is outlined in many studies of behaviour, motivation and knowledge, though in other sectors. Although a minority of texts reviewed have detailed positivist or even quantitative analyses, the majority have adopted inductive and theory building styles, addressing attitude, behaviour and cultural issues and factors.

Building a "rich picture" of these attitudes and behaviours allowed the authors to explore meanings in depth. The underlying drivers of these answers to unspoken questions created by unstructured interviews, creates "a combination of exploratory and conclusive research strategies"[69]. The study was underpinned throughout by the belief that "knowledge and the processes that lead to its production are context specific"[70]. Lyons and Coyle go on to discuss how the collection and analysis of qualitative, non-numeric data can provide rich detail, and much description, together with possible explanations of how meaning-making occurs – "how they make sense of the world and experience certain events"[71]. Citing Willig they note how qualitative researchers "aim to understand (…) how people negotiate relationships (…)"[72], quoting family life and work as examples. This approach has been used throughout.

8.1.2 Interpretative Phenomenological Analysis

"IPA is a qualitative research approach committed to the examination of how people make sense of their major life experiences"[73]. As such it is ideally suited to the authors' purpose here. A second quote also illustrates this good match: "IPA researchers are especially interested in what happens when the everyday flow of lived experience takes on a particular significance for people"[74]. Thus, in this book the authors asked people about motivation to be in their community of practice, and inevitably the responses focused on the most important reason, usually a life-changing experience. This demonstrates the value of IPA in this context.

On the same point, Smith JA et al. quote how "someone makes sense of a major transition in their life"[75]. In addressing their 2nd major theoretical axis, an interpretative endeavour informed by hermeneutics, the theory of interpretation, they assert that, as sense-making creatures, the narrative that interviewees provide reflect their attempts to make sense of the events, that these authors are studying. The authors further defend this choice of

---

[68] Bryman, A., Bell, E. *Business Research Methods,* Oxford University Press. 2003, p. 86.
[69] Robson, C., *Real World Research*, Blackwell, Oxford 2002, p. 31.
[70] Lyons, E., Coyle, A., *Analysing Qualitative Data in Psychology*, Sage 2007, p. 4.
[71] Ibidem, p. 4.
[72] Willig, C., *Introducing Qualitative Research in Psychology*, McGraw-Hill Education 2008; Willig, C., Stainton-Rogers, W. (eds.) *The Sage Handbook of Qualitative Research in Psychology,* Sage, London 2008.
[73] Smith J. A., Flowers, P., Larkin, M., *Interpretative Phenomenological Analysis: Theory, Method and Research*, Sage, London 2009, p. 1.
[74] Ibidem, p. 3.
[75] Ibidem.

approach by further quoting "IPA is committed to the detailed examination of the particular case. (...) IPA studies usually have a small number of participants (...). (...) the aim is to reveal something of the experience of each (...). As part of this the study may explore in detail the similarities and differences of each case (...). The aim is to find a reasonably homogeneous sample to examine convergence and divergence in some detail (...). Immediate claims are therefore bounded by the group but an extension can be considered through theoretical generalizability (...)". Again, reinforcing the above point: "IPA's core interest group is people concerned with the human predicament...engaging with the world"[76]

As already stated when considering generic qualitative techniques, the authors note that this interpretative approach, albeit with considerable variation in detail, is outlined in many of the papers and books reviewed. For example Smith, Flowers and Larkin state, quoting Husserl: "The founding principle of phenomenological inquiry is that experience should be examined in the way it occurs (...). (...) then Husserl reasoned that these essential features of an experience (...) and might then illuminate a given experience for others too"[77].

Thus, to experience the perceptions of the participants under study, and look for meaning, as the participants' experience it, interpretative phenomenological analysis was chosen. The authors assert that it allows outsiders to understand the motivation to become involved in, and eventually manage and contribute to, the members situated learning, and subsequent knowledge base. It permits each individual's perceptions and recollections of their initial motivations, and the subsequent interactions between members, to be explored. The technique shows discovery of new knowledge by CoP members, and transition from new peripheral membership to eventual mature core legitimacy. This can include managerial roles, and several forms of hegemony, as described elsewhere[78]. This aspect was a prominent feature of many interviews and can be extensively evaluated via this technique. This aspect, and their situated learning, both in the community of practice under study, and in their earlier life, and how it helped them, clearly shows that phenomenology is the obvious and appropriative choice for this type of study, because it allows an "orienting framework".

The actual processes, as used by these authors, are described in depth in the methodology chapter, so are not reviewed here, except by exampling the perceived meaning of the terms used. So, the criteria for identifying a "meaning unit" are taken directly from Langridge's text: "When trying to determine the units of meaning, the analyst should be limited by two horizons to the meaning that they construe (...) to discern meaning units, it is necessary to do this with an eye for where the experience relates to issues appropriate (...). So one might notice motions (...) but not organisation dynamics, unless they impact directly (...). That is if one were researching the experience of acute illness, then that would be the focus (...)"[79]. Similarly, the processes of noting initial thoughts and then compiling them into

---

[76] Smith J. A., Flowers, P., Larkin, M., *Interpretative Phenomenological Analysis...*, op. cit, p. 3.

[77] Ibidem., p. 12.

[78] Humphreys, A., Brown, B., *Narratives of Organizational Identity and Identification: A Case Study of Hegemony and Resistance*, "Organizational Studies" 2002, Vol. 23, No. 3, pp. 421-447.

[79] Langridge, D., *Phenomenological Psychology, Theory Research and Method*, Pearson Prentice Hall 2007, pp. 88 onwards.

emergent themes are described in depth in the methodology chapter. Here, suffice it to say, that the process is easy to use, rigorous and extremely useful.

Moving on to how to analyse the data that interpretative phenomenological analysis generates, research by Greeno suggested that knowledge cannot be separated from action, because it is situated in activities driven by social and cultural contexts[80]. Another work by Greeno[81] has been reviewed more recently by Robbins and Aydede and suggests that "knowing" is situated and cannot stand alone[82].

This point was considered by Lave and Wenger[83], and is very much based on theories of human behaviour. Knowing, therefore, emerges as individuals develop intention, through directed activities within the cultural contexts of their community of practice. The direction of this leads them to the accomplishment of their desired goals. Their situated learning is thus expressed by their ability to act as an increasingly competent participant. As they participate more fully within their communities of practice, their knowing continuously evolves. New individuals then become more active in their community of learners. Lave and Wenger also introduced the concept of legitimate peripheral participation (LPP), and this is discussed under the review of communities of practice later in this section. Later in this chapter, work on motivation and behaviour is cited, which expands on this.

More recent work often focuses on developing communities and the idea of "learning organisations", for example Aggeslam asks "chicken or egg?", when discussing knowledge management[84] and evaluating cultural evolution. Here the authors have analysed how that culture evolved, its motives and processes. Borowiecki and Dziura gave many useful insights on Eastern European organisations[85]. Their edited book includes a paper by the editors which gives a useful definition: "(..) all economic activities conducted by enterprises (...) whose ethics (...) place service to members ahead of profit (...) are independent"[86]. Buła, Fudaliński and Szarucki state that: "(...) we are looking (...) for a natural tendency of societies to act for the benefit of socially useful objectives"[87].

---

[80] Greeno, J. G., *On claims that answer the wrong question*, "Educational Research" 1997, Vol. 26, No. 1, pp. 5-17.

[81] Greeno, J. G., *Middle School Mathematics Through Applications Project Group. The situativity of knowing, learning, and research*, „American Psychologist" 1998, Vol. 53, No. 1, pp. 5-26.

[82] Robbins, P., Aydede, M., *The Cambridge Handbook of Situated Cognition*, Cambridge University Press 2008.

[83] Lave, J., Wenger, E., *Situated Learning: Legitimate Peripheral Participation*, Cambridge University Press 1991.

[84] Aggeslam, L., *Learning Organization or Knowledge Management - what came first, the Chicken or the Egg?*, "Information Technology and Control" 2006, Vol. 35, No. 3A, pp. 295-302.

[85] Borowiecki, R., Dziura, M (eds.), *Third Sector: Theoretical and Empirical Approach*, Crakow University of Economics, Cracow 2014.

[86] Borowiecki, R, Dziura, M., *From the third sector to the social economy*. In: Borowiecki, R. Dziura, M. (eds.), *Third Sector: Theoretical and Empirical Approach*, Crakow University of Economics, Cracow 2014, p. 36.

[87] Buła, P., Fudaliński, J., Szarucki, M., *Determinants of the process of social management of social economy entities on the example social cooperative activity*. In: Borowiecki, R., Dziura, M. (eds.), *Third Sector: Theoretical and Empirical Approach*, Crakow University of Economics, Cracow 2014, p. 54.

8.1.3 Emergent Theme Analysis Tools

The authors quickly identified a need to reduce the data collected. Once "meaning units" were identified, and "initial thoughts" noted, there was a need to identify emergent themes[88]. So, labels were sought to at least begin to categorise the data. A very extensive literature review, of which only a small part can be referenced here, led to the selection of some classification labels to reduce the mass of IPA output, so the emergent themes were labeled using some of the concepts below. This final outcome allowed comparisons between CoPs and countries.

One useful tool was supplied by Collins, Brown and Newman, who identify 6 features of a "cognitive apprenticeship" that included: observation, coaching, scaffolding, modeling, fading, and reflection[89]. Their work advocated a "master/apprentice" model, which has many parallels with the "LPP to maturity" concept used by Lave and Wenger[90], and this is acknowledged. However, the cognitive apprenticeship idea actually helps in consideration of how and where, when and whereby, this move from LPP actually happens. "Apprenticeship embeds the learning of skills and knowledge in their social and functional context"[91]. The next quote sums it up well: "Active listeners or readers, who test their understanding and pursue the issues that are raised in their minds, learn things that apprenticeship can never teach. To the degree that readers or listeners are passive, however, they will not learn as much as they would by apprenticeship, because apprenticeship forces them to use their knowledge. Moreover, few people learn to be active readers and listeners on their own, and that is where cognitive apprenticeship is critical–observing the processes by which an expert listener or reader thinks and practicing these skills under the guidance of the expert can teach students to learn on their own more skilfully"[92].

The authors have tried to give useful definitions and explanations of the terms, outlined briefly here and in the analysis section of this book. The definitions are drawn from, but not exactly the literature reviewed. Thus, cited sources underpin but do not limit the usage here:

Observation: Observing others, often with varying degrees of skill, encourages "apprentices" (here meaning beginners or those undergoing LPP) to view learning as an incremental or staged process. Observation also aids learners develop a conceptual model of the target task or process, before attempting to execute it themselves;

Coaching: "Apprenticeship" - see above comment, embeds the learning of skills and knowledge in their social and functional context. It can also reinforce success, that which is done well, and so encourages beginners to use their new found skills to observe other activities, new ideas etc. and apply them in their own context;

Scaffolding: This means (as used here), co-operative learning and problem solving with

[88] As recommended under the IPA section, mainly in: Smith, J. A., Flowers, P., Larkin, M., *Interpretative Phenomenological Analysis: Theory, Method and Research*, Sage, London 2009 and Langridge, D. *Phenomenological Psychology, Theory Research and Method*, Pearson Prentice Hall 2007.

[89] Collins, A., Brown, J. S. and Newman, S. E., *Cognitive apprenticeship: Teaching the crafts of reading, writing, and mathematics.* In: Resnick, L. B. (ed.) *Knowing, learning, and instruction: Essays in honor of Robert Glaser*, Hillsdale, NJ: Lawrence Erlbaum Associates. 1989, pp. 453-494.

[90] Lave, J., Wenger, E., *Situated learning...*, op. cit.

[91] Collins, A., Brown, J. S., Newman, S. E., *Cognitive apprenticeship...*, op. cit., p. 454.

[92] Ibidem, p. 459.

others to "scaffold/frame/support" their learning activity. It provides students with an additional source of knowledge and processes, already distributed throughout the group.

Modeling: „Access to models of expertise-in-use against which to refine their understanding of complex skills. Moreover, it is not uncommon for apprentices to have access to several masters and thus to a variety of models of expertise"[93];

Fading: This is used here to suggest the gradual removal of supports to allow independence and maturity. The move to Maturity from LPP;

Reflection: This skill enables students to compare their own problem-solving processes with those of an expert, another student, and ultimately, an internal cognitive model of expertise.

All the above ideas were taken from several literature sources and compiled by the authors. The single most useful is work of Collins, Brown and Newman. Discussing Schoenfield they cover most of the above "labels" very well, outlining the learning processes occurring. Their table and descriptions guided these authors in their application of these classifications. As a single example they state that situated learning allows students to learn and actively apply their learning in their own situation and context. They also discuss intrinsic motivation in a way that is very relevant to the usage in this book[94].

Another helpful group of "labels" was taken from the work of Fairclough. This distinguishes four "research objects": emergence, hegemony, recontextualization and operationalization[95], and relates them to strategic critique.

To summarize them, **emergence** is understood as, and applied by the authors as: the emerging into the discourse - or mainstream knowledge and awareness of the peripheral members, of how the community of practice acts, behaves and expresses its values. The emergence can, and in some cases does include, explicit knowledge, whether expressed as public papers, Facebook pages, web publication, or internal documentation. It can also include tacit knowledge held by the CoP, expressed in discourse and identified by common understanding but not documented.

Hegemony is considered by the authors to be a key concept in any analysis of relationships and behaviour. It was stressed by Lave and Wenger, and many others already discussed, so is addressed in depth here. It is seen by the authors as the power relationships present in the dyadic relationship of social structure amongst the community of practice formed and working to operationalize the new knowledge, contacts or process. It is also relevant to the hegemony or power hierarchy of the available literature on the topic in question.

The first point, in the authors world-view, is based around the assumption that each member will have core competencies that need to be transferred, at least in part to the other. For example it is reasonable to expect that, in an existing group (which all those studied, by choice, are) the "mature" CoP members will be providing expertise, and thus demonstrating

---

[93] Collins, A., Brown, J. S., Newman, S. E., *Cognitive apprenticeship...*, op. cit., p. 456.
[94] Ibidem, pp.: 473-474, 476, 487, 489.
[95] Fairclough, N., *Peripheral Vision. Discourse Analysis in Organization Studies: The Case for Critical Realism*, "Organization Studies" 2005, Vol. 26, No. 6, pp. 915-939.

hegemonic status. Whereas the learner will be of inferior knowledge of the topic in question, but potentially able to operationalise it. So they may well both exert hegemonic power in differing contexts. Clearly the concept of LPP fits here.

The second point relates to the value placed on sources of information- which may be tacit, implicit, anecdotal, web based, published or other knowledge held by a fellow member or associate. Regardless of format, it is necessary to integrate and establish the real value of the knowledge, as perceived by the relevant community, of each piece of data. All this must be synthesized into a whole, as seen by the stakeholders in the community. As noted by Fairclough, the "inter discursive" articulation of each concept needs analysis, to establish the level of social practice, and its acceptability or contestation. Stake-holder mapping and analysis is of obvious utility here, available in several forms, and has been used extensively[96]

Moving on, **recontextualization** is the presence or absence of dialogue, discussion and debate between stake-holders as to the utility, application, value and realities of the new learning that is occurring, its usage in the field and from the perception or world-view of the potential user.

Operationalization is seen by the authors as in part, the conversion of a situated learner into a mature community of practice member. However, in this study it may also relate to the change in attitude and behaviour of the group: new ways of acting and interacting. Fairclough, as a consequence of exposure to the semiosis emanating from the learners inputs. Kolb's "Learning Cycle" comes to mind here and finds obvious application[97]. So, it can be viewed as the realization or operationalization of the "imaginaries" created as the initial vision of the learner changes, and is implemented by their later actions. In this context the acceptance of the new good or process by its peers is then "incorporated into successful strategies"[98]. So, these terms (with their associated definitions) are relevant to the analysis of primary data undertaken in this book.

8.1.4 Working in 2 Languages

The interviews, transcriptions and interpretative phenomenological analysis, were all conducted in the interviewee's native language, by the author whose native language was the same. This created a translation need. Colleagues were consulted, in both languages, and an extensive literature search undertaken to ensure rigour. Only 3 sources are selected here, but they summarise the issues well.

Filep discusses interview and translation strategies, with a Central European focus, ideal for a Polish analysis[99]. He states in the introduction to his paper: „it is important for us researchers to get balanced interview data, and consequently we very often have to conduct

---

[96] Mitchell, R. K., Agle, B., R., Wood, D., J., *Toward a Theory of Stakeholder Identification and Salience: Defining the Principle of Who and What really Counts*, „Academy of Management Review" 1997, Vol. 22, No. 4, pp. 853 – 888; Mendelow, A., *Stakeholder Mapping*, „Proceedings of the 2nd International Conference on Information Systems", Cambridge, MA, 1991.
[97] Kolb, D. A., *Experiential Learning*, Englewood Cliffs, Prentice Hall 1984.
[98] Ibidem.
[99] Filep, B., *Interview and translation strategies: coping with multilingual settings and data*, „Social Geography" 2009, Vol. 4, pp. 59-70.

interviews in several different languages (…). In order to avoid "communication problems" or even conflictual (interview) situations, which might damage the outcome of the research, we are thus challenged to find appropriate communication strategies for any of these situations (…). He goes on to say: „Many words and phrases that exist in one language do not have an exact equivalent in another. Therefore we have to find a solution for translating these expressions and concepts in a way that their meanings do not get lost by translation". Later he states that „We often face the question of whether or not one should translate the text literally (…)." He states „the sentences in the language of data collection involve grammatical and syntactical structures that do not exist in English. The question here is whether the sense of the sentences can be adequately translated into English once the rules of English structure are applied, or if the risk of the introduction of pseudo-information or the loss of information is too high".

Squires discusses the issues well, with a focus on medical work and translation[100], she states: „Changes to language occur during the process of translation. When a translator performs a translation, they translate not only the literal meaning of the word, but also how the word relates conceptually in the context" (citing Gee, 1990). She goes on to say: "Conceptual equivalence means that a translator provides a technically and conceptually accurate translated communication of a concept spoken by the study's participant (…)". Later, discussing content analysis and its methods, she says: "The analysis proceeded under the assumption that researchers conducting cross-language qualitative research viewed translators, their roles, and translation processes potential effects on data as methodological factors in their study".

Choi *et al.* state „up front", in their abstract: „Achieving conceptual equivalence between two languages is a challenge in cross-cultural, cross-language research, as the research is conducted in a language that is not the researcher's or research team's first language. Therefore, translation provides an additional challenge in cross-cultural research. The comprehension and interpretation of the meaning of data is central in cross-cultural qualitative analysis[101]". The authors of this book avoided most of these challenges by interviewing in the native language of the interviewer. However, the authors have known each other and worked together for some time, each is not fully fluent in the other language, and both are at similar academic and social levels. This ensures comparability of analyses.

Many other sources were consulted but these are adequate to justify the process used. Polish and English are structured very differently. Polish has no definite or indefinite article (a, the), and a much more structured approach where verbs cannot be used as nouns etc. This makes translation interesting.

---

[100] Squires, A., *Methodological challenges in cross-language qualitative research: a research review*, "International Journal of Nursing Studies" 2009, Vol. 46, No. 2, pp. 277-287.
[101] Choi, J., Kushner, K. E., Mill, J., Lal, D. W. L., *Understanding the Language, the Culture, and the Experience: Translation in Cross-Cultural Research*, „International Journal of Quantitative Methods" 2012, Vol. 11, No. 5, pp. 652-665.

8.2 Underlying Concepts

8.2.1 Social Enterprise and Organisations

The terms "social enterprise" and "social organisation" are widely used but these authors found appropriate definitions hard to find. Grassl gives a really helpful pointer "Terminological profusion and confusion, and underlying conceptual vagueness, still plague the field of social entrepreneurship to a point where different groups of practitioners, and even more so researchers, have developed their own preferred designations. Terms like <<social enterprise>>, <<philanthropy>>, <<non-governmental organisations>>, <<non-profits>>, <<charities>>, and <<third sector>> are often used interchangeably, or with only small differences in meaning"[102]. Other papers that helped in categorisation included work by Kerlin[103], and Zahra et al.[104].

Here the authors suggest that social enterprise or organisation participants are individuals that form and/or join groups, that then labour to develop social products or services, then give them away, or just recover their costs[105]. However, in some cases their labour is directed to fundraising for money that is then donated to the "cause", or "technical purpose" - thus "social enterprise" is the best label. In other cases their labour is solely directed to knowledge acquisition and sharing, thus "social organisation" is a better label. Salamon and Sokolowski, looked at a broad range of entities that meet the following five key criteria:

- They have some kind of formal organisational structure (e.g., a set of rules, formal or informal, that define goals, activities, membership, selection and competencies of officers, the use of resources, etc.);
- They are self-governing (i.e., are not a subordinate part or agency of another organisation);
- They are not profit distributing (i.e., any income or surplus generated by their operations is ploughed back into the organisation, not distributed among the organisation's officers or owners);
- They are private (i.e., are not a part or an agency of their government);
- They are voluntary (i.e., membership is not coerced or mandated by law, and they customarily receive donations of money, other property, or labour to be used for the social good) [106].

Useful material on rural and 3rd world development qualitative study has been found, for example Eversole et al., who state "social change processes involving real people and

---

[102] Grassl, W., *Business Models of Social Enterprise: A Design Approach to Hybridity*, „ACRN Journal of Entrepreneurship Perspectives" 2012, Vol. 1, Iss. 1, pp. 37–60.

[103] Kerlin, J., *Social Enterprise in the United States and Europe: Understanding and learning from the differences*, "VOLUNTAS: International Journal of Voluntary and Nonprofit Organizations" 2006, No. 17, pp. 246-262.

[104] Zahra, S. A., Gedajlovic, E., Neubaum, D. O., Shulman, J. M., *A Typology of Social Entrepreneurs: Motives, Search Processes and Ethical Challenges*, "Journal of Business Venturing" 2009, Vol. 24, No. 5, pp. 519-532.

[105] Authors definition, built from the work cited and other reading.

[106] Salamon, L. M., Sokolowski, W., *Volunteering in Cross-National Perspective: Evidence From 24 Countries*, "Working Papers of the Johns Hopkins Comparative Nonprofit Sector Project", No. 40, The Johns Hopkins Center for Civil Society Studies, Baltimore 2001.

institutions in and across real places who work (or do not work) together and who seek or resist particular kinds of change"[107]. They also quote many useful texts such as Evans & Syrett[108], Kay[109] and many others not referenced here.

Krzemiński reviews non-profit organisations in Polish healthcare. He reviews the changes in Poland which followed the political changes in 1989, and discusses the gaps in healthcare that exist today. This is relevant to the CoPs analysed in this book, labelled as "L", a healthcare community of practice, in the UK, "M", a Polish orphanage support group, and in part all the other Polish groups. He notes the often local nature of these NGO's, their innovation, spontaneity and flexibility. He stresses the "local community involvement" and also gives many useful statistics[110].

Some academic work points to "phases" of social organisations. Most of the papers reviewed indicate that only financed work exists, and that groups operating without structured income from donations, work or sale of product or services are "beginners". Some academics suggest that enterprise - meaning in this book, financial work towards a social good, is the natural last stage of an organisation. Others discuss the challenges required to move into a financed but still not for profit enterprise: "Sourcing, financing, staff retention, adjusting to different roles in managing the enterprise and measuring the scale and impact of their business are the primary challenges encountered (...)"[111].

Haugh endorses this viewpoint. Her abstract states: "Non-profit social ventures pursue economic, social, or environmental aims, generating at least part of their income from trading. They fill market gaps between private enterprise and public sector provision, and, increasingly, policy makers consider them to be valuable agents in social, economic, and environmental regeneration and renewal" [112]. Working with Docherty and Lyon, their paper discusses "organisations that combine enterprise with an embedded social purpose", going on to discuss hybridity in depth[113]. Most of this is outside the scope of these authors, so not considered further here, but is recommended as a very good overview.

The authors here fairly quickly formed the view that early SE research had to to define distinctive characteristics and explain the emergence phenomenon before actually analysing what was going on. Later studies seen investigated SE management and performance but sometimes was not well underpinned. However, possibly because of this more recent

[107] Eversole, R., Barraket, J., Luke, B., *Social Enterprises in Rural Community Development*, „Community Development Journal" 2014, Vol. 49, No. 2, pp. 245-261.
[108] Evans, M. and Syrett, S., *Generating social capital? The social economy and local economic development*, „European Urban and Regional Studies" 2007, Vol. 14, No. 1, pp. 55-74.
[109] Kay, A., *Social capital, the social economy and community development*, „Community Development Journal" 2006, Vol. 41, No. 2, pp. 160-173.
[110] Krzemiński, P., *Non-profit Organizations Operating in Healthcare sector in Polad in 1989-2010*, In: Borowiecki, R., Dziura, M. (eds.), *Third Sector: Theoretical and Empirical Approach*, Crakow University of Economics, Crakow 2014, p. 165.
[111] Hynes, B., *Growing the social enterprise – issues and challenges*, „Social Enterprise Journal" 2009, Vol. 5, No. 2, pp. 114-125.
[112] Haugh, H., *Community-Led Social Venture Creation*, „Entrepreneurship Theory and Practice" 2007, Vol. 31, Iss. 2, pp. 161-182.
[113] Doherty, B., Haugh, H., Lyon, F., *Social Enterprises as Hybrid Organizations: A Review and Research Agenda*, „International Journal of Management Reviews" 2014, No. 16, pp. 417-436.

research has advanced new theories to explain their emergence. These points are discussed elsewhere.

Grassl helps enormously, discussing how the terms vary between countries and continents: "An approach is developed that does not rest on dichotomous distinctions by sectors or profit orientation"[114]. Darby and Jenkins assessed sustainability indicators to social enterprise models, using a case study approach. This paper is also recommended as essential reading, as it outlines many useful pointers and concepts. It concludes: "No one method of social accounting has been universally accepted in the UK. This requires greater co-ordination by those developing such models and a common research agenda on this area for SEs in the UK" [115]. Docherty and Thompson profile 11 cases from around the world, highlighting "the diverse world of social enterprise" [116]. They conclude that one size does not fit all. Overall, these authors found it difficult to find realistic models that could be applied to their findings. Thus, they claim originality.

8.2.2 Communities of Practice

A quarter of a century ago, Lave and Wenger introduced the concept of a community of practice, with situated learning, legitimate peripheral participation, growth to maturity in cognitive apprenticeships and other ideas used here[117]. However, more recently it has been extended significantly by many other workers, including Cox[118]. Wenger et al. describe a community of practice as being made from a group or network of people, and sometimes organisations, often working informally, and sharing their knowledge[119]. They state that these groups share common interests, which, with their concern about social issues, processes and practices, create a context. They define practice as co-ordinated activities of people undertaking tasks, and informed by a particular organisational context. These activities are always related to a particular purpose, topic or theme, with a common style of activities and tasks referred to as "shared practice".

Wenger et al. state that CoPs are "Communities of practice are groups of people who share a concern or a passion for something they do and learn how to do it better as they interact regularly"[120]. These key definitions, although paraphrased here, form the basis of this usage of the groups under study, as CoPs.

[114] Grassl, W., *Business Models of Social Enterprise: A Design Approach to Hybridity*, „ACRN Journal of Entrepreneurship Perspectives" 2012, Vol. 1, Iss. 1, pp. 37-60.

[115] Darby, L., Jenkins, H., *Applying sustainability indicators to the social enterprise business model: The development and application of an indicator set for Newport Wastesavers, Wales*, „International Journal of Social Economics" 2006, Vol. 33, Iss: 5/6, pp. 411-431.

[116] Thompson, J., Doherty, B., *The diverse world of social enterprise: A collection of social enterprise stories*, „International Journal of Social Economics" 2006, Vol. 33, Iss: 5/6, pp. 361-375.

[117] Lave, J., *Cognition in Practice: Mind, mathematics, and culture in everyday life*, Cambridge University Press. Cambridge 1988.

[118] Cox, A., *What are communities of practice? A comparative review of four seminal works*, „Journal of Information Science" 2005, Vol. 31, No. 6, pp. 527-540

[119] Wenger, E, McDermott, R, Snyder, W. M., *Cultivating Communities of Practice: A Guide to Managing Knowledge*, Harvard Business Press 2002.

[120] Smith, M. K., *Jean Lave, Etienne Wenger and communities of practice'*, "The encyclopedia of informal education" 2003, 2009, www.infed.org/biblio/communities_of_practice.htm, Accessed 5 June 2016.

Moving on to analysis of action in a community of practice, Lin and Beyerlein state that "an appropriate level of analysis for collaboration research would be social interaction and the optimal unit of analysis would be communities of practice. Such a socio-cultural approach departs from the traditional positivist approach"[121]. Wood and Gray reviewed different definitions of collaboration, identified elements, and proposed that "collaboration occurs when a group of autonomous stake-holders of a problem domain engage in an interactive process, using shared rules, norms, and structures to act or decide on issues related to that domain" [122]. They claim that the "level of analysis" should be that of "social interaction". The authors agree, and have taken their direction from this, by choosing this initial definition.

From this starting point, they commenced their study of social enterprises, where the problem domain is the shared social enterprise purpose (for example the "L Support Group") and the shared rules are the community of practice culture. The Wood and Gray review covers much of the general interest in this topic. Specifically, they discuss five critical elements of communities of practice: practice, community, meaning, learning, and identity. Wood and Gray define practice, in part as "the way we do things round here". They go on to define community as where the practice resides, stating that: "A community forms when people who share the same practice interact with each other. Unlike institutions, a community usually takes shape without deliberate construction. Membership is naturally developed, depending on whether one speaks the same language as others in the community and the competence he/she has"[123]. There is clear evidence that this occurs in the primary data collected for this book. For example, each of the communities of practice studied here was shaped from within by its members and none were "deliberately constructed" from outside. These concepts are all addressed directly in the discussion of the primary data collected and analysed in the preceding chapters.

Finally, Wood and Gray also quote: "Such a new approach sees communities of practice as containers of both collaboration and learning. Communities of practice provide the environment where shared mental models (...) develop". They also say that collaboration and learning are needed jointly[124].

Ribeiro et. al. propose to define the community of practice in terms of three aspects. Firstly, the nature of phenomena: "A special platform of activity, organized from the bottom up and accumulating knowledge resources. It is a joint activity that evolves and is continually renegotiated and refined by its members". Secondly, the course of action. People join the community of practice, because of shared interests and experiences. They are involved in convergent and commonly themed activities, and so co-create a single social entity. Finally, the effects. The members form a set of resources and services over time[125].

[121] Lin, Y., Beyerlein, M. M., *Communities of practice: A critical perspective on collaboration*, In: Beyerlein, M. M., Beyerlein, S. T., Kennedy, F. A. (ed.), *Innovation through Collaboration*, (Advances in Interdisciplinary Studies of Work Teams, Volume 12), Emerald Group Publishing Limited, pp. 53-79.
[122] Wood, D. J.,Gray, B., *Towards a comprehensive theory of collaboration*, "The Journal of Applied Behavioral Science", Vol. 27, No. 3, p. 46.
[123] Wood, D. J.,Gray, B., *Towards a comprehensive theory of collaboration*, op.cit., p. 58.
[124] Ibidem, p. 70.
[125] Ribeiro, R., Kimble, Ch., Cairns, P., *Quantum phenomena in Communities of Practice*, "International Journal of

These are both "explicit" effects (e.g. documents and other items stored) and "tacit" (developed organisational culture, new or improved patterns of behaviour, etc.).

Moving on, Ruuska and Vartiainen developed six characteristics, at different levels of organisation, which refer to the results or outcomes of the community of practice at different organisational levels. They argue that community structure can be divided into informal, semi-formal and formal. communities usually set their ideas and purposes around knowledge needs, so a community of practice is cemented together by their shared interests in a domain. The main activities are shared actions, discussions and an exchange of experiences, mutual learning and discussions about difficult cases[126]. Supporting this, Lave and Wenger differentiated two forms of practice: "talking about" (e.g., exchange of information needed for the activation of the current activities) and "talking within" (e.g., stories, discussions)[127].

Table 16. The key elements in Wikipedia that produce a community of practice

Key Elements	Influence on the Construction of Community of Practice
Individuals	"Individuals" refers both to the people using, and those editing Wikipedia. As users, or readers, individuals are attracted by the content. Motivated users can use the available technology to start generating content. "As they practice, they peripherally participate within the community of practice. As the Community of Practice starts to form, these individuals can be further motivated to practice by affiliation, belonging, and recognition" from the Wikipedia development community.
Practice	"Practice refers to the activities that people engage in", when creating Wikipedia content. Generating new or improved Wikipedia content involves several different practices: Some practices can be conducted at the individual level, such as composing a single page; other practices, such as co-ordinating a project need to be conducted by the community at large. So, practice generates content and also promotes a platform for individuals' interaction.
Content	Content is essential to the community of Wikipedia, because it is a collection of articles and documents. First, creating the collection serves as the purpose of the community, as every action within Wikipedia revolves around the purpose of building the content. Second, it provides value to attract newcomers – Wikipedia would not be able to recruit new members if the content already met their needs for information.
Interaction	"Interactions can foster individuals' attachment to other members and to the community processes, including policies, co-ordination and differentiated roles".
Community	"Community is at the centre of the model, which is a result of the interaction of the four elements above. The community -argued to be a community of practice, is defined by social practice, has a shared goal of

Information Management" 2010, No 30, p. 22.
[126] Ruuska, I., Vartiainen, M., *Characteristics of knowledge sharing communities in project organizations*, "International Journal of Project Management" 2005, No. 23, pp. 375-376.
[127] Lave, J., Wenger, E., *Situated learning...*, op. cit.

Key Elements	Influence on the Construction of Community of Practice
	content building, and is built on interactions. As the community forms, it creates a sense of belonging for individuals, who then build identities and reputations, whilst participating in community practices, and are further motivated to contribute by their recognition and membership of the community".
Technology	"Technology supports all elements above and surrounds them".

Source: X. Zhao, M.J. Bishop, *Understanding and supporting online communities of practice: lessons learned from Wikipedia,* "Educational Technology Research and Development" 2011, No. 59, p. 729-730.

Xiao and Bishop[128] give the Wikipedia project as an example of a global organisation that bears the marks of a community of practice. They examined it "more closely, to try to identify the factors that lead to the creation and evolution of a successful online community of practice"[129]. Their analysis of key factors gave six elements, which occurred repetitively: individuals, practice, content, interactions, community and technology. Table 16 extracted from a paper by Zhao and Bishop (modified in a few details) illustrates the concepts used in this book very well. The authors here have marked key concepts with italics.

This example of knowledge sharing in a Wikipedia, operating as a community of practice is also discussed by Łukasik[130]. He introduces his paper by stating „in recent years knowledge management and knowledge sharing became one of the most popular topics in management literature, referencing Mikuła[131]. He also discusses „Open clinical", which specializes in knowledge management for clinical care, again relevant to the role of the „L" group reported in this book. He goes on to discuss communities of practice, and his definitions have been very useful: „core group, active group and peripheral group"[132].

8.2.3 Motivation

This book has as its core „why"? Why do people give up their time, money and opportunities elsewhere, to create and deliver a social good. What motivates them? A very extensive literature review sought some answers. Most of the material found related to job or work satisfaction, not voluntary social volunteering. However there are clear and obvious parallels with membership of a community of practice, and was used by the authors in their analysis, so the material is presented here. One initial conclusion was that much of the work published is old. The authors make no apologies for citing it here, as it forms the foundation for all that has been studied since. Newer papers are cited where appropriate and needed.

Barnard claimed that organisations are made from collections of individuals, each with their own motivations, and that the function of managers was to formulate and make explicit these goals in a clear and communicable way[133]. This suggested that hegemony and other

[128] Zhao., X., Bishop, M. J., *Understanding and supporting on-line communities of practice: lessons learned from Wikipedia,* "Educational Technology Research and Development" 2011, No. 59, pp. 729-730.
[129] Zhao., X., Bishop, M. J., *Understanding and supporting...,* op. cit., p. 715.
[130] Łukasik, P., *The social sharing of the knowledge,* In: Borowiecki, R. Dziura, M. (eds.), *Third Sector: Theoretical and Empirical Approach,* Cracow University of Economics, Cracow 2014, pp. 131-145.
[131] Mikuła, B. *Organizacje oparte na wiedzy,* Wydawnictwo Akademii Ekonomicznej w Krakowie, Kraków 2006.
[132] Łukasik, *The social sharing of the knowledge,* op. cit., p. 141.

power structures should be considered. It is addressed in this chapter under the tools used for analysis, but the core concepts are repeated here for clarity. Lave and Wenger,[134] and many others cited, discussed it. Fairclough describes it as power relationships in groups of individuals working to operationalize new ideas[135]. These can include knowledge, contacts or process.

Herzberg coined the concept of job enrichment and discussed the need for, and means of creating motivation. He suggests a 2-factor theory, separating job satisfaction from job dissatisfaction. Intrinsic factors affect satisfaction. Extrinsic factors such as administrative procedures, supervision methods and other "hygiene issues" affect dissatisfaction[136]. These are possibly less important in a group with voluntary membership, but could lead to dissatisfaction and leaving. Conversely, dissatisfaction at work or home could operate as satisfiers. Job involvement was also stated to be closely related to intrinsic aspects by McKelvey and Sekaran[137]. However Wall and Stephenson[138], and House and Wigdor[139] criticise Herzberg's methodology. Their view was that it is an over-simplification, but that intrinsic factors are most relevant to motivation.

McGregor formulated the idea of "theory x & y managers", and postulates that their style affects motivation[140]. He goes on to theorise that there is no intrinsic dislike of work, and that employees will exercise self-direction and control in the service of objectives to which they are committed. The authors here argue that a community of practice creating a social good creates commitment and rewards. McGregor goes on to say that the degree of commitment is a function of rewards seen to result from the commitment -thus a "self-fulfilling prophecy" or circle is created, and thus people maintain involvement. Within this, higher (self-actualisation) rewards are most significant. Such rewards are intrinsic, no external mechanisms are needed. Thus, if the conditions are right the individual will seek responsibility.

Cassidy and Lynn identified 6 motivational drivers: the work ethic, pursuit of excellence, status aspiration, competitiveness, acquisitiveness and mastery (against set standards)[141]. Although these do not map well onto social enterprise groups, it can be argued that the drivers are intrinsic, part of human nature and so applicable in this context. Thus, creation of a social good requires a „work ethic", to give up time (an „opportunity cost"),

---

[133] Barnard, C., *Functions of the* executive, 30th Anniversary Edition, Harvard University Press 1968.

[134] Lave, J., Wenger, E., *Situated learning...*, op. cit.

[135] Jorgensen, M., Phillips, L. J., *Discourse Analysis as Theory and Method*, SAGE Publications, London- Thousand Oaks- New Delhi 2001, p. 172.

[136] Herzberg, F., *One more time: how do you motivate employees?*, "Harvard Business Review" 1968, vol. 46, No. 1, pp. 53-62.

[137] McKelven, B., Sekoran, U., *A Career Based Theory of Job Involvement*, "Admin Science Quarterly" 1977, Vol. 22, pp. 281-305.

[138] Wall T. D., Stephenson, G. M., *Herzberg's two-factor theory of job attitudes: a critical evaluation and some fresh evidence*, "Industrial Relations Journal" Vol. 1, Iss. 3, pp. 41-65.

[139] House R. J., Wigdor L. A., *Herzberg's dual-factor theory of job satisfaction and motivation: a review of the evidence and a criticism*, "Personnel Psychology", 1967, Vol. 20, Iss. 4, pp. 369-390.

[140] McGregor, D., *The human side of enterprise*, McGrow-Hill, New York 1960.

[141] Cassidy, T., Lynn, R., *A multifactorial approach to achievement motivation: The development of a comprehensive measure*, "Journal of Occupational Psychology" 1989, Vol. 62, pp. 301-312.

improve status in the community of practice and master new skills - in other words go from LPP to mastery. This "6-driver theory" has parallels with expectancy theory.

Vroom tries to explain which course of action follows a situation requiring choice, as a result of an evaluation of possible options. For each, he asserts that expectancy (can I do it?), instrumentality (will it work?), and valence (is it worth it?) must all be met with a "yes" (i.e. multiplied together) to lead to a positive decision to proceed. Again, this can be applied to life in a community of practice[142].

McClelland tried to quantify motivation, by postulating three needs, achievement, power and affiliation. He suggests that high achievers have identifiable characteristics. They prefer to be able to take personal responsibility, and that the satisfaction resulting from achievement is internal. They like a challenge, but it must be achievable. Moderate goals and calculated risks motivate, whereas uncontrolled gambling doesn't. A high need for variety is often exhibited. Finally they must have concrete feedback. This clearly maps onto people giving up their time for social goods[143].

McClelland also claims that, in any individual, the balance between these needs gives rise to two basic groupings of people, those who are challenged by opportunity (high achievers), and those who don't care. He produced a hierarchy of needs, after Maslow[144] that suggests that structured and focused training will help self-actualisation. It can be argued that this training can be in the form of situated learning in a community of practice, or knowledge sharing as a result of earlier training. Thus, the paid work environment parallels the voluntary presence in a community of practice.

Many others also stated that "need for achievement" is required. Murray discussed this, as do many others cited here[145]. Bronowski, in a paper edited by Maslow claimed that behaviour is dominated by the lowest group of needs remaining unsatisfied[146]. Two factors clearly of relevance here are esteem and self-actualization, however survival -the lowest and most fundamental, is also a factor in the medical group (L), and arguably the vegan one (V).

8.2.4 Situated Learning, Cognition and Knowledge Transfer

This is also addressed under the section on communities of practice. Situated cognition and situated learning are theoretical concepts that suggest learning is "naturally tied to authentic activity, context, and culture"[147]. Lave argues that learning is a function of the activity, context and culture in which it occurs, so, is situated. This differs from training or classroom learning activities which are theoretical, abstract and out of context[148].

So, social interaction is an essential part of situated learning, because learners become

---

[142] Vroom, V. H., *Work and motivation*, Wiley, 1994.
[143] McClelland, D. C., *Assessing human motivation*, General Learning Press, Morristown 1971.
[144] Maslow, A. H., *A theory of human motivation*, "Psychological Review" 1943, Vol. 50, No. 4, pp. 370-396.
[145] Murray, H. A., *Explorations in personality: A clinical and experimental study of fifty men of college age*, Oxford University Press, New York 1938.
[146] Bronowski, J., *The values of science*, In: *Maslow, A. H. (ed.), New Knowledge in Human Values*, Harper & Row, New York 1959.
[147] Brown, J. S., Collins, A., Duguid, S., *Situated cognition and the culture of learning*, „Educational Researcher" 1989, Vol. 18, No. 1, pp. 32-42.
[148] Lave, J., *Cognition in Practice...*, op. cit.

involved in a community of practice which provides context and beliefs and behaviours. When a new member moves from the periphery of this community to its heart, they become more active and deeply engaged within the culture and become mature members. At this stage hegemonic relationships are often cited. Situated learning often occurs tacitly, rather than explicitly. This is the process of what Lave and Wenger call the process of "legitimate peripheral participation" (LPP) [149].

Fitts[150] suggested 3 stages of skill acquisition: cognitive assimilation of information, associative strengthening of understanding by repeating the connections, and finally, autonomous actions. Others have created similar models, for individuals and groups, i.e. Kolb's learning cycle[151], and Tuckman and Jensen's "Forming, Norming, Storming and Performing"[152].

Pavitt[153], Pralahad & Hamel[154], and Cohen & Levinthal[155] all take a theoretical view of organisations abilities to develop new capabilities. Allen[156] describes the role of „gatekeepers" in change processes. He goes on to discuss knowledge transfer processes in some depth. Although focused on for-profit business, the insights gained are relevant to knowledge acquisition and transfer in communities of practice.

Checkland and Scholes propose his "soft systems methodology" as a tool from which to manage the processes required to implement change. Within this he details the use of "rich pictures" to map conflict and other issues[157]. This clearly maps onto the rich pictures that interpretative phenomenological analysis creates from community of practice interview transcripts. The soft systems he describes are clearly present in the communities analysed here.

Blackler and Osborne discuss in depth the advantages of involving the end user as early as possible in managing change[158]. This is relevant in communities of practice creating a social good, because there is a clear need to accept knowledge transfer among all stake-holders.

---

[149] Lave, J., Wenger, E., *Situated Learning: Legitimate Periperal Participation*, op. cit.
[150] Fitts, P. M., *Factors in complex skills training*, In: Glaser, R. (ed.), *Training research and education*, University of Pittsburgh, reprinted Wiley, New York 1965.
[151] Kolb, D. A., Fry, R., *Toward an applied theory of experiential learning*, In: Cooper, C. (ed.), *Theories of group process*, John Wiley, London 1975; Kolb, D. A., *Experiential Learning*, op. cit.
[152] Tuckman, B. W., Jensen, M.A. *Stages of Small Group Development Revisited*, "Group and Organisational Studies" 1977, No. 2, pp. 419-427.
[153] Pavitt, K., *What We Know about the Strategic Management of Technology*, "California Management Review", Vol, 32, No. 3, pp. 17-26.
[154] Prahalad, C. K., Hamel, G., *The Core Competence of the Corporation*, "Harvard Business Review" 1990, Vol. 68, No. 3, pp. 79-91.
[155] Cohen, W. M., Leventhal D. A., *Absorptive Capacity: A New Perspective on Learning and Innovation*, "Administrative Science Quarterly" 1990, Vol. 5, No. 1, pp. 128-152.
[156] Allen, T. J., *Managing the Flow of Technology*, MIT Press, Cambridge MA 1977; Allen, T. J., *Performance of Communication Channels in Transfer of Technology*, "Industrial Management Review" 1966, Vol. 8, pp. 87-98; Allen T. J., *Information Flow in R&D labs.*, "Administrative Science Quarterly" 1969, Vol. 14, pp. 12-19.
[157] Checkland, P., Scholes, J., *Soft Systems Methodology in Action*, Wiley 1990.
[158] Blackler, F., Osborne, D., *Information Technology and People*, British Psychological Society 1987.

8.2.5 Knowledge Management and Usage

Knowledge Management, as a label or term was first popularly used around 25 years ago, in the 1990s. Davenport offered a definition: "Knowledge management is the process of capturing, distributing, and effectively using knowledge" [159]. This clearly has relevance to the subsequent use of situated learning. Duhon suggests a more detailed version: "Knowledge management is a discipline that promotes an integrated approach to identifying, capturing, evaluating, retrieving, and sharing all of an enterprise's information assets. These assets may include databases, documents, policies, procedures, and previously un-captured expertise and experience in individual workers"[160].

However, contemporary management of enterprises and organisations is based largely on the acquisition of knowledge, and its use in business, in current and strategic operations[161]. The knowledge becomes a key organisational resource, but formal departments and operational groups within many organisations seem not to be able to successfully create, spread and use the knowledge[162]. Possibly, communities of practice, with their informal, situated knowledge acquisition processes may do it better[163].

Traditional approaches to knowledge management, as already stated, have been mainly studied in for-profit organisations, often try to capture existing knowledge in formal systems, procedures and databases[164]. However, the knowledge, and especially its tacit dimension, is always first embedded in people and must be transformed into organisational knowledge -this is the base of knowledge management. Tacit knowledge is hard to codify and transfer without personal interactions between the knowledge source and receiver[165]. So, explicit information or knowledge is set out in tangible form. Tacit information or knowledge is extremely difficult to set out in tangible form[166].

All these sources are from business however. Less information exists on knowledge management in communities of practice. From the material found useful, Iverson and McPhee makes the point that "for people-based approaches, knowledge is inherently tied to social and contextual phenomena"[167]. It is therefore tacit. Other material reviewed makes similar points, but most focuses on communities of practice in the first or second sectors. Thus, this book breaks new ground.

---

[159] Davenport, T. H., *Saving IT's Soul: Human Centered Information Management*, "Harvard Business Review" 1994, Vol. 72, No. 2., pp. 119-131.

[160] Duhon, B., *It's All in our Heads*, "Inform" 1998, Vol. 12. No. 8, pp. 8-13.

[161] Hildreth, P. J., Kimble, Ch., *The duality of knowledge*, op. cit.; Inkpen, A. C., Dinur, A., *Knowledge management processes and international joint ventures*, "Organization Science" 1998, Vol. 9, pp. 454-468.

[162] Ruuska, I., Vartiainen, M., *Characteristics of knowledge sharing communities in project organizations*, "International Journal of Project Management" 2005, Vol. 23, pp. 374-379.

[163] Łukasik, P., *The social sharing of the knowledge*, op. cit., pp. 131-145.

[164] Teigland, R., Wasko, M., *Knowledge transfer in MNCs: Examining how intrinsic motivations and knowledge sourcing impact individual centrality and performance*, "Journal of International Management" 2009, Vol.15, pp. 15–31.

[165] Inkpen, A C. Dinur, A, *Knowledge management processes...*, op. cit.; Feghali, T., El-Den, J., *Knowledge transformation among virtually cooperating group members*, "Journal of Knowledge Management" 2008, Vol. 12, Iss. 1, pp. 92 – 105.

[166] Koenig, M. E. D., *What is KM: Knowledge management explained*, http://www.kmworld.com/Articles/ Editorial/ What-Is-.../What-is-KM-Knowledge-Management-Explained-82405.aspx, Accessed 2 June 2017.

[167] Iverson, J. O., McPhee, R. D., *Knowledge management in communities of practice*, "Management Communication Quarterly" 2002, Vol. 16, No. 2, pp. 259-266.

8.3 Research Underpinnings Summary

The text above contains only the key points the authors consider required to justify and expand on the concepts used. Therefore, it follows the „thought structure" of the book, going from ideas and methodologies to analysis and then core concepts. The key ideas are used as sub-headings, and expanded appropriately. Thus, motivation, communities of practice and forms of knowledge acquisition and transfer feature heavily. More abstract concepts of knowledge management were less important to the interviewees, and examples from the 3rd sector are not well covered in the literature found by the authors, so are not addressed here in depth. The processes used for the study were clearly important, so are detailed, with many quotes from the books and papers the authors used.

There is a significant focus on work motivation here. This is because there is much more material and analysis on motivation in the workplace. Parallels can be drawn and the studies of job satisfaction, intrinsic factors and achievement map well onto the studies in this book. Although unpaid and almost certainly creating an opportunity cost, the commitment shown by all interviewed would have been welcomed by an employer.

Bibliography

Aggeslam, L., *Learning Organisation or Knowledge Management -what came first, the Chicken or the Egg?*, "Information Technology and Control" 2006, Vol. 35, No. 3A, pp. 295-302.

Allen T. J., *Information Flow in R&D labs.*, "Administrative Science Quarterly" 1969, Vol. 14, pp. 12-19.

Allen, T. J., *Managing the Flow of Technology*, MIT Press, Cambridge MA 1977.

Allen, T. J., *Performance of Communication Channels in Transfer of Technology*, "Industrial Management Review" 1966, Vol. 8, pp. 87-98.

Barnard, C., *Functions of the executive*, 30th Anniversary Edition, Harvard University Press 1968.

Blackler, F., Osborne, D., *Information Technology and People*, British Psychological Society 1987.

Borowiecki, R, Dziura, M., *From the third sector to the social economy*. In: Borowiecki, R. Dziura, M. (eds.), *Third Sector: Theoretical and Empirical Approach*, Crakow University of Economics, Cracow 2014, pp. 23-51.

Borowiecki, R., Dziura, M (eds.), *Third Sector: Theoretical and Empirical Approach*, Crakow University of Economics, Cracow 2014.

Bronowski, J., *The values of science*, In: Maslow, A. H. (ed.), *New Knowledge in Human Values*, Harper & Row, New York 1959.

Brown, J. S., Collins, A., Duguid, S., *Situated cognition and the culture of learning*, „Educational Researcher" 1989, Vol. 18, No. 1, pp. 32-42.

Bryman, A., Bell, E. *Business Research Methods*, Oxford University Press. 2003.

Buła, P., Fudaliński, J., Szarucki, M., *Determinants of the process of social management of socialeconomy entities on the example social cooperative activity*. In: Borowiecki, R., Dziura, M. (eds.), *Third Sector: Theoretical and Empirical Approach*, Crakow University of Economics, Cracow 2014, pp. 53-73.

Cassidy, T., Lynn, R., *A multifactorial approach to achievement motivation: The development of a comprehensive measure*, „Journal of Occupational Psychology" 1989, Vol. 62, pp. 301-312.

Checkland, P., Scholes, J., *Soft Systems Methodology in Action*, Wiley 1990.

Choi, J., Kushner, K. E., Mill, J., Lal, D. W. L., *Understanding the Language, the Culture, and the Experience: Translation in Cross-Cultural Research*, „International Journal of Quantitative Methods" 2012, Vol. 11, No. 5, pp. 652-665.

Cohen, W. M., Leventhal D. A., *Absorptive Capacity: A New Perspective on Learning and Innovation*, "Administrative Science Quarterly" 1990, Vol. 5, No. 1, pp. 128-152.

Collins, A, Brown, J. S., Newman, S. E., *Cognitive apprenticeship: Teaching the crafts of reading, writing, and mathematics*. In: Resnick, L. B. (ed.), *Knowing, learning, and instruction: Essays in honor of Robert Glaser* Hillsdale, NJ: Lawrence Erlbaum Associates, 1989, pp. 453-494.

Collins, A., Brawn J. S., Holum A., *Cognitive apprenticeship: Making thinking visible*, „American Educator" 1991, No. 15, pp. 6-11.

Cox, A., *What are communities of practice? A comparative review of four seminal works*, „Journal of Information Science" 2005, Vol. 31, No. 6, pp. 527-540.

Cresswell, J. *Qualitative Inquiry and Research Design: Choosing among Five Traditions*, Sage 1998.

Darby, L., Jenkins, H., *Applying sustainability indicators to the social enterprise business model: The development and application of an indicator set for Newport Wastesavers, Wales*, „International Journal of Social Economics" 2006, Vol. 33, Iss: 5/6, pp. 411-431.

Davenport, T. H., *Saving IT's Soul: Human Centered Information Management*, "Harvard Business Review" 1994, Vol. 72, No. 2., pp. 119-131.

Doherty, B., Haugh, H., Lyon, F., *Social Enterprises as Hybrid Organisations: A Review and Research Agenda*, „International Journal of Management Reviews" 2014, No. 16, pp. 417-436.

Duhon, B., *It's All in our Heads*, "Inform" 1998, Vol. 12. No. 8, pp. 8-13.

Evans, M. and Syrett, S., *Generating social capital? The social economy and local economic development*, „European Urban and Regional Studies" 2007, Vol. 14, No. 1, pp. 55-74.

Eversole, R., Barraket, J., Luke, B., *Social Enterprises in Rural Community Development*, „Community Development Journal" 2014, Vol. 49, No. 2, pp. 245-261.

Fairclough, N. *Critical discourse analysis,* „Marges Linguistiques" 2005, No. 9, pp.76-94.

Fairclough, N. Jessop, R., Sayer, A., *Critical realism and semiosis.* In: Joseph. J., Roberts. J. (eds.), *Realism discourse and Deconstruction*, Routledge, London 2004.

Fairclough, N., *Analyzing Discourse and Text: Textual Analysis for Social Research*, Routledge, London 2003.

Fairclough, N., *Peripheral Vision. Discourse Analysis in Organisation Studies: The Case for Critical Realism*, "Organisation Studies" 2005, Vol. 26, No. 6, pp. 915-939.

Fairclough, N., Wodak, R., *Critical discourse analysis.* In: van Dijk, T., *Discourse as Social Interaction*, Sage, London: 1997.

Feghali, T., El-Den, J., *Knowledge transformation among virtually-cooperating group members*, "Journal of Knowledge Management" 2008, Vol. 12, Iss. 1, pp. 92-105.

Filep, B., *Interview and translation strategies: coping with multilingual settings and data*, „Social Geography" 2009, Vol. 4, pp. 59-70.

Fitts, P. M., *Factors in complex skills training*, In: Glaser, R. (ed.), *Training research and education*, University of Pittsburgh, reprinted Wiley, New York 1965.

Grassl, W., *Business Models of Social Enterprise: A Design Approach to Hybridity*, „ACRN Journal of Entrepreneurship Perspectives" 2012, Vol. 1, Iss. 1, pp. 37–60.

Greeno, J. G., *Middle School Mathematics Through Applications Project Group. The situativity of knowing, learning, and research*, „American Psychologist" 1998, Vol. 53, No. 1, pp. 5-26.

Greeno, J. G.., *On claims that answer the wrong question*, "Educational Research" 1997, Vol. 26, No. 1, pp. 5-17.

Haugh, H., *Community-Led Social Venture Creation*, „Entrepreneurship Theory and Practice" 2007, Vol. 31, Iss. 2, pp. 161-182.

Herzberg, F., *One more time: how do you motivate employees?*, "Harvard Business Review" 1968, vol. 46, No. 1, pp. 53-62.

Hildreth, P. J., Kimble, Ch., *The duality of knowledge*, "Information Research" 2002, Vol. 8, No. 1, pp. 142-149.

Hildreth, P., M., Kimble, C., *Knowledge Networks: Innovation through Communities of Practice*, Idea Group, Hershey 2004.

Hougaard, G.. R., *Legitimate Peripheral Participation as a Framework for Conversation Analytic Work in Second Language Learning*, „Forum: Qualitative Social Research" 2009, No. 10(2), Art.4., http://www.qualitative-research.net/index.php/fqs/article/view/1280/2750, Accessed 25 May 2017.

House R. J., Wigdor L. A., *Herzberg's dual-factor theory of job satisfaction and motivation: a review of the evidence and a criticism*, "Personnel Psychology", 1967, Vol. 20, Iss. 4, pp. 369-390.

http://fundraising.co.uk/2015/09/10/why-charities-should-make-a-big-deal-of-being-small/#.V0gt2vn9lph, Accessed 27 May 2017.

http://onin.com/hhh/hhhexpl.html, Accessed 10.6.2017

http://www.theguardian.com/voluntary-sector-network/2015/mar/15/why-i-believe-small-charities-are-better-than-big-ones, Accessed 27 May 2017.

http://www.worldharrierorganisation.com/, Accessed 3 June 2017.

http://www.yorkshireairambulance.org.uk/files/file/content/YAA-annual-report-accounts-13-14.pdf, Accessed April 2017.

http://www.yorkshireairambulance.org.uk/info/volunteers, Accessed 1 April 2017.

https://en.wikipedia.org/wiki/Hash_House_Harriers, Accessed 3 June 2017.

https://www.nationaltrust.org.uk/features/about-the-national-trust, Accessed 18 May 2017.

Humphreys, A., Brown, B., *Narratives of Organisational Identity and Identification: A Case Study of Hegemony and Resistance*, "Organisational Studies" 2002, Vol. 23, No. 3, pp. 421-447.

Hynes, B., *Growing the social enterprise - issues and challenges*, „Social Enterprise Journal" 2009, Vol. 5, No. 2, pp. 114-125.

Inkpen, A. C., Dinur, A., *Knowledge management processes and international joint ventures*, "Organisation Science" 1998, Vol. 9, pp. 454-468.

Iverson, J. O., McPhee, R. D., *Knowledge management in communities of practice*, "Management Communication Quarterly" 2002, Vol. 16, No. 2, pp. 259-266.

Jorgensen, M., Phillips, L. J., *Discourse Analysis as Theory and Method*, SAGE Publications, London-Thousand Oaks-New Delhi 2001.

Kay, A., *Social capital, the social economy and community development*, „Community Development Journal" 2006, Vol. 41, No. 2, pp. 160-173.

Kerlin, J., *Social Enterprise in the United States and Europe: Understanding and learning from the differences*, "VOLUNTAS: International Journal of Voluntary and Nonprofit Organisations" 2006, No. 17, pp. 246-262.

Koenig, M. E. D., *What is KM: Knowledge mangement explained*, http://www.kmworld.com /Articles/ Editorial/ What-Is-.../What-is-KM-Knowledge-Management-Explained-82405.aspx, Accessed 2 June 2017.

Kolb, D. A., *Experiential Learning*, Englewood Cliffs, Prentice Hall 1984.

Kolb, D. A., Fry, R., *Toward an applied theory of experiential learning*, In: Cooper, C. (ed.), *Theories of group process,* John Wiley, London 1975.

Krzemiński, P., *Non-profit Organisations Operating in Healthcare sector in Polad in 1989-2010*, In: Borowiecki, R., Dziura, M. (eds.), *Third Sector: Theoretical and Empirical Approach*, Crakow University of Economics, Crakow 2014, p. 163-179.

Langridge, D. *Phenomenological Psychology, Theory Research and Method*, Pearson Prentice Hall 2007.

Lave, J., *Cognition in Practice: Mind, mathematics, and culture in everyday life*, Cambridge University Press. Cambridge 1988.

Lave, J., E. Wenger, *Situated learning: Legitimate peripheral participation*. Cambridge University Press, 1991.

Lin, Y., Beyerlein, M. M., *Communities of practice: A critical perspective on collaboration*, In: Beyerlein, M. M., Beyerlein, S. T., Kennedy, F. A. (ed.), *Innovation through Collaboration*, (Advances in Interdisciplinary Studies of Work Teams, Volume 12), Emerald Group Publishing Limited, pp. 53-79.

Łukasik, P., *The social sharing of the knowledge*, In: Borowiecki, R. Dziura, M. (eds.), *Third Sector: Theoretical and Empirical Approach*, Cracow University of Economics, Cracow 2014, pp. 131-145.

Lyons, E. and Coyle, A. *Analysing Qualitative Data in Psychology*, Sage 2007.

Maslow, A. H., *A theory of human motivation*, "Psychological Review" 1943, Vol. 50, No. 4, pp. 370-396.

McClelland, D. C., *Assessing human motivation*, General Learning Press, Morristown 1971.

McGregor, D., *The human side of enterprise*, McGrow-Hill, New York 1960.

McKelven, B., Sekoran, U., *A Career Based Theory of Job Involvement*, "Admin Science Quarterly" 1977, Vol. 22, pp. 281-305.

Mendelow, A., *Stakeholder Mapping*, „Proceedings of the 2nd International Conference on Information Systems", Cambridge, MA, 1991.

Mikuła, B. *Organizacje oparte na wiedzy*, Wydawnictwo Akademii Ekonomicznej w Krakowie, Kraków 2006.

Mitchell, R. K., Agle, B., R., Wood, D., J., *Toward a Theory of Stakeholder Identification and Salience: Defining the Principle of Who and What really Counts*, „Academy of Management Review" 1997, Vol. 22, No. 4, pp. 853 – 888.

Murray, H. A., *Explorations in personality: A clinical and experimental study of fifty men of college age*, Oxford University Press, New York 1938.

Nonaka, I., Takeuchi, H., *The Knowledge Creating Company*, Oxford University Press 1995.

Parscal, T., Hencmann, M., Cognitive Apprecenships in Online Learning, @4th Annual Conference on Distance Teaching & Learning, University of Winconsin, 2008, http://www.uwex.edu/disted/conference/resource_library/proceedings/08_12686.pdf, Accessed 5 June 2017.

Pavitt, K., *What We Know about the Strategic Management of Technology*, "California Management Review", Vol, 32, No. 3, pp. 17-26.

Pavlin, S., *Community of practice in a small research institute*, "Journal of Knowledge Management" 2006, Vol. 10, No. 4, pp. 136-137.

Prahalad, C. K., Hamel, G., *The Core Competence of the Corporation*, "Harvard Business Review" 1990, Vol. 68, No. 3, pp. 79-91.

Ribeiro, R., Kimble, Ch., Cairns, P., *Quantum phenomena in Communities of Practice*, "International Journal of Information Management" 2010, No 30, p. 21-27.

Robbins, P., Aydede, M., *The Cambridge Handbook of Situated Cognition*, Cambridge University Press 2008.

Robson, C., *Real World Research*, Blackwell, Oxford 2002.

Ruuska, I., Vartiainen, M., *Characteristics of knowledge sharing communities in project organisations*, "International Journal of Project Management" 2005, No. 23, pp. 375-376.

Salamon, L. M., Sokolowski, W., *Volunteering in Cross-National Perspective: Evidence From 24 Countries*, "Working Papers of the Johns Hopkins Comparative Nonprofit Sector Project", No. 40, The Johns Hopkins Center for Civil Society Studies, Baltimore 2001.

Smith J. A., Flowers, P., Larkin, M., *Interpretative Phenomenological Analysis: Theory, Method and Research*, Sage, London 2009.

Smith, M. K. *Jean Lave, Etienne Wenger and communities of practice*, „The encyclopedia of informal education" 2003, 2009, www.infed.org/biblio/communities_of_practice.htm. Accessed 18 May 2017.

Squires, A., *Methodological challenges in cross-language qualitative research: a research review*, "International Journal of Nursing Studies" 2009, Vol. 46, No. 2, pp. 277-287.

Teigland, R., Wasko, M., *Knowledge transfer in MNCs: Examining how intrinsic motivations and knowledge sourcing impact individual centrality and performance*, "Journal of International Management" 2009, Vol.15, pp. 15–31.

Thompson, J., Doherty, B., *The diverse world of social enterprise: A collection of social enterprise stories*, „International Journal of Social Economics" 2006, Vol. 33, Iss: 5/6, pp. 361-375.

Tuckman, B. W., Jensen, M.A. *Stages of Small Group Development Revisited*, "Group and Organisational Studies" 1977, No. 2, pp. 419-427.

Vroom, V. H., *Work and motivation*, Wiley, 1994.

Wall T. D., Stephenson, G. M., *Herzberg's two-factor theory of job attitudes: a critical evaluation and some fresh evidence*, "Industrial Relations Journal" Vol. 1, Iss. 3, pp. 41-65.

Wenger, E, McDermott, R, Snyder, W. M., *Cultivating Communities of Practice: A Guide to Managing Knowledge*, Harvard Business Press 2002.

Wenger, E., *Communities of Practice: Learning, Meaning and Identity*, Cambridge University Press, Cambridge 1998.

Wenger, E., Wenger-Trayner, B., *Introduction to communities of practice: A brief overview of the concept and its uses*, http://wenger-trayner.com/introduction-to-communities-of-practice/. Accessed 18 August 2017.

Willig, C. *Introducing Qualitative Research in Psychology*. McGraw-Hill Education 2008; Willig, C., Stainton-Rogers, W. (eds) *The Sage Handbook of Qualitative Research in Psychology*. London: Sage 2008.

Wood, D. J.,Gray, B., *Towards a comprehensive theory of collaboration*, "The Journal of Applied Behavioral Science", Vol. 27, No. 3, p. 46.

Zahra, S. A., Gedajlovic, E., Neubaum, D. O., Shulman, J. M., *A Typology of Social Entrepreneurs: Motives, Search Processes and Ethical Challenges*, "Journal of Business Venturing" 2009, Vol. 24, No. 5, pp. 519-532.

Zhao., X., Bishop, M. J., *Understanding and supporting on-line communities of practice: lessons learned from Wikipedia*, "Educational Technology Research and Development" 2011, No. 59, pp. 711-735.

Appendix: Examples of transcripts and IPA analyses

The UK Medical Support Charity

Interview with L1 - Transcript with full interpretative phenomenological analysis

Initial thoughts	Interview L1	Emergent themes
Held: July 2009. 37 minutes. 3500 words. ***Ethics form signed and stored, with full permission. Standard introduction used.*** L1 is Female. Covers 1991-2009.		
Awareness Need publicity Motivation	Right, I agreed to be identified due to the fact that lxxx is a relatively small group and it <u>requires as much um public... sort of knowledge as</u> ....<u>it can</u>	Motivation
Competition Rationale, Need for group	because if you understand <u>it has a hard time trying to battle with major charities,</u>	Explanations Justification
Explanation Rationale	and as such it is not a charity, <u>it is there to help the poor.... um people who suffer from lxxx.</u>	
Explanations Motivation	and in my personal experience ....my mother was a sufferer, and <u>seeing my mother go through life in absolute agony, day after day, seven hours a day-er 7 days a week, 24 hours a day, is ...difficult,</u>	Motivation
Explanation Need for help	<u>And you just wish you could turn to somebody and gain some knowledge of how to make that person's life a bit more livable and help in any way you can.</u>	Need for help, Need for KT & CoP
Clarification	And <u>therefore the Lxxx group was set up with that in mind,</u>	
Clarification of Strategic Direction	not as a charitable existence as regarding um...<u>to get, you know funds. That was never its intention,</u>	
Rationale / driver CoP	<u>it was there as a support and to help these people</u>	CoP Rationale
Explanation Motivation	you know, they do have good days and they have bad days. And <u>the majority of the time its bad days, you know there is no pain relief whatsoever</u>	Motivation
Saw advert Group was marketing to attract new members	...and asking, in my experience of the Lxxx group, coming on to that now I became a member of the group, well, me and my family became a member of the group, solely because <u>we happened to, funnily enough, um, my dad was loaned a car for. And in that car was a bookmark ... you know, the ...general organisation, um...advertising about Lxxx weekend, by a very good</u>	Storytelling and SL LPP

149

Initial thoughts	Interview L1	Emergent themes
	friend of his	
Handling process Storttelling	so we rang the number that was on the bookmark and we were informed we were asked which area we lived in ,and we were put in touch with the local ...group,	LPP
Reflection on Ignorance of support availability	which we didn't know existed, because ...we had no knowledge of it.	No KT!
Explanation	Doctors have no knowledge of it, no-one else has any knowledge about it,	No KT!
	it isn't advertised in the newspaper, it was never published	
Competition Analysis Rationale	because the Lxxx organisation as a whole has a very hard time trying to compete with other organisations.	Need for marketing skills- KT
Lack of Knowledge	So the only way we found out was through ringing the number on the bookmark and they put us in touch with the our local group	CoP existence not known
Got involved Pro-active	So we went along to the first meeting, which	LPP
Explanation	...in the lxxx group is mainly social activities where lxxx sufferers were able to go and meet other sufferers who were in the same position who were suffering of the same disease and same condition,	SL
	and also they could compare their, you know, their medical treatment, their hospital treatment	KT. SL CoP
Networking Help	and also it was a place for the lxxx sufferers to actually sort of talk to other lxxx sufferers to find out how they feel, what they went through, it was an aid to um, really it was an aid to sort of feel not alone because this condition, it...	CoP SL
Solitude Awareness	because of its sort of...anonymous...anonymously, you know not many people know about it, that	
Analysis Solitude Suffer alone	it was the only place they could they could sort of talk to, talk to um people, and um not feel alone	Networking CoP
Analysis Explanation Solitude Suffer alone	because I mean, lxxx sufferers, they are really, you know they can only suffer within the family and all they got to talk to is the family	Change

Initial thoughts	Interview L1	Emergent themes
Networking (need)		
Need help Limits to State help	They go and talk to the consultant and <u>the consultant just helps them with their problem, they don't help them with the actual emotional side of the disease,</u>	Limits of NHS
Reflection Solitude Suffer alone	and um, you know, as I said people, people, people are …<u>you know, they are alone, they feel alone.</u>	Lack of knowledge. Need for SL from a CoP
Motivation	And um so <u>the reason I got involved with this group,</u> was purely through my mum, because <u>I wanted to do something was to help my mother</u>	Motivation to help
Motivation	and um, because <u>I hated to see her suffering every day</u>	Motivation
Solitude Suffer alone	<u>she was alone, she was in the house all day, she was housebound, she couldn't get out, she was you know restricted</u>	Storytelling
Solitude Suffer alone	<u>and she couldn't talk to anyone about it,</u>	No knowledge of CoP
Solitude Suffer alone	<u>and I was at work, my father was at work, she was alone ,</u>	
Solitude Suffer alone	but in constant pain all the time and <u>she had no…nowhere to let that pain out, really basically.</u>	No help from outside
Networking Enjoyment (of membership)	So we went to the first Yorkshire Lxxx group meeting…. and we found, <u>my mum enjoyed it,</u> because <u>it was a social event, it wasn't a meeting,</u> it was held in a social capacity, in that, you know like was a coffee morning or you know it was a social event	Networking and opportunity for SL
Networking Public Awareness CoP Enjoyment (of membership)	like for example making a social event as in <u>people getting together, you know, like minded people getting together and talking,</u>	SL
Contributing	and so we got, <u>we started getting involved,</u>	CoP formation
Motivation	and the first thing I did for Lxxx was, I mean , <u>because I wanted… had the determination</u> and I wanted to help so much,	Motivation Move from LPP to mature
Public Awareness	to <u>get it pushed to the limelight</u>	Marketing, KT outwards
Public Awareness	that I helped in the first event which was that that ,um <u>I wanted to um… help make the public aware.</u>	Need to market KT outwards

Initial thoughts	Interview L1	Emergent themes
Marketing		
	And the way we did this first of all was to actually have a um... because it happened to be an event arranged by the um... professional Lxxx organisation, called Lxxx week which is where the professional organisation, that is Lxxx UK	Found umbrella org
Public Awareness	<u>wanted to make people aware and the general public aware of this disease</u> and how cruel this disease is because it's a killer.	Need for KT outwards
Explanation	And it can affect anybody, the majority of which are women	
Lack of Support	and because we found we didn't have any, <u>we didn't have any sort of, backing from anybody, nobody wanted to know us, the government didn't want to know us, you know,</u>	No external support No knowledge in medical profession
Public Awareness	<u>nobody knew anything about it.</u>	Need fo KT out
Public Awareness	<u>So the first public event we held was actually in</u> Leeds railway station under the title of Lxxx week, where we set up a table in the station, and it was, it was a day event and we ...sort of , <u>we had leaflets,</u>	KT out
Public Awareness Promotion	<u>we had published leaflets about the disease</u>, about the organisation,	KT out Marketing
Fundraising	um and we also um <u>wanted to raise funds as well</u>, so we had a gift box as well, we went round.	Fundraising (not main priority)
Takes guts! Motivation	<u>I remember walking to total strangers in the train station, walking up to them and saying right "please read this"</u>, you know " it's important, "have you heard about lxxx, do you know what lxxx is "and you know, and	KT out Mature member
Public Awareness Confidence	what I found was that quite a few of the people, when I did my little stint, <u>quite a few of the people, were ignorant, they didn't know anything about it</u>	KT out. SL
Wry reflection	And some people weren't interested obviously	
Public Awareness	And the majority of the people, especially woman, took the leaflet, because they... <u>began to realise that it could affect me, you know</u>, it could affect any woman,	SL

Initial thoughts	Interview L1	Emergent themes
	especially of childbearing age.	
Motivation	Then, um, so we did that and we found... we, we got a good response from that, and so we <u>decided we would do it every year.</u>	SL
Public Awareness	Then the next sort of major um, public... you know, it also, this, this helping, it encouraged the members of the group, because we thought we were doing something, achieving something, we were making, the most important thing of all, <u>we were making the public aware.</u>	KT out
Public Awareness	That this disease exists, and it's not a pleasant one. And um, we were hoping... even if they didn't take any knowledge or any leaflets, or whatever <u>at least we made them aware.</u>	KT out
Public Awareness	<u>We were determined, we had the determination there because we wanted to put across... so much about this disease. A</u>nd hoping to transfer that learning and that <u>knowledge.</u>	Motivations KT
Explanation	The next incident I had with ...um lxxx was that <u>I also found out that a very close friend of mine, um childhood friend of mine, that his wife had also contracted lxxx.</u>	No KT
Reflection Public Awareness Analysis	And um she went through numerous tests till it was found to be actually having lxxx and it was all just because of a little infection she got and she developed lxxx and they say that you know it affects women of childbearing age, and she became pregnant, and she became pregnant with twins and she was nursed at St Thomas's hospital in London and <u>they knew everything about it</u>	KT in
Lack of Medical Awareness	which coming on to that point we felt, <u>we felt the GP's didn't know anything about the disease, the consultant didn't know anything about the disease,</u> we found that people had <u>a lack of knowledge in the medical profession.</u>	No KT in normally No knowledge in medical profession
Lack of Medical Awareness	So, also, having been with my mother for 12 years <u>she was.... misdiagnosed</u> as having rheumatoid arthritis, and it turned out, I mean, she was <u>misdiagnosed, mistreated,</u>	Need for KT SL No knowledge in medical profession
Lack of Medical Awareness	she was put on steroids, which they say that is the only ...sort of medical, um medical sort of medication they can take as lxxx sufferers, <u>but nobody knew about lxxx.</u>	No knowledge in medical profession

Initial thoughts	Interview L1	Emergent themes
Lack of Medical Awareness	<u>They were very limited,</u> my mum was first diagnosed ,in about, oh it wasn't till about the ninety's, before that she was treated for um rheumatoid arthritis, and <u>she went 12 years of pure neglect.</u>	No knowledge in medical profession
Changed Situation	And we found this out because my mum changed consultants and went to see a consultant rheumatologist in Leeds.	Knowledge sporadic in medical profession
Lack of Medical Awareness	Who very kindly went through loads of tests and <u>they found out she actually had lxxx,</u> that <u>that she had been treated wrongly,</u> um <u>because of lack of knowledge ...on behalf of the medical profession.</u>	Finally, expertise
Lack of Medical Awareness	<u>Doctors seem not to be trained very much about lxxx,</u>	No knowledge in medical profession
Analysis Public Awareness Creation Lack of Medical Awareness	so we thought the next thing to do to make people more aware about the disease was to actually, um actually sort of ...um...make, <u>we sent GP notes, we sent GP information,</u> so that GPs could put them in the surgery informing patients of their own about lxxx,	No knowledge in medical profession so creating amateur KT Mature
Public Awareness Creation Lack of Medical Awareness Action advertising CoP	<u>so we made little booklets out,</u> <u>We made a booklet out for the GP</u> to understand the disease, and <u>we made a booklet out for the patients and the GPs, in the GP group, um in the GP surgery and practices.</u>	No knowledge in medical profession so creating amateur KT
Action Public Awareness Creation	<u>Then we started giving talks,</u> we go to various hospital establishments, to inform the medical staff about the disease,	No knowledge in medical profession so creating amateur KT
KT Public Awareness Creation	and so that's how we ...<u>tried to transfer our knowledge...</u> to them, about a relatively unknown disease	No knowledge in medical profession so creating amateur KT
Public Awareness Creation	And also, not only that, we... its Lxxx UK as usual, but they have supporting branches in the local group, like of course I'm a member of the Yorkshire Lxxx's group, which is a small group, but we are doing our best, <u>we</u>	No knowledge in medical profession so creating

Initial thoughts	Interview L1	Emergent themes
	promote it, we promote Lxxx at every opportunity we can.	amateur KT
Public Awareness Creation	We hold fêtes in recognition of lxxx, we hold, um, we hold sort of events in aid of lxxx, all with the point of view to make the public aware, to... educate people, to inform people so that um...they, they sort of ...so they know, so people are aware, and that it's not a disease to be sniffed at.	SL Mature so creating LPP in others
Reflection Analysis Knowledge SL	You know, this is a serious disease, you know, and unfortunately it's not the disease that's the killer, It's the actual...Because it destroys the immune system its actually the infections that is the killer, but because the lxxx sufferers do not have any sort of immune system, the immunity towards the infection, the infection is ten times worse.	Knowledge, SL
Reflection SL Understanding	And therefore, for example, for example, if a Lxxx sufferer gets a cold its pneumonia to them, its life threatening ...you know, it's horrible, its, it's not a pleasant thing to have,	Motivation to help
Motivation	and that is why solely, this group was set up.	Motivation
Reflection Analysis	It was not set up like... majority of major charities where, you know they are out to, you know, for example there is the Royal Society for the Deaf, Where they send Jxxx, my aunt, who is profoundly deaf, um, you know, they send her a leaflet saying give us ten pounds, why should she give ten pounds?	Reflection
Reflection	We are not like that, you know, what's that ten pounds going to do, you know, we welcome any amount of money, how small, doesn't really matter.	Reflection
Public Awareness Education	We don't dictate, to people, we are there, just solely to become, so people are aware and also to highlight what a cruel disease this is, and it can happen to anyone, and it's not, there is no cure for it,...	Reflection
Public Awareness Creation	and these, these raising...these public awareness meetings that we hold.	
Public Awareness Creation CoP	It also, not only educates, it's our way of trying to... you know, add sufferers and helpers of sufferers, of trying to, you know, establish that...it's you know, want to, raise, we want to more, more than anything else we want to raise the fact that this should be looked into, that there should be research into this... disease, you	Offering KT out

Initial thoughts	Interview L1	Emergent themes
	know	
Public Awareness Creation	and that people are,...people are, you know, aware of it, and, you know, with hope to find an eventual cure, cos there is no cure..., and this, they are working on it as we speak nowadays	Offering KT out
Funding research	and that's why every penny, we raise, does not go to the government, it goes solely to research, into the disease. We do not do not take it for	
Rationale	ourselves as Lxxx people, but yes, it is to benefit ...the Lxxx people, a way, in a way of finding out a cure...	Motivation
	(CW) That's great, that's really good, that's, that's excellent, you have told me a lot about your motivation, attitudes, and the experiences... So how did you find out about all this stuff? You know a huge amount about it ...um, you know, you have talked about its implications, and all the rest of it... ...That the NHS were useless - I think that was your words? So, where did you find out all this stuff - stuff you are now passing on to others? How did you find out about it, tell me about that.	
Clarification	How did I find out about the disease, or how did I find out about the group?	
	(CW) Well both...	
	Because firstly about the disease, Really, the way I found out about the disease, was going round with my mum, to the consultant, sitting in on her... um... appointments, so that I would understand the disease.	SL
Ignorance	I was only ...a teenager at the time, and... I knew nothing, my mum knew nothing, my dad knew nothing about the disease at all,	SL No knowledge in medical profession so creating amateur KT
NHS weakness Need to Learn Finding Expertise SL	and it was solely because we hit the right person, you know, who specialised in lxxx, you know, lxxx was one of his specialities, It just wasn't, you know, it just wasn't concentrated, on just knowing...you know...it wasn't something he had studied in a textbook, he'd specialised in it.	Change SL
Use of Funds	So, also, not only that, at the group, we also, with the funds that we raised, we also, um we also, aided in a Lxxx nurse, paid by us, you know, by the funds that we	Creating CoP

Initial thoughts	Interview L1	Emergent themes
	raised. We, in Chapel Allerton, we have been able to fund a, a Lxxx nurse, where and also, at one time, we also, had a Lxxx room, which I think we still have at Chapel Allerton, where it was a place for Lxxx patients to go.	
Knowledge Sharing	And also, with the health of the group as well, because, talking to the various people in the group, listening about their experiences, you were able to, sort of, match what you were going through, what my mum was going through, what my dad went through, you know, that we were able to talk about it, we talked about it amongst ourselves	KT SL CoP
NHS weakness	and, as I said, the NHS were useless, because lack of knowledge. And the doct... the GPs were useless, they just gave the prescriptions for the pills, they didn't really know very much about it,	No knowledge in medical profession so creating amateur KT
Need for Knowledge KT Self-starting to find if CoP existed	and... basically it was, really, the way I found out about lxxx, was reading up about it, in sort of like, going to the library, trying to find out information there. Also, um... looking on websites, as well,	SL Motivations own efforts for KT
International Dimension	because it's all over the world is lxxx, it's not just contained here in England.	
	It's just that, you know, we are lucky to have such a charity, well, not a charity but an organisation,	CoP value
SL KT Self Starting CoP	and also, not only that, I subscribed to a monthly magazine called Lxxx UK, which is the main organisation that takes care of lxxx.	
SL KT Joined CoP	So we subscribe, became members, of the Lxxx UK, where we were given, um, 3 monthly magazines, which also um…, which also... told you about the development, the medical development, um...[long pause], you know, the lxxx... about the disease itself, what organs it affects, what it can cause to the organs, how people can feel, and we gained information from that.	SL from umbrella but not actually controlling CoP
Networking	Not only that, we also, you had con... also, in the group itself, you had contacts, which you could turn to...	KT in
Networking Support CoP	You could turn to people in the Lxxx group and say right "can I talk to you about this, I'm not feeling very good today, but I would like to talk to... I'd like to talk	SL

Initial thoughts	Interview L1	Emergent themes
	to you about how I feel, how can I, how can I, you know, what do I do, you know".	
SL CoP	And they... I trained myself, to be a young, um, young Lxxx contact... and we, we sort of did it that way really. And, um... um... we sort of, that's how we sort of got to know.	SL
Education	We educated ourselves basically. We found out what we could, and then .we, we developed a library as well, you know, a library of our own, and we have a librarian, who collects books and ,um, any sort of publications regarding lxxx, which, you know, hopefully um...will aid in the um, in m...gaining a little bit more knowledge.	SL CoP
Networking SL CoP	And also talking to other people. Other Lxxx sufferers, other families... of Lxxx sufferers, and we all sort of, got together and shared our knowledge and sort of tried to, sort of, make, make ourselves understood, about it.	SL
Support Recognition	And also, thanks to Dr XX, down in um.. St Thomas's hospital, in London, who was the major sort of pinnacle, um, consultant, in Lxxx, um.	
Sources of Knowledge	He...he... he, he used to put articles in the Lxxx magazine. which used to highlight, you know, the different, the medical aspects of lxx.	SL KT
Proactive	And therefore educating ourselves into the disease. So really, basically, it was a magazine that helped.	
Confirmed all are proactive	*(CW) Thanks...um. So it sounds to me as though you were very proactive, you went out and got on with it, now, is that because you are you, or is that because you think that everybody in the group tends to be.*	KT SL
Awareness Networking Motivation	Everyone else is the same because the fact is this disease is so unknown, that people will do anything to help, you know, I mean, ...we are all active in the group	CoP Mutual support
Supporting Friendship Enjoyment Networking	...we are not, we're not... sort of, you know, we have a good time... at the end of the day we have all become very good friends, you know, and you know they are there and you can talk to them.	SL Mutual support
Friendship CoP	And we have all become friends, not as , not as a sort of group entity as in we don't, you know, all right, "see you next week",	Mutual support
Networking CoP	we know that we can meet outside, we can ring each other up, we're not, we are not distant, you know, a...	Mutual support

Initial thoughts	Interview L1	Emergent themes
CoP	and <u>we are all of the same boat,</u>	Mutual support SL
Common interest Motivation	we're all, you know. all <u>the lxxx sufferers are all suffering</u>, and you know,	Mutual support
Need friends	and they get lonely, lonely through the pain and <u>they just want someone to talk to,</u>	Mutual support
CoP	and <u>so everyone knows everybody else</u>, and they are always interested, you know, and this is, this is what, <u>this is what is the major thing about the group, we help each other,</u>	CoP Mutual support
CoP against the world	you know, because... because of who we are,... of the disease, we are having to sort of, do what we can for it, because nobody else gives a toss, you know, nobody else outside the world wants to know about it, or they just pretend it doesn't exist.	SL Mutual support
	(CW) OK That's great, I have got a very clear view of motivation... that's great. What about the way that you learnt, um, you say that you looked on the web, (6 words unclear) ...How much of what you know is written down, tell me a bit about that, is it - tacit and explicit is the technical term? Tacit knowledge, stuff that's in your head, or explicit knowledge, you know, stuff that I could go to a book for, tell me a bit about that.	
SL not CoP	<u>I picked up more of my knowledge through actually being with my mother</u>, because, how she suffered, and that's how I gained my knowledge really, from the physical side, not particularly.	SL Mutual support
Proactive Motivation Education	<u>I backed it up by reading books</u>, um, because I was interested, because I wanted to know more, and because <u>I wanted to help my mum</u> and...	SL KT in by positive effort
SL	but, <u>a lot of it was gained from actually, physically, seeing it myself</u>, seeing my mum deteriorate as time went by,	SL
Motivation	and <u>you just felt you wanted to do something</u>, you had the determination, you know, because you just felt...	Motivation
Motivation	I hate , you know, as anyone would, you know, you hate to see someone suffering.	
	And you tried to do the best you could.	Motivation
Education	<u>Mine really has just come from doing it basically.</u>	SL

Initial thoughts	Interview L1	Emergent themes
	Not by, sort of, it's more, sort of... it's not the theoretical, its more the physical, it's more you know, sort of touching... and <u>more being with that person, listening to that person</u> and spending you know, 24 hours a day, 7 days a week, with a person who was constantly in pain, feeding her medication, you know, <u>you learn. You begin to learn.</u>	SL
	<u>And also, listening to the specialist, you know, asking questions of the specialist.</u>	SL KT in because of positive effort
Proaction to improve CoP	And also, not only that, <u>in the group itself, we also have, we've had actual um...</u> specialists, in the different areas of lxxx, coming to the group and <u>actually educating the group themselves.</u>	SL
Inviting specialist to CoP	About, you know and about, the, sort of, the different aspects of the disease, you know, We've even had, we've had Gxxx, <u>at our meetings, telling us about, telling us about what's going on, keeping us informed,</u> keeping us in the picture, you know... telling us about the new drugs that might help, you know...	SL
	<u>the group was informed by these speakers</u>, and they would come and they would speak, and the Lxxx people were allowed to ask questions after, and, you know, put their side across, and say, look-how can I be helped.	SL
	(CW) Whose idea was it to have these people come?	
	It was us as a group, we, we decided that, um, because, in the group itself, as I said, like any other group, we have a Chairman, we have a Chairperson, um and we have a financial person, and we have a um... err..., um, social secretary, contact people, and err, treasury, obviously.	Storytelling about CoP
Motivation	And, but, because the husband and his, err the Vice-chair as well, she lost her sister to lxxx and the Treasurer is the husband of her sister, and he wanted to do something. <u>The Chairman wanted to do something as well, um, because his wife suffers from lxxx.</u>	Motivation
	These people, all right, they are well, but <u>they got the determination, to fight for a good cause.</u>	Motivation Maure participant
Motivation Socialisation	And also, not only that, it was also the fact that, um, my um, it was also not only that <u>lxxx sufferers themselves are members of the committee as well</u>, those that are	CoP SL

Initial thoughts	Interview L1	Emergent themes
	able to, you know, that are not too debilitated, do take part in the committee, and we are welcome as members, to attend these meetings, you know, they are not just solely committee meetings, they are meetings for everybody, you know, that we can talk about issues.	
Networking. KT	And also same at the Annual General Meeting. We have an Annual General Meeting and we meet up there, we meet up with other groups within the Yorkshire area, You know, South Yorkshire, East Yorkshire, North Yorkshire. We all get together and we sort of, we sort of communicate with other groups as well.	CoP KT SL
	(CW) That's great, great, Last bit I think, then I will finish. I know time to go. How many years, tell me, just tell me, how long have you been involved with the group, some dates.	
	Right, I've been involved with the group, since, um, I think I was involved since I was about, let me see, What would it be, I was involved since about 1991.(18 years)	
	(CW) 18 years, ok yes - So your mum was diagnosed....	
No medical knowledge (1970's)	My mum was actually diagnosed, well she had, she actually started with it, when I was born, but nobody knew about it, nobody could diagnose it, because nobody knew anything about it, the disease, the doctors didn't know anything,	Medical ignorance (to 1991)
1981 recognised	and um, she actually, um, properly um began with the disease in about …it was actually medically recognised in 1981 and then she started treatment for lxxx	No medical Prof knowledge
	but unfortunately she'd been mistreated, and therefore unfortunately she gained osteoporosis due to the use of steroids.	
	(CW) Ok, so you were born in 1970, your mum was diagnosed in 1981, you got involved in the group 10 years later (1991)	
Ignorance	Yes, because there was nothing around , we didn't know, we didn't know this group existed, we knew nothing about it.	Need for CoP and SL KT
Motivation	I have been active in it ever since. The reason I want to be active in it is for my mum, because it's about time somebody, you know - hooray for Yorkshire Lxxx doing something about it because, to be honest,	Motivation
Ignorance	in all the time without that group, we were alone, we	Mutual support

Initial thoughts	Interview L1	Emergent themes
before found CoP	<u>were uneducated, we were alone,</u> We were um, …we <u>were very much, having to sort of, scrabble about, with you know, little bits of information, you know, that was, you know, nine times out often, useless.</u>	Motivation
	(CW) Thanks, that's great, unless there is anything else you want to add?	
	No – that's fine.	

Summary: 36 min. 3600 words. Covers 1990 – 2009. Many references to motivating factors. Many for lack of knowledge in medical profession and public, so need for KT both ways and providing help - maybe this was early on? Many refs to gaining SL and mutual support via CoP. Lots about need to promote and market medical and care knowledge to potential audience. Many refs to needing to be a self-starter. No state/medical support available in early days. Had to go and look. Although Internet was available later no refs to using it, so probably not computer aware (2009). Mutual support quoted often, CoP providing this. Obvious SL and inward KT occurring via CoP. Also evidence of KT out via CoP. Marketing and KT out stressed, but no mention of professional expertise. Mature member but stressed early LPP. Mainly storytelling but lots of reflection and awareness of how SL led her to mature membership of CoP. (CoP Member 18 years from 1991-2009).

The Air Ambulance (AA)

This is the only UK group specifically named. This is at the request of the interviewee, because he stated he was passionately motivated to use all possible ways to promote his Social Enterprise. Only 1 interview was held - transcript with full interpretative phenomenological analysis

Initial thoughts	Interview AA	Emergent themes
Held via Skype: 3 Feb 2014. 37 minutes. 1700 words. ***Ethics form signed and stored, with full permission. Standard introduction used.*** AA is male.		
Explanation and story	Right, OK, I will start from the beginning. Way, way back in...2003 I think it was, Chris, <u>A friend of mine was on his motorbike and come off.</u> And, err, he and his bike became separated, at high speed. Err,	
Explanation and story	<u>He was picked up by the Cornish Air Ambulance, but unfortunately didn't survive....</u>	
Explanation and story	At his funeral, his mum and dad knew that I spent a lot of time down in that part of the country, because at that time I was working for the MOD.	
Explanation and story	And, the next time I was in Truro, would I call into the Cornwall Air Ambulance office and give them the money they had from the collection they had at the funeral.	
Reflection	Now..., <u>I must have stood there with a puzzled look on my face</u> because I was – <u>why are you giving money to the Air Ambulance service? Is there a charity that D. was part of that … would appreciate the money you got then?</u>	Reflection SL
Explanation and story	And that's the point where <u>I was stunned to learn that the Air Ambulance services in the UK, are all charity based.</u>	SL
Explanation and story	So I did as I was asked, I took the money to Truro next time I was down that way, and <u>I got chatting to the folks there.</u> And then I was told all about it and that's where I thought, well	SL
Motivation	I can find out what goes on back at home.	Motivation
Reflection	<u>And that is how I came to find out about the Yorkshire Air Ambulance.</u>	Reflections SL
Motivation	So <u>I err, I approached them, and said, y'know, is there anything I can to to help.</u>	Motivation
Storytelling	And you will be surprised to know they said yes. <u>What would you like to do?</u> (pause).	Initial Involvement

Initial thoughts	Interview AA	Emergent themes
	(CW) Right, OK	
Storytelling Reflection	It is... The whole story seems to be that you can do as little or as much as you like.	
Reflection	You have known me for long enough now, <u>I will just dive into anything...</u> (pause).	Motivation to help
Storytelling Involvement	As things develop, I guess you could almost say that what I do is almost seasonal. In summer, I turn up at various village fairs, and err sporting occasions, and ....motorbike rallies etc. etc. With a gazebo in the car. A trestle table. Umm.... Boxes full of pin badges and pens, leaflets and information.	
	<u>More than happy to stand there.</u>	Motivation
KT	One way of <u>making people aware of the fact that I wasn't aware of, that the Air Ambulance is, is charity funded.</u>	Motivation KT
	(CW) OK	
Storytelling	In the winter its slightly different. It's more likely to be, <u>I will pile along to a WI meeting, or Brownies, or the Guides, or the Cubs, and give them an actual, formal Power Point presentation.</u>	
	<u>On the background to the Air Ambulance. What they do, where they are based, how much it costs etc.etc.</u>	KT
Reflection CoP qualifies!	Emm... (Pause) <u>Formal training. Very little to be honest mate.</u>	Reflection
Reflection	<u>Training is there if you need it,</u> but to be honest, I have had enough experience of life, in talking to people. That ...err I have not really needed it.	Reflections past SL used
Reflection Networking KT	<u>Cos that's all it is, talking to people, which, you have known me long enough. I am not backwards at coming forwards, when it comes to talking to people.</u> (Pause).	Reflections SL KT
	CW. Right, OK	
Reflection	Especially if they are cute and female, that's just an added bonus...	Reflection
	(CW) OK, I believe that, yeah OK.	
Storytelling	<u>So, that is basically how I got involved, and what I do.</u>	
	And basically, if <u>I am available I will do anything that is needed.</u>	Motivation
Storytelling	<u>If somebody wants me to go along to a ball "suited and</u>	Motivation

Initial thoughts	Interview AA	Emergent themes
	booted" I will go to a ball suited and booted.	
Money!!!	And on more than 1 occasion I have picked up a huge "comedy cheque" and had a photograph taken and, err say a few words.	CoP about Money- Enterprise!
Motivation - enjoys events	Have a small sherry and a vol-au-vent, it's great. (Long pause).	Motivation Reward
	(CW) Right, and how many people do what you do?	
Storytelling Reflection	Err... (long pause) In West Yorkshire I would say there is probably... (longer pause) 10 really regular people that do... what I do on a very regular basis, and another, similar number, of 10, maybe 12 that seem to drift in and drift out, on a, you know, almost a cyclical basis.	
Reflection	OK, they get distracted by other things, life gets in the way, You don't see them for a few months on end, and then all of a sudden they pop back.	LPP
	There is almost a hard core there of people who are doing it week in, week out. (pause)	Core Maturity
	(CW) OK, and do you... talk to each other?	
KT	Oh, very much so, yeah. We have a regular get together, every 3 months or so. The charity has an intra-net as well, where it can keep in touch with what everybody is up to, and we have all got each other's phone numbers so yeah, in regular contact...	KT SL
	(CW) So nothing formal?	
Eligible as CoP	Except for the regular "get together". The regular get together is formal. That's organised by the charity- you know? But that's purely in West Yorkshire. There is nothing err. Yorkshire wide.	Reflection
	Obviously the North and East and South Yorkshire have their similar teams as well....	
	(CW) OK, do you, umm, let's see now, do you learn from the others, do you teach the others, how does it ...	
LPP	Yes, it's very, very organic in that way Chris, you pick things up from each other, particularly ...the ways, of...putting things over in an effective way.	SL KT
LPP	Err, and obviously, people who are new to it are quite nervous. Maybe not quite sure of what they are doing, what they are saying.	LPP

Initial thoughts	Interview AA	Emergent themes
LPP	So yeah, but there is no (pause).... There is a err, actual formal training session for the actual, formal Power Point presentation, but when it comes to standing in a gazebo in the middle of a wet field it err, in a rainy July, then, <u>there is only one way to learn. That is to get in there and do it...</u>	SL
	(CW) OK....umm.... Age of the people that do it? Sex, age?	
Reflection	Err...Mature.... (pause) I would say that the split between the sexes is pretty much 50:50.	
Reflection	Age wise, I am one of the younger ones. Lucky to be …. To be fair. Umm, I would say I am certainly in the bottom 10%. There is one guy of 85 who potters about and does his bit…	
	(CW) Marvellous, err	
	Yeah, <u>But I am very conscious that we need to get some new blood in.</u>	
	I keep banging on about it, and maybe one day something will get done	Motivation
	It's a perception with the kids, isn't it?	
	(CW) Well, that right. I didn't know anything about it until my son had his accident. Same story.	
	Very similar yeah.	
	(CW) Right, I think you have answered all my questions to be honest. Anything else? Any funny stories, anything you want to share? Anything I can help with?	
	Well, <u>you can always help.</u>	
	If there is any "ex-pats" you know out there who want to get involved always happy to look at that.	Motivation
	That's something I am looking to do. With friends I have got over in Australia, Canada. Especially those from Yorkshire.	
Reflection	And there is a lot of interest. Just a, sort of, go… on the benefits to me.	
Reflection	Err, <u>the reason that I prefer working for Yorkshire Air Ambulance is, ...I guess you would almost call it a selfish reason in that I can see exactly where the money is going.</u>	Reflections Motivation Analysis

Initial thoughts	Interview AA	Emergent themes
	<u>I can see where my efforts are making a difference.</u> Cos, you see the yellow helicopter flying in and out of Leeds General Infirmary and other hospitals.	Motivation
Social contact	And, <u>because of what I do I get to meet people</u>, that's picked up. And I have met people whose lives have been saved by... the efforts that I put in, and... you just can't buy that, can you?	Social Element Rewards
Reflection	And (pause) it gets me (pause), to go to places that normally, Chris, I just wouldn't even think of going to.	Rewards
Reflection	<u>I go to events that normally I wouldn't even think about going to.</u>	Rewards
Storytelling	Like, err, a couple of weekends <u>ago I went to a wrestling match</u> in Castleford. <u>Previously I</u> would never have even thought of going to something like that.	Reward Reflection
	But <u>we had a right old time. It were grand!</u>	Reward
Storytelling Reflection	Umm, you know, you, err, We regularly now go to the Bramham Horse Trials, <u>not something I would go to.</u>	
Reflection	<u>But, you know there is a huge link there.</u> And, yeah, you can see, as I am sure you can appreciate the link between people who ride horses and the Air Ambulance.	
	(CW) Yeah.	
Reflection	The number of emm who, like, both you and I used to think, "that's part of the National Health Service", its huge.	Reflection
	And, even now, even with all the work that's been done through the TV programme, err, Richard, I don't know if you remember Richard Hammond had an accident a few years ago. He was picked up by the Air Ambulance and that got us a huge amount of publicity.	Reflection
Reflection	<u>Even after all that, there is still a lot of people out there who just don't realise. The need to raise 10,000 pounds every day of the year.</u>	Motivation SL
	(CW) Is it so much?	
	Yeah, 3.6 million pounds a year. <u>That keeps 2 helicopters flying.</u> If you say it quickly it's not too bad.	Situated Learning
	(CW) Someone once told me it costs 500 pounds per hour to fly a helicopter.	

Initial thoughts	Interview AA	Emergent themes
Reflection	I can see that being there, being about thereabouts. It's about 5 pounds a minute so... 300 pounds an hour. There or thereabouts. Depends obviously on how far you fly... (Long pause).	
	(CW) That's fine. Thanks. I will turn the recording off...	

Index